Making History

Making History

Czech Voices of Dissent and the Revolution of 1989

MICHAEL LONG

To Cindy, Donald and Catherine!
Best Wishes,
Michael Long
4.17.05

ROWMAN & LITTLEFIELD PUBLISHERS, INC.
Lanham • Boulder • New York • Toronto • Oxford

ROWMAN & LITTLEFIELD PUBLISHERS, INC.

Published in the United States of America
by Rowman & Littlefield Publishers, Inc.
A wholly owned subsidary of The Rowman & Littlefield Publishing Group, Inc.
4501 Forbes Boulevard, Suite 200, Lanham, MD 20706
www.rowmanlittlefield.com

P.O. Box 317, Oxford OX2 9RU, UK

British Library Cataloguing in Publication Information Available

Library of Congress Cataloging-in-Publication Data

Long, Michael, 1957–
  Making history : Czech voices of dissent and the revolution of 1989 / Michael Long.
     p. cm.
  Includes bibliographical references and index.
  ISBN 0-7425-3650-5 (cloth : alk. paper)—ISBN 0-7425-3651-3 (pbk. : alk. paper)
  1. Dissidents—Czechoslovakia—Interviews. 2. Czechoslovakia—Politics and government—1968–1989. I. Title.
  DB2230.L66   2005
  943.704'3'0922—dc22

                                                        2004019619

Printed in the United States of America

♾™ The paper used in this publication meets the minimum requirements of American National Standard for Information Sciences—Permanence of Paper for Printed Library Materials, ANSI/NISO Z39.48-1992.

for Ann and Catriona

Contents

CONTENTS

Acknowledgments

I would like to thank the Institute for Oral History at Baylor University for the grant which made this project possible. Both audiotapes and transcripts of each interview are available for further research at the Institute for Oral History at Baylor University in Waco, Texas. I would also like to thank the dean of the College of Arts and Sciences at Baylor University for recognizing the value of this project and awarding me release time and financial support, in order to bring the project to completion.

I owe a great debt to my friend and colleague Ivana Doležalová (Prague) for her help in arranging the interviews, her advice, and for answering my numerous e-mails concerning various facts and topics related to this project. Katka Prajznerová (Brno) deserves special gratitude for her expert transcriptions and translations from Czech to English of five of the interviews. I want to also express my thanks and appreciation to a number of individuals who either reviewed the manuscript before it was received by the publisher or aided in its final preparation: Kelly Bemis, Anne Davis, Ivana Doležalová, Justin Jones, Andrew Konitzer-Smirnov, Jonathan Lindsey, Ann McGlashan, Chris Marsh, Matthew Schobert, and Sylvia Stockton. I must give special thanks to Katie Cook who formatted the manuscript for publication. Finally, I owe a great debt of gratitude to each of the interviewees who granted me their time and willingly shared their insight and memories with me: Ivan Havel, Věra Jirousová, Michael Kocáb, Eda Kriseová, Daniel Kummerman, Dana Němcová, Martin Palouš, Jiřina Šiklová, Petruška Šustrová, Petr Uhl, and Jan Urban.

Finally, I want to thank my wife Ann McGlashan and my daughter Catriona McGlashan Long for allowing me the time and providing encouragement to complete this project.

Introduction

The idea of an oral history project based on memoirs of former Czech dissidents emerged as a result of my research into the life of Václav Havel, the president of the Czech Republic from December 1989 to February 2003. The collapse of Czechoslovakia's Communist government during what is now known as the Velvet Revolution of 1989 catapulted Havel to the presidency. When I began my research on Havel, I was primarily interested in converting what I had learned into a screenplay for a feature film. Of course, my research on Havel yielded much more material than I could use in a script for a two-hour film. After all, the story should focus on Havel's life, not the complete life experiences of all of his associates in the twenty years since 1968.

My research on Havel revealed to me the depth and breadth of the dissident movement in Czechoslovakia since 1968—the year when tanks of the Warsaw Pact nations rolled into Prague in the attempt to crush developing liberal socialism. During the repressive years of the postinvasion Communist regime of Czechoslovakia, Havel's voice was one among many comprising the chorus calling for the state to acknowledge and protect internationally recognized basic human rights. In reading the works of other scholars—historians, political analysts, journalists, as well as Havel's essays and published interviews—I developed a deep respect and admiration for those other voices, the voices of those who struggled alongside Havel but who lacked his international celebrity.

The dissident community in Czechoslovakia between 1968 and 1989 was a diverse group of individuals. Among them were a large number of writers—novelists, poets, journalists—as well as other artists—actors, theater and film directors, painters, photographers, and musicians. These individuals resisted the regime, at least initially, primarily due to restrictions imposed by the state on their creative, artistic freedom. Other dissidents were reform-minded Communists, some of whom had held positions in government and civil service, who, having been tainted by the "liberalism" of the Dubček regime prior to 1968, found themselves ostracized from political life in the invasion's aftermath.

Academics from various fields comprised another category of dissident. Many of these individuals, some also committed Communists, found themselves at odds with the regime after 1968 and were removed from their positions in higher education, or left their positions voluntarily in protest against politics by invasion.

Still others, devout persons from both the clergy and the laity, found their way into the community of dissidents due to their religious convictions and opposition to the regime's policy toward religion and religious organizations. A final category of dissident was comprised of individuals from various backgrounds, who for whatever reason, refused to capitulate to the regime and simply chose to live "underground."

All of these people, with differing points of conflict with the regime, came together united with one purpose: to reform or remove the socialist government of Czechoslovakia. The various groups had no formal affiliations among themselves but associated and cooperated with each other freely in dealing with issues where they shared common interests and beliefs.

My goal for this project, therefore, was to interview some of the former dissidents. To be honest, this project was motivated, at least partially, by my own desire to meet these outstanding human beings. I also had the conviction that their stories needed to be told, needed to become known to a larger audience; and who better to tell the story than the people themselves, without interpretation and analysis.

In addition, the timing of this project seemed right. At the time of the interviews in 1998, almost ten years had passed since the opening of the Berlin Wall in November 1989, and the subsequent breaking of the Communist stranglehold on the nations of so-called "eastern" Europe, including Czechoslovakia. Human beings have an inherent need to mark the passage of time. Virtually all human cultures, no matter how primitive or advanced, observe anniversaries of births, marriages, deaths, and life-changing events, e.g., battles, armistices, epidemics, and the like. Czechoslovakia's Velvet Revolution in 1989 was a life-changing event, both a birth and a death at once. The old, repressive regime met its death, making way for the birth of a new nation.

Contained in this volume are the personal narratives of eleven individuals who had some part in this life-changing event of a nation. The narratives are based on interviews I conducted in Prague and Berlin in July and October 1998. In addition to presenting cold historical fact, the interviews provide a format for reassessing and evaluating the events of fall 1989 in intensely personal terms. Together, the narratives present an oral history of events prior to, during, and after the Velvet Revolution.

The concept of "oral history" is not well known or understood in the Czech Republic. After a brief explanation of the purpose of the interview, virtually all persons contacted for an interview consented without hesitation. On a few occasions, interviewees commented how interesting it was that a foreigner, an

American, was delving into this particular chapter in their lives and the life of their nation, while most Czechs were uninterested, indifferent, or ambivalent. Only on one occasion did a potential interviewee demand monetary compensation before consenting to the interview. Not having funding for that purpose, I declined the request and moved on.

Of course any number of persons could have been interviewed for this project. A variety of factors affected the selection of this particular set of interviewees. I knew some of their names from previous reading and research on the Communist era of Czechoslovakia and my research on Havel. Others were recommended by my contacts in Prague. The availability and willingness of each person to be interviewed were, however, the deciding factors. The omission of any person who might have made a significant contribution to this project is neither by design nor purpose.

The interviews are structured around three primary questions. I asked each person to begin his or her narrative with a brief biographical sketch—to talk about family history, childhood, and education. This question put most of the interviewees at ease and allowed them a large amount of control in the interview, which is important when trying to obtain a memoir rather than a rehearsed answer. In some cases, the answer to the first question led seamlessly into the answer to the second and third questions.

Following the biographical sketch, I asked each person to focus on his or her life and experiences leading up to and during the Velvet Revolution. Finally, I asked each person to reflect on the years since the revolution and to evaluate it in terms of its accomplishments and perceived failures. This question allowed the interviewees the chance to provide their own analysis of the political, social, economic, and cultural development of the Czech Republic in its transformation to a market economy and democratic form of government. In follow-up questions I invited the interviewee to comment further on topics particular to that person's narrative.

As a Slavist who has studied socialism as practiced in the Soviet Bloc for more than two decades, I have always been intrigued by how a person growing up in such a society began to feel in conflict with the regime and made the decision to act in opposition to the regime. How is it, for example, that some citizens blindly accepted everything the state-controlled media told them about capitalism and Western societies in general, while others at some point began to lose their blinders and open themselves to doubt. In other words, what incident or event turned the thinking of a potential dissident, eventually leading that person to live in defiance of the regime and join the underground? During my interviews, this topic or episode in the person's life often emerged spontaneously. When it did not, I posed the question directly.

Chapter one is an introductory essay in which I attempt to fill in some of the gaps of information not explicitly covered in the interview narratives. The essay focuses on a few key moments in Czechoslovakia's history between 1968 and 1989, including the Prague Spring, the 1968 Warsaw Pact invasion, the emergence of the dissident movement, Charter 77, and finally, some of the significant events of 1989. The interview narratives comprise chapters two through twelve, each devoted to the memoir of a single individual. In chapter thirteen, I discuss the phenomenon of dissent in Czechoslovakia and make some comparisons between the opinions of the interviewees with the views of the Czech public in regard to the transition to democracy, the market economy, and other issues.

The narratives are edited versions of the printed transcripts of the interviews. In editing the interviews for publication I followed two main principles: first, to preserve each person's unique voice and style of discourse; and second, to make the narratives conform to idiomatic English insofar as I did not violate the first principle. I have retained the Czech language titles of newspapers, magazines, journals, and names of organizations as they were mentioned followed by the English translation. I have also added a few footnotes to provide identification of persons mentioned by name, as well as the names of various organizations.

In preparing this volume, I entertained a couple of ideas for its structure. One idea—and it was indeed suggested to me by colleagues and others—was to organize the chapters around specific themes, e.g., Prague Spring, life as a dissident, the Velvet Revolution, combining perspectives from various interviewees relevant to the given topic. This type of structure would seem logical and appropriate, but in practice it did not serve one of the most important aims of the entire work: to preserve the voice and narration of each individual interviewed. In the thematic structure, the interviewee, i.e., the person, the storyteller, virtually disappeared. After writing two chapters in this manner, I abandoned the thematic structure in favor of a structure in which each chapter is comprised of a single person's narrative. This type of structure preserves each narrator's voice, and at the same time provides a comprehensive view of events from a single perspective. This method served a second aim for the volume, which was to limit my own intrusion into the narratives, to present each narrative without analysis and without editorializing.

I ask the reader to bear in mind that this volume represents for the most part an oral memoir. The exactness of historical fact should not be the main criterion in evaluating the information contained in the narratives. As an oral history, it is based on memory, and it is well documented that the memory of human beings is faulty. Human beings forget facts, but what they do not forget are their personal feelings, emotions, and reactions to historic events and facts. Evaluate the narratives on that basis, and your intellectual curiosity will be rewarded.

Complete printed transcripts and audiotapes of the interviews are available for further research in the Institute for Oral History at Baylor University.

Waco, Texas, April 2004

1

Dissidence in Czechoslovakia, 1968-1989

We believe that Charter 77 will help to enable all the citizens of Czechoslovakia to work and live as free human beings.
—Charter 77 Declaration, 1977[1]

The interviews presented in the following chapters contain a number of references to events, personalities, and organizations that played major roles in shaping the lives not only of the interviewees, but of other dissidents, as well as the general Czech-Slovak population. A straightforward presentation of the interviews without a historical context would assume a large amount of historical knowledge on the part of the reader and deprive the interviews of their full significance and impact.

Indeed, the interviewees often refer to a key event only by the year in which it occurred and to organizations only by initials and acronyms. Without a historical perspective, a reader unversed in the history of Czechoslovakia between 1968 and 1989 would remain confused and deprived of a means of interpreting the information imparted in the interviews.

What follows, therefore, is a brief summary of certain key events which shaped the development of a political opposition and an active dissident community in Czechoslovakia between 1968 and 1989.

Prague Spring

In the story of the revolution in Czechoslovakia in 1989 and the individuals who helped bring it about, the events of 1968 played a pivotal and profound role. In the spring of that year, the Czechoslovak Communist Party (CCP), under the leadership of General Secretary Alexander Dubček, implemented a number of reforms intended to liberalize Czechoslovak society. The reforms undertaken by

1

the Communist leadership and the resulting effect on Czechoslovak society are now collectively referred to as the "Prague Spring."

As outlined in the "action program" of the CCP in April 1968, the reforms encompassed greater freedoms for the press and assembly; expanded trade with Western countries and the parameters of private enterprise; and the revision of electoral laws, among other things. The program also pledged to achieve federal status for Slovakia and to codify this change in status in a new constitution by the end of 1969. In addition, the Central Committee pledged to rehabilitate all persons persecuted unjustly from 1949 to 1954. Premier Oldřich Černík presented the program to the National Assembly on 24 April.[2]

One minor reform that seemed more than any other to incite harsh criticism from other East Bloc nations, was the abolition of advance or prepublication censorship. Passed in June 1968, the law made editors and managers of newspapers, journals, and radio and television broadcasts responsible for the content of their publications and programming. As a result, the editors of the prestigious *Literární listy*[3] [*Literary pages*] seized on the opportunity to publish on 27 June the "Two Thousand Words to Workers, Scientists, Artists and Everyone," authored by Ludvík Vaculík. The "Two Thousand Words Manifesto," as the document is commonly known, presented an eloquent rebuke of the Communist Party for losing sight of the people's interests in exchange for maintaining power: "The leaderships' incorrect line turned the party from a political party and ideological alliance into a power organization which became very attractive to egoists avid for rule, calculating cowards, and people with bad consciences."[4] However, the manifesto claimed support for the party as long as the party remained true to the process of democratization and offered suggestions as to how the process might be carried out.

The timing of the law to abolish advance censorship together with the publication of the "Two Thousand Words Manifesto" could not have been more inopportune. Following the visit of a high-level Soviet military delegation in May, the Czech government announced that Warsaw Pact[5] nations would conduct joint military exercises in Czechoslovakia 20-30 June. While estimates of Soviet troop strength in the exercises range widely, it is clear that several thousand remained in the country despite the passing of various deadlines for their departure; they finally left as late as 3 August.[6] In hindsight, the military exercises had the quality of a dress rehearsal for the full-scale invasion which occurred only seventeen days later.

Fearing the Czech reforms would stir up envy and unrest among their own populations, governments of the other Warsaw Pact nations resoundingly denounced the 1968 reforms. Indeed, Polish university students had already staged protests demanding reforms in line with the Prague Spring.[7] Communist Party officials in neighboring countries used every opportunity to heap vitriolic criticism onto Dubček and the Czechoslovak Communist Party leadership and government. The Czech press answered the criticisms swiftly, warning Czechoslovakia's neighbors to refrain from interference in Czech internal affairs.

In spite of attempts by the Dubček government to reassure its neighbors that the country was neither allying itself with the Federal Republic of Germany (FRG), nor abandoning its commitment to the Warsaw Pact, tensions continued to rise. The Soviet Union finally proposed a meeting between the Soviet Politburo and the Czechoslovak Party Presidium. After some negotiation, Dubček agreed to a meeting in the far eastern corner of Czechoslovakia in Čierna-nad-Tisou, a small railway junction near the Soviet border, beginning 29 July and ending on 1 August 1968.

Journalists from both East and West were barred from reporting on the proceedings. From the scant reports which leaked from the "talks," the Czech delegation apparently held its ground against strong Soviet pressure to turn back the clock on democratization and allow the stationing of Soviet troops on Czech soil along the border with the FRG. The final communiqué addressing the outcome of the conference was issued from Bratislava on 3 August, after ratification by representatives from Bulgaria, Poland, East Germany, and Hungary. The communiqué stressed that the creation of a socialist society would continue in Czechoslovakia "on the basis of the principles of equality, respect for sovereignty, and national independence, territorial integrity, fraternal mutual assistance and solidarity."[8]

The Czech delegation left Čierna with virtually the entire reform program intact, confident they had finally achieved some measure of autonomy and assurances that Pact member-states would refrain from further criticism and would cease meddling in Czechoslovak internal affairs. Their confidence was short-lived.

Warsaw Pact Intervention

During the night of 20 August 1968, combined armies from the Soviet Union, Poland, Hungary, East Germany, and Bulgaria moved across the borders into Czechoslovakia, swiftly occupied Prague, and effectively ended the experiment in liberalizing socialism known as the Prague Spring.

The Czechoslovak citizenry met the invasion at first in a state of bewilderment and stunned disbelief, but encouraged and supported by Dubček and the party leadership quickly sprang into an active campaign of nonviolent resistance. Knowing armed resistance was futile and fearing a bloodbath similar to that of the Hungarian uprising of 1956, the Dubček government encouraged the population to adopt a program of passive resistance. At about 1:00 A.M. on 21 August, the Presidium of the Czechoslovak Communist Party Central Committee issued a proclamation which called upon "all citizens of the Republic to keep the peace and not resist the advancing armies, because the defense of our state borders is now impossible."[9] Although the proclamation was broadcast several times, the transmitter had been turned off on the orders of the director of central communications, so that the majority of listeners never heard the complete statement.

Václav Havel, the future president, was visiting friends in Liberec in north-western Bohemia when the invasion took place. In *Disturbing the Peace*, Havel relates that during the first week following the invasion, he wrote commentary which was read on local radio broadcasts by actor Jan Tříska. Together, Havel and Tříska kept the population within their broadcast range informed of events and read government proclamations carried over the still-functioning wire services.[10]

Resistance to the invasion and occupation took many forms. Ordinary Czech citizens—workers, shoppers, housewives, students—confronted soldiers directly in the streets and attempted to reason with them, to persuade them to turn their tanks around and head home. Mass demonstrations were held in the center of Prague. Students and others erected barricades and attacked the tanks with Molotov cocktails[11] and virtually any other object that could be lifted and thrown, including bottles, stones, and even mattresses. Resisters sabotaged railways to halt the transport of military equipment and supplies from the Soviet Union and either painted over or removed road and street signs to confuse the invading troops.

Dramatic scenes of Czech citizens in confrontation with confused soldiers of the invading armies played on television screens around the world. Jan Němec, an aspiring young Czech filmmaker, captured the invasion and acts of resistance and confrontation in his moving documentary film *Oratorio for Prague*.[12] Initially, the invasion forces seemed reluctant to use force against the local population. As the days passed, however, frustrated and embattled tank commanders assumed a more forceful attitude. A report issued on 12 September 1968, by the Paris Bureau of the Assembly of Captive Nations in Europe, concluded 186 citizens were killed and 362 seriously wounded in the first week of the invasion.[13]

On the day of the invasion, Soviet agents arrested Dubček and four other members of the Czechoslovak government and Communist Party Presidium at Central Committee headquarters and forcibly shuttled them out of the country to Moscow for "talks." The detainees were later joined in Moscow by president of the republic Ludvík Svoboda, vice chairman of the government Gustáv Husák, and several other party and government functionaries.

Negotiations between the Czechoslovak delegation and their Soviet counterparts continued until 26 August, and the Czechoslovak delegation returned to Prague on 27 August. The actual terms of the agreement reached in Moscow were revealed only partially in notes secretly smuggled home by members of the Czechoslovak delegation and in later speeches by government officials. One curious provision of the agreement was that its terms should remain secret. While Dubček and Svoboda still pledged the party's commitment to the democratization process, they had to make several key concessions, including the stationing of Soviet troops along Czechoslovakia's border with the FRG and the restoration of press censorship.[14]

Recently unsealed and declassified documents reveal that the Soviet military and its Pact allies were already making preparations for an invasion of

Czechoslovakia even while the Čierna conference was being planned. General Karoly Csemi, chief of the Hungarian People's Army General Staff, met with Soviet generals Konstantin Provalov and Fedor Marushchak on 24 July. The purpose of the meeting, according to Csemi's notes, was to secure Hungary's commitment of one division to the invasion, in order to "help the Czechoslovak people to [*sic*] defeat the counterrevolution."[15]

1968 and the Impact on the Collective Psyche

The 1968 invasion of Czechoslovakia dealt a devastating blow to the collective psyche of its people. For many citizens, the invasion was a life-changing event. For those loyal to Dubček and supportive of the reform process, the invasion defied reasonable explanation, shattered the notion of "socialist brotherhood," and spelled disillusionment and disappointment. For others, namely, the nation's academic, cultural, and artistic elite, it meant the abandonment of hope for an intellectual life free from government interference.

Both the bulk of the reforms associated with the Prague Spring and the invasion took place in the same year, 1968. Contemporary Czechs and Slovaks reference the two events differently. "Prague Spring" is the label applied in reference to the positive reform aspects of cultural and political life experienced in 1968 in Czechoslovakia. In reference to the invasion and the painful memories of 1968, the term "sixty-eight" is used.

Among Czechs and Slovaks, the mere mention of "sixty-eight" in conversation evokes memories of an era of intense emotion, feelings of elation and celebration juxtaposed with disappointment and betrayal. Much as Americans of a certain age retain a distinct memory of when and where they heard the news of President John F. Kennedy's assassination, Czechs and Slovaks retain vivid memories of the first days of the invasion. Indeed "sixty-eight" proved an emotional and philosophical turning point in the lives of the eleven people whose personal narratives are collected in this volume. The narratives presented in the following chapters show that the long-term effects of the invasion and its aftermath are incalculable and have ramifications into the present. It is no wonder that in the early days of the Velvet Revolution in 1989, the opposition contemplated and weighed virtually every move, every strategy, against the events and outcome of 1968.

The Prague Spring proved to be a watershed for Czechoslovak culture and gained admiration and encouragement for the country's leaders from the West. Artists, filmmakers, and writers, who had steadily gained international recognition and acclaim through the mid-1960s, were finally able to enjoy their celebrity in their homeland. Czech New Wave film directors set trends and garnered Academy Award nominations and Oscars. Ján Kadár's film *The Shop on Main Street* dealt with the Jewish Holocaust in Slovakia and won the Oscar for Best Foreign Language film in 1965. Miloš Forman's "coming of age" story *Loves of a Blond* received an Oscar nomination in the same category in 1966. Jiří Menzel followed with a win in the same category in 1967 for his film adaptation of *Closely Watched Trains*, based on the Bohumil Hrabal novel of the same name, both now considered classics of Czech film and literature. Václav Havel, the playwright, enjoyed the success of his play *The Memorandum* in an Off-Broadway production starring Olympia Dukakis and won an Obie for the Best Foreign Language Play in 1968.[16] Czechoslovak rock bands and jazz ensembles gained a national and international following and were widely regarded as avant-garde.

If the Prague Spring represents a time of euphoria in the political and social history of Czechoslovakia, then the following two decades were in many ways a time of depression.

Normalization

The immediate aftermath of the August invasion involved the "realignment" of Czechoslovakia with the Soviet Union and its Warsaw Pact allies, a process termed "Normalization" in the political parlance of the time. Having embarked on an independent path of reforming socialism, Czechoslovakia had behaved much like an impudent and disobedient child; now the nation would have to be disciplined.

Pravda, the official newspaper of the Communist Party of the Soviet Union, defined Normalization as "the complete exposure of the right-wing, anti-Socialist forces; the elimination of their influence on a part of the population, and especially the youth; the resolute strengthening of the leading role of the Communist Party in the activities of the state agencies, in the ideological and public sphere, in the whole life of the country."[17] On the state level, Normalization required the reshuffling of the government in order to accommodate Soviet demands and the installation of a leadership loyal to Soviet hegemony. While Dubček retained his position until April 1969, when first secretary of the Slovak Communist Party Gustáv Husák replaced him, several events transpired leading up to his demise, which had far-reaching consequences for the nation.

The governments of the Soviet Union and Czechoslovakia established by treaty the withdrawal of non-Soviet Warsaw Pact troops and the "temporary" stationing of Soviet troops on Czechoslovak soil "with the aim of consolidating defenses against growing revanchist efforts by West German militarist forces."[18] The treaty, consisting of fifteen articles, was ratified both by the Czechoslovak National Assembly and the Presidium of the Supreme Soviet of the USSR on 18 October 1968. Soviet troops were to remain in Czechoslovakia until their withdrawal was negotiated in the heady days of the Velvet Revolution in 1989, behind-the-scenes details of which are provided by Michael Kocáb (chapter four).

Normalization and the Emergence of Dissidence

The quasi-permanent stationing of Soviet troops in the country provoked enormous protest among the population which demanded the complete withdrawal of troops, and also at times, the restoration of key points of the reform program, namely the relaxation of censorship and freedom of assembly. An active and vocal student movement emerged which took an uncompromising stand against the curtailment of hard-won freedoms by mounting strikes and passing out leaflets and flyers. For their stance, many students, including Petruška Šustrová (chapter ten), lost their right to study and endured prison sentences.

The single most important event associated with the Soviet occupation transpired on 16 January 1969. Jan Palach, a student at Charles University, set himself on fire on Prague's central Wenceslas Square. Palach died three days later. His death initiated a wave of protests, demonstrations, public appeals, and other acts of civil disobedience. The apparent inability of the Dubček regime to control the situation convinced the Soviets that the Czechoslovak government needed a stronger hand. Dubček, forced to tender his resignation, disappeared from public life until 1989, when he reemerged for a brief return to politics.[19] Husák assumed the party's leadership position and remained in power until December 1989. Thus began for the intellectual life of the nation what Václav Havel has called a "long period of moribund silence."[20]

Palach's act of self-sacrifice, though it did not lead to the immediate withdrawal of Soviet troops, provided an emotional center for the oppressed political opposition, which continued to have an impact up to the revolution of 1989. Palach assumed his position in the pantheon of Czech national heroes alongside Bohemia's tenth-century king Svatý Václav [St. Wenceslas] and the fourteenth-century preacher and reformer Jan Hus,[21] both martyred for their faith and acts of resistance. During the long years of Normalization, Palach's death gave the opposition a cause around which they could hold public memorial demonstrations, and no government dared refuse permission. Indeed, the eventful year of 1989 began in Prague with the arrest of several dissidents due to their—in some cases alleged—participation in events associated with an official "Palach Week" in January.

In practical terms, Normalization meant that no one who had embraced and promoted the reform movement in any public activity—politicians, journalists, filmmakers, academics, writers, and students, among others—could be allowed to continue in those activities. Consequently, hundreds of people found themselves either officially excluded from practicing their profession, or at least forced into the position of compromising their personal ethics and professional integrity in order to survive in the new political reality. The proverbial "housecleaning" undertaken by the regime, mandated by Legislative Measure 99/1969, meant that "at least three-quarters of a million citizens, or about 2 million people if their households are included, lost their jobs or were demoted or seriously discriminated against."[22] Conformity with the postinvasion ideology was a choice many intellectuals, including those whose stories appear in this volume, were not prepared to accept.

Nonconformity with the process of Normalization in all of its phases and guises almost certainly meant leading a life in professional isolation, outside of official society. Living a life of nonconformity with regard to the prevailing political dogma meant, therefore, leading the life of a dissident. The only other option was emigration.

The dissident community that emerged and evolved during the period of Normalization, processes which continued right up to the Velvet Revolution, was multifaceted and developed its own ethics and standards of behavior, as well as its own culture, which are illuminated through the narratives presented here. The term "dissident" is politically charged, and many of the individuals now considered to have been dissidents during the Husák era resist acceptance of the label. Václav Havel remarks that he and others sometimes used the term themselves, "although it is done with distaste, rather ironically, and almost always in quotation marks." "In fact, a 'dissident'," Havel continues, "is simply a physicist, a sociologist, a worker, a poet, individuals who are merely doing what they feel they must and, consequently, find themselves in open conflict with the regime."[23] In the case of the Czechoslovak opposition, the so-called "dissidents" made it a point to act strictly within the law. This was especially true after the Helsinki Conference of 1975 and the founding of Charter 77, topics I will explore in more detail below. Nevertheless, and with all due respect to Havel's point of view, I use the term here for lack of a better one and with no emphasis on the objectionable connotations of its meaning.

The Underground

Those persons who suddenly found themselves ostracized, punished, or discriminated against by the regime through the process of Normalization, or, one might say, in a "dissident" position with regard to the regime, responded to the new, postinvasion politics in a number of ways. Many, such as Václav Havel and others who either found their work banned or found themselves banned from working, went into a self-imposed exile, finding professional or personal fulfillment in other ways. Havel worked several months in a brewery. Eda Kriseová (chapter five), a popular journalist before the invasion, found fulfillment assisting the medical staff of a provincial institution for the mentally ill. Others earned a living—not always by choice—in menial jobs as bricklayers, furnace stokers, security guards, window washers, groundskeepers, janitors, and the like.

At the same time, groups emerged centered around intellectual or cultural activities that dissidents were otherwise officially banned from pursuing. Writers banned from publishing, actors and others attended miniconferences hosted by Václav Havel and his wife Olga at their country cottage, and at times even staged productions of Havel's plays. Literary works gathered partially from those presented at the writers' conferences and from other sources were copied, bound, and distributed in two *samizdat*[24] series: the aptly named *Edice Petlice* known in English as *Padlock Press*, initiated by Ludvík Vaculík in 1972, and *Edice Expedice* [*Expedition Edition*] started by Havel in 1975. The duplication and distribution of the two *samizdat* collections required careful supervision and entailed a certain amount of risk. In the late 1970s, Ivan Havel (chapter two) and his wife Daša Havlová assumed the responsibility for the reproduction and distribution of the *Expedition Edition*. Vaculík continued publication of *Edice Petlice* until 1979, when he relinquished the majority of the responsibilities to the authors themselves.[25]

The dissemination of *samizdat* material abroad, first to Great Britain and from there further afield, was primarily arranged by the Czech émigré community. Jan Kavan, who had been active in the student movement of 1968, established Palach Press, Ltd. in 1976 in London.[26] Kavan managed to organize a network of secret couriers and drivers in disguised vehicles to transport a variety of materials—*samizdat* literature, as well as letters and other messages—to and from Czechoslovakia throughout the late 1970s and 1980s. Jiřina Šiklová (chapter nine) functioned for several years as an underground courier between Palach Press and the Czech dissident community until her arrest in 1981.

In addition to writers' gatherings, the Havels also hosted musical events. The Plastic People of the Universe played concerts in the barn belonging to theater director Andrej Krob, a neighbor of the Havels. The Plastics were one of a number of avant-garde rock and jazz bands of increasing popularity through the 1970s, including the groups DG 307, Alea jazz, Adept, and Michael Kocáb's group *Pražský výběr* [Prague's Choice].

In the musical underground of the early 1970s, Plastics manager Ivan "Magor" Jirous was the acknowledged expert on the underground music scene and the author of the unpublished *Report on the Third Czech Musical Revival*.[27] Václav Havel became acquainted with Jirous and the music of the Plastics in early 1976, thus beginning a long association which was to play a historic role in the future lives of dissidents, the lives of the Plastics, and ultimately in the future of the Communist regime.

The Plastics formed in 1969 and was comprised of a number of musicians over the next ten years. Their style of composition and performance was diametrically opposed to the sentimental, romantic style of the "officially" sanctioned crooner Karel Gott and other popular singers and bands. Nor did the Plastics' music find much in common with mainstream jazz of the same period. The Plastics' compositions are characterized by dissonant, percussion-driven music—often without an obvious melodic line and little harmony—supported by blaring and, at times, jarring tones from brass and wind instruments. The Plastics made a name for themselves by setting literary texts of unconventional writers to music, e.g., Egon Bondy (pseudonym of Zbyněk Fišer) and Kurt Vonnegut, their irreverence toward socialist values, and their use of slang and mild profanity. While I do not intend to introduce here a comprehensive analysis of the Plastics' music, a couple of examples of their songs prove illustrative. An example of a typical Plastics song is *"Komu je dnes dvacet"* ["The Twenty-year-old Today"]:

Komu je dnes dvacet	Whoever is twenty today,
chce se mu hnusem zvracet	Feels like throwing up from disgust,
Ale těm co je čtyřicet	But those in their forties
je toho vyblít ještě vice	Want to puke even more.
Jen ten co mu je šedesát	Only the sixty-year-old
může jít se sklerózou klidně spát	Can nurse his sclerosis in bed.
Když je člověku dnes dvacet	But whoever is twenty today,
chce se mu hnusem zvracet	Only hurls with disgust.[28]

While at first glance the lyrics might seem mildly raucous or indelicate to the outsider, the subtle political references were obvious to Czech listeners of the 1960s and 1970s. Twenty-, forty-, and sixty-year-olds are indexical references to critical moments in Czechoslovakia's history. Considering the time of the song's writing, the generation of twenty-year-olds bore witness to 1968 and Normalization. Their parents, the forty-year-olds, were themselves youths when Czechoslovakia became Communist after the elections of 1948. The sixty-year-olds were the youth of the nation when Czechoslovakia became a Protectorate of the Third Reich in 1938. Indeed, each generation had seen its hopes and dreams demolished by political forces beyond its control.

In another song, *"Mír"* ["Peace"] which lasts one minute twenty-three seconds, the two lines of lyric are sung in the last five seconds:

Mír, mír, mír	Peace, peace, peace
Jako hajzlpapír.	Is like shit-house paper.[29]

In Czech, the word *mír*, "peace," finds its rhyme with the final syllable of *hajzlpapír*, "shit-house paper." The ridicule of official propaganda and Communist jingoism expressed in these two lines of "Peace" is unmistakable. Combining unconventional texts and music with unconventional performance, the Plastics struck a chord (pardon the pun) with disenchanted youth—the twenty-year-olds—who flocked to their concerts.

The State versus Plastic People of the Universe

The State Security Police, *Státní Bezpečnost* or *StB*, began taking an interest in the Plastics at the end of 1971 and the beginning of 1972.[30] The Plastics failed to achieve official sanction for their public performances after auditions before a jury of the Prague Cultural Center in 1973. There is evidence to suggest that officials of the Prague Cultural Center, in making their final decision, might have yielded to pressure from either state authorities or Communist Party officials. While the center initially recognized the Plastics' "professional qualifications," the band received the final rejection notice fifteen days after the audition.[31] The lack of official endorsement from the Prague Cultural Center did not prevent the band from performing per se but made their bookings more complicated. Ultimately the band was banned from performing inside the Prague city limits and only at ostensibly private events, such as weddings, baptisms, birthday parties, and the like, or in small-town pubs, often sharing the stage with other groups. Very often the venue merely served as a pretext for a concert. *StB* harassment increased over time; on more than one occasion, police broke up concerts and harassed concertgoers and fans. In March 1976, the StB broke up a Plastics concert and arrested a total of nineteen musicians and fans. While the StB released most of the original detainees, the state prosecuted band members Svatopluk Karásek, Vratislav Brabenec, and Pavel Zajíček along with their manager, Ivan Jirous. The trial took place in September 1976. Jirous was sentenced to eighteen months in prison, Zajíček twelve months, and Karásek and Brabenec eight months suspended for time served in pretrial detention.[32]

The state's case against the Plastics was flimsy at best, even according to totalitarian standards. Band member Milan Hlavsa, one of those arrested in March 1976, relates the following incident that took place before his release from jail. A state procurator inquired of him whether his detention had been properly conducted. When he replied that it was "child's play," she informed him the arrest was the result of an alleged disturbance caused by the Plastics at a concert two weeks earlier in Bojanovice. When Hlavsa answered he had no knowledge of a disturbance, the procurator replied, "But Mr. Hlavsa, you sang some songs. And wasn't the word *prdel* [ass] used, for example?" Hlavsa replied affirmatively. "That's enough for me," answered the procurator and signed the order remanding him to prison to await trial.[33]

The arrest and eventual trial of the Plastics proved to be a needed catalyst to unite dissidents of various backgrounds and points of view. Věra Jirousová (chapter three), then wife of Ivan Jirous, and Dana Němcová (chapter seven), wife of Plastics supporter and underground activist Jiří Němec, acted as managers for the Plastics while Jirous was in prison at various times.

The dissident community responded to the Plastics' arrest and trial swiftly and decisively. Václav Havel viewed the persecution of the Plastics as an assault on the entire society and an indicator of the regime's capacity for cruelty:

> The objects of this attack were not veterans of old political battles; they had no political past, or even any well-defined political positions. They were simply young people who wanted to live in their own way, to make music they liked, to sing what they wanted to sing, to live in harmony with themselves, and to express themselves in a truthful way. A judicial attack against them, especially one that went unnoticed, could become the precedent for something truly evil: the regime could well start locking up everyone who thought independently and who expressed himself independently, even if he did so only in private. So these arrests were genuinely alarming: they were an attack on the spiritual and intellectual freedom of man, camouflaged as an attack on criminality, and therefore designed to gain support from a disinformed public.[34]

Havel and Němec quickly organized a public campaign for the defense of the Plastics through the circulation of a petition protesting the detention of the band's members. The campaign not only achieved the immediate goal of attracting international media attention to the case of the Plastics, but, as Havel states, "through newly established contacts and friendships . . . the main opposition circles, hitherto isolated from each other, came together informally."[35] Thus, the campaign had the unforeseen effect of uniting the dissident community around a common cause, which could be developed or molded into real opposition to the regime.

During the Plastics' trial, supporters and well-wishers packed the corridors and stairwells outside the courtroom. Those gathered shouted greetings and assurances to the prisoners as they filed past in handcuffs into the courtroom. In the corridors of the district courthouse on Prague's Karmelitská Street, the Plastics' supporters—dissidents from across the spectrum of experience and opinion—in muffled conversation planned their strategy for further cooperation, for as Havel states, "something had happened here, something that should not be allowed simply to evaporate and disappear but which ought to be transformed into some kind of action that would have a more permanent impact, one that would bring this something out of the air onto solid ground."[36]

The involvement of Havel and other dissidents in the case of the Plastics changed the nature of "dissidence" in Czechoslovakia. Prior to the Plastics' trial, dissidence had been primarily a solitary mode of existence, i.e., an individual engaged in his or her personal conflict with the state. The Plastics' arrest gave dissidents an issue, a cause for which they could exercise collective protest and take collective action against the state. Thus, dissidence moved out of the strictly private, personal arena into the broader struggle for the protection of human rights in the public arena.

Charter 77 and Collective Dissidence

The "action" of which Havel speaks was the establishment of Charter 77. At the conclusion of the Plastics' trial, several persons who had worked to publicize the injustice done to a handful of musicians began meeting to formulate what was eventually to become Charter 77. Among attendees at these meetings were, besides Havel and Němec, Zdeněk Mlynář, Pavel Kohout, Petr Uhl, Jiří Hájek, and Ludvík Vaculík. Zdeněk Mlynář, a political scientist, was in 1968 a member of the Presidium of the Central Committee of the Communist Party of Czechoslovakia. Pavel Kohout was a playwright, political writer, and translator. Petr Uhl (chapter eleven) was a journalist and leftist reformer, a self-proclaimed "Trotskyist." Jiří Hájek, in addition to being a politician and diplomat, had served the Dubček regime as minister of foreign affairs at the time of the invasion. This core group—with the advice and counsel of many others—agreed on the aims and structure of Charter 77 and produced a manifesto in which those aims were spelled out.

The Charter 77 Declaration was a simple, straightforward document. The declaration started from the basic precept that the Czechoslovak government was a signatory to both the International Covenant on Civil and Political Rights and the International Covenant on Economic, Social and Cultural Rights. These international covenants—confirmed at the Helsinki Conference on Security and Cooperation in Europe in 1975—were part of Czechoslovakia's legal code and in force since 23 March 1976.[37] The declaration states categorically that "Charter 77 is not an organization; it has no rules, permanent bodies or formal membership."[38] Charter 77 is described as a citizens' initiative working on behalf of the public interest with the aim of conducting constructive dialogue with the political and state authorities, preparing documentation, and suggesting solutions in particular cases where human or civil rights were violated, and acting as a mediator in conflict situations.

The declaration enumerated a number of specific articles of the two named international covenants which state authorities routinely violated, including the "freedom of public expression," i.e., the continued censorship of any view that deviated from the official ideology, and the "freedom of religious confession." Moreover, the declaration cited the Ministry of the Interior's repeated violation of the prohibitions against interference in the privacy of the family, home, or correspondence by the practices of electronic eavesdropping, opening the mail of private citizens, conducting home searches, and establishing networks of neighborhood informants.

The framers of Charter 77 decided on a loose structure of administration, only choosing three persons who would function as *mluvčí*, or "speaker," for the charter. Václav Havel, Jiří Hájek, and Jan Patočka volunteered as the first speakers and were so identified in the declaration. The declaration gave the speakers full authority to represent the charter and its signatories in relations with state authorities and with the public and to attest with their signature to the authenticity of documents prepared and issued in the charter's name.

The State versus Charter 77

Having completed the text of the declaration, the framers carried out a campaign of collecting signatures in support of the declaration. In the first round, 243 signatures were collected. Havel and actor Pavel Landovský were to deliver the text of the declaration with a list of signatories to the Federal Assembly and government offices, and at the same time mail a copy of the declaration to each signatory. On the appointed delivery date, 6 January 1977, Havel, Landovský, and Vaculík, who just happened to drop in on Havel that morning, set out with the documents. But the StB, tipped off to the plan, was fully prepared to intercept the delivery. When Havel et al. departed, StB agents pursued them in a car chase through Prague, worthy of the best Hollywood action films. The StB ultimately prevailed; the three were arrested, interrogated, then released, and the copies of the declaration were confiscated. Over the next several days, Havel,

Hájek, Patočka, and others were repeatedly summoned back to StB headquarters in Bartolomějská Street for further questioning.[39]

The interrogations, sometimes lasting as long as ten hours, took their toll. The StB investigators targeted the three speakers especially. Of the three, Patočka suffered the most, due to his age, for which the StB showed no regard. Jan Patočka was a philosopher of tremendous renown in Czechoslovakia. Born in 1907, he started his teaching career at Charles University in 1936. After their takeover in 1948, the Communists expelled him from the university. Patočka returned to Charles University for a brief period in 1968 but was finally forced into retirement in 1972 under the pressures of Normalization. Patočka was held in high esteem, not only by the organizers of the charter, but also by hundreds of former students, as well as the dissident community at large. He had played an enormous and influential role in the ongoing private seminars of the so-called flying university described later. He had consented to be a charter speaker only after repeated visits and personal appeals by Havel and Jiří Němec.

The StB finally arrested Havel on 14 January 1977, and continued to interrogate the other speakers. In March, after a particularly grueling interrogation that lasted several hours, Patočka apparently suffered a stroke; he died a few days later. Although Havel's arrest and Patočka's death constituted a tremendous blow to the morale of the signatories of the charter, the StB failed in its attempt to intimidate the chartists and crush the building momentum of the opposition. The remaining chartists continued to collect signatures and even stepped in to fill the role of speaker in the place of Havel and Patočka. The practice soon emerged of chartists rotating in the office of speaker, while still maintaining the three-person structure. Dana Němcová (chapter seven), Martin Palouš (chapter eight), Petruška Šustrová (chapter ten), Petr Uhl (chapter eleven), and Jan Urban (chapter twelve) each served a term as charter speaker.

A smaller committee, known by its Czech acronym VONS, for *Výbor na obranu nespravedlivě stíhaných*, or "Committee for the Defense of the Unjustly Prosecuted," formed in early 1978. Largely an offshoot of the charter and made up of chartists, VONS aimed to provide assistance—financial and material, as well as spiritual—to the families of those who had been illegally prosecuted for alleged crimes against the state. Václav Havel, along with Petr Uhl, Dana Němcová, and several others formed the core of VONS. On 16 May 1979, the *StB* arrested sixteen members of VONS and carried out searches of each of their homes. Nine were charged with "subversion of the Republic" according to Article 98 of the criminal code, but were later released. Six of the nine, including Havel, Němcová, Uhl, Václav Benda, Otta Bednářová, and Jiří Dienstbier remained imprisoned to await trial.[40]

The trial against VONS took place 22-23 October 1979. Just like the show-trials held during the party purges of the 1950s, state authorities had already decided the outcome before the VONS trial commenced. The defendants and their attorneys argued before the court that the charge of conspiracy was unfounded: the committee's actions were guaranteed by the constitution and protected by various court rulings, and the committee had conducted its affairs openly, even sending its signed communiqués to state authorities. In his statement before the court, Havel maintained that since he had turned down the offer by government officials to emigrate while he sat in prison awaiting trial, his appearance at the trial was of his own volition, and therefore proved he bore no hostility toward his country. Although the authorities failed to prove a single accusation against any of the six defendants, the court brushed aside all arguments and proceeded to pronounce its guilty verdict and sentence: Václav Havel, four and one-half years; Petr Uhl, five years; Václav Benda, four years; Otta Bednářová and Jiří Dienstbier, each three years; Dana Němcová, two years, suspended for five years.[41]

In spite of interrogations, home searches, beatings, arrests, and prison sentences, VONS and the charter continued to function, surviving up to the eve of the Velvet Revolution of 1989 and beyond. The prison terms added new chapters to the lives of the VONS defendants, inspired them to persevere in their conflict with the regime, and hardened their determination not to give up the struggle for the establishment of a free, democratic government that would honor its commitments to the protection of human and civil rights.

The "Gray Zone"

A discussion of the political opposition in Czechoslovakia after 1968 would not be complete without mention of the so-called gray zone, or shadow zone. Working behind the scenes, semiofficially in many cases and sometimes quietly aiding the actions of dissident groups, were thousands of people who were neither openly dissident nor members of the Communist Party. These persons were "technical, legal, and academic experts who had never overtly challenged the regime before but who had played by the rules while quietly dabbling in political and economic unorthodoxies in research institutes, publishing houses, or cultural institutions."[42] In other words, persons in the gray zone did not sign Charter 77, although they may have agreed with the charter's principles, and when they could, acted in accordance with those principles.

Václav Klaus, who became prime minister in 1992, is an example of an inhabitant of the gray zone. Klaus held a position at the Economics Institute of the Academy of Sciences in 1968. Although he was never an open dissident, Klaus nevertheless was not spared in the reprisals of Normalization, and was demoted to a lesser position at the state bank. He was reinstated at the Academy of Sciences in 1988, and at the time of the Velvet Revolution in 1989, he held a position in the Institute for Prognosis. Klaus, "a silver-grey-haired [*sic*] man with glinting metal spectacles, as arrogant as he is clever,"[43] readily participated in the activities of Civic Forum in 1989 and championed the liberal ideas of economic theorist Milton Friedman in the forum's deliberations.

The people of the gray zone were then and are now either admired, at least somewhat, or vilified by the dissident community. Many dissidents, who put their own lives and those of their families at risk to effect change, sometimes spending years in prison for their efforts, resented the relative safety and comfort of those in the gray zone. Other, more charitable former dissidents are at least willing to recognize that certain people in the gray zone, who, though never sticking their necks out too far, nevertheless committed small dissident acts in some areas, only in a different way from that of prominent dissidents. Jiřina Šiklová adopts a conciliatory stance toward inhabitants of the gray zone, noting that they "differ from dissidents mainly in the sphere of courage, taking a stand, in their unwillingness or inability to confront power. They are spectators to what is happening, not players themselves. Like fans, they occasionally cheer aloud and applaud visibly."[44] Šiklová goes even further to note that dissidents, at least those of the older generation, had their origins in the gray zone: "Up until we crossed a certain line, every one of us was in the gray zone. It is only the youngest generation within the opposition who genuinely chose to join the dissent."[45]

Flying University

While the state carried out its persecution of chartists and VONS, a new entity began to emerge at the end of the 1970s which formed another source of irritation. Disenfranchised academics and the children of dissidents, who were shut out of formal higher education, organized a number of "home seminars." Collectively, the home seminars are known by a variety of names, including the "flying university," and the "Patočka university." Topics covered in these seminars ranged from philosophy and theology to mathematics and theater. Martin Palouš and his close friend Daniel Kroupa organized a seminar known as the *Kampakademie* [Kampa Academy] meetings of which were held in the Palouš home on the Kampa island in Prague. Ivan Havel, cyberneticist and logician, began another seminar in 1977. Crowds of students gathered to listen to Jan Patočka lecture on philosophy until his death in 1977.

In 1979, the Sub-Faculty of Philosophy at Oxford University began an association with the home seminars, which existed well into the 1980s. In April 1981, the Jan Hus Foundation was registered in London as a charitable organization with the aim of raising funds to support and cover expenses for cultural activities and research stipends, including grants to Czechs for academic pursuits.[46] In the mid-1980s, with support from the Hus Foundation, the home seminars spread into Moravia and Slovakia as well. Petr Oslzlý, the internationally renowned director of Brno's *Divadlo na provazku* [Theater on a String] and his wife Eva ran a successful seminar in their home beginning in 1984. In Bratislava, Ján Čarnogurský, a devout Roman Catholic and lawyer—who lost the right to practice in 1981 for defending a Charter 77 signatory—helped to organize and hosted a seminar on law and history from 1987.

Both attendees and organizers of the home seminars felt the pressures of the StB. Secret police sometimes trailed foreign lecturers to the seminars and on a few occasions actually conducted raids on the seminars. In one notorious incident in December 1981, French philosopher Jacques Derrida was detained at the airport on his attempted return to Paris after lecturing for a seminar organized by Ladislav Hejdánek, a philosopher and two-term speaker for Charter 77. Customs police accused and charged Derrida with "the production and traffic of drugs," then after interrogation drove him to Ruzyně prison, where he was processed as a common criminal. After five days of interrogation and detention, it was only after direct intervention of the French government with Husák that authorities released Derrida and put him on a train bound for Paris. It is now clear that the Derrida incident was part of a strategy devised by the Czech authorities to discredit the chartists. The whole operation backfired, however, and rather than intimidate the operators and students of the home seminars, it had the effect of creating "greater solidarity between the Czechs and their foreign lecturers, and especially in France, stimulated academics to travel behind the Iron Curtain."[47]

The seminars played a profound role in the intellectual lives of dissidents and their families. Not only were Havel and Palouš, whose personal stories are collected in this volume, involved in the organization of home seminars, but others also attended the seminars, especially those of Patočka, as did a number of children of the dissidents mentioned in this essay. The seminars provided a means by which chartists, their children, and others who had been marginalized by the system, could receive education and intellectual stimulation not only from visitors from the West, but also from their own homegrown specialists, e.g., Patočka, who themselves had been marginalized.

1989

Revolution came to the Soviet satellite states of Central and Eastern Europe rather unexpectedly. The sudden breakdown of Soviet hegemony over the region at the end of the twentieth century—in stark contrast to its hammer-and-fist approach to the region in the post-World War II era—took most people by complete surprise. Most accounts attribute much of the credit for the about-face of Soviet policy toward the region to Mikhail Sergeevich Gorbachev, general secretary of the Communist Party of the Soviet Union (CPSU) (1985-1991). In the remainder of this introductory essay, I will point out a few key historical moments which marked Czechoslovakia's path from subservience to freedom and independence.

Gorbachev Emboldens Opposition

One of the key factors in the story of the transformation of the political landscape of Central and Eastern Europe is Gorbachev himself. Almost immediately after his rise to the post of general secretary of the CPSU in 1985, it was clear to observers both Western and Soviet, that Gorbachev was something new in Soviet political life. Unlike his predecessors in CPSU leadership, who had adopted a posture of secrecy and isolation, only making selective and well-orchestrated public appearances, Gorbachev—often accompanied by his wife Raisa—enjoyed mingling with the masses and "pressing the flesh" in the style of Western European and American politicians. On official, or even impromptu, visits to factories, schools, or collective farms, Gorbachev spoke extemporaneously in a nothing-to-hide-nothing-to-fear manner. On state visits abroad, Gorbachev put his hosts at ease with his easygoing style and unrehearsed remarks.

In 1988, three years into his tenure as general secretary, Gorbachev introduced two new concepts into Soviet life and politics: perestroika, "restructuring," and glasnost, "openness." Placing the blame for the country's social ills squarely on the shoulders of the institutions of the state and the Communist Party, Gorbachev recognized the need for "sweeping reforms," or complete "restructuring," in order to address the problems. Through glasnost, Gorbachev gave teeth to perestroika by calling party functionaries, factory managers, and ministers of state departments to public accountability by allowing open criticism and debate on the issues in public forums and the media.[48]

Naturally, perestroika and glasnost made some members of the *nomenklatura*—the elite class of party and state officials grown accustomed to comforts unattainable by the masses—nervous. While Gorbachev won many friends in the West, his liberal ideas met with less than enthusiastic acceptance in the leadership circles of the satellite nations of Central and Eastern Europe. Indeed Czechoslovakia, with its "distinctive history of the 'normalization' period," was "in the 1980s one of the regimes most resistant to Gorbachev's perestroika and glasnost."[49] Gorbachev's pledge to reduce Soviet troop strength throughout the East Bloc, however, no doubt encouraged opposition groups to exert even more pressure on conservative, stagnated regimes.[50]

Against the backdrop of Gorbachev's reform direction in Soviet politics, and bolstered by his anti-interventionist rhetoric, opposition groups across the East Bloc poised for action in 1989. Czechoslovakia was no exception. In January 1989, certain chartists and other activists planned a series of activities under the rubric of "Palach Week" to mark the twentieth anniversary of Jan Palach's self-immolation in protest against the Soviet-led invasion of 1968. Palach Week was to culminate in a march to Wenceslas Square to lay flowers at the spot where Palach committed suicide. Read "between the lines," Palach Week was also the "official" means by which to "unofficially" mark the anniversary of the invasion of 1968. The event resulted in a number of arrests, including that of Václav Havel and Dana Němcová, although Havel was not a participant in the event but only a bystander. The arrests in January 1989 led to more protests that "went well beyond the circle of established dissidents to draw in a much larger group of intellectuals and artists who had not previously taken public action," and spawned even more opposition groups in the country.[51]

In the following months of 1989, historic events transpiring in Poland, Hungary, and East Germany no doubt mutually encouraged the opposition and dissident groups throughout the region. In May 1989, Hungarian and Austrian officials ceremoniously dismantled the border fences between the two countries. The open border between East and West was an open invitation to any East Bloc tourist in Hungary to emigrate. In a more symbolic act, in June the Hungarian government allowed a state funeral and the reburial of Imre Nagy and his complete official rehabilitation.[52] In Poland, the historic June 1989 elections saw Solidarity enter the *Sejm*, or "parliament," in a power-sharing arrangement with the Communist Party. Achieved after more than a decade of struggle and months of intense negotiations, the trade union movement, which began in the shipyards of Gdańsk, became the first organization or political bloc to break the Communist Party's choke hold on power in any socialist country.

The open border between Hungary and Austria proved to be an irresistible gateway for East Germans looking for an escape route to the West. The closed borders between East and West had been the only concrete obstacle between East Germans and full citizenship in the Federal Republic of Germany. By October, approximately 50,000 East German citizens crossed the Hungarian border into Austria. Prague citizens witnessed hundreds of East Germans scaling the fences surrounding the West German embassy. In a matter of days, the number of people occupying the embassy garden reached critical proportions, causing concern on the part of Prague and West German officials for the health and safety of the asylum seekers demanding passage to the FRG. West German, Hungarian, and Austrian officials negotiated transfer by train for the refugees to resettlement in the Federal Republic. At the same time, massive demonstrations took place in Leipzig and (East) Berlin, calling for the legalization of opposition groups. The uncontainable and unstoppable protests culminated in the opening of the Berlin Wall on 9 November 1989, an event unforeseen and unimagined since the wall's construction in August 1961. By October 1990, East Germany had ceased to exist and the two Germanies reunited to form one sovereign state. A significant portion of the citizens of the other socialist countries watched the German demonstrations and the opening of the Berlin Wall on television by means of continuously replayed video, which could not but encourage them to take action in their own countries.

The "Velvet Revolution"

A mere eight days following the "fall of the Berlin Wall," Czech students took the initiative in bringing revolution to Czechoslovakia. On 17 November, students gathered legally at a Prague cemetery to mark the fiftieth anniversary of the death of Jan Opletal, a student who was murdered by the Nazis. The students gave speeches, chanted, then decided to move the demonstration to Wenceslas Square, where they encountered riot police. At the intersection of Národní Avenue and the square, the students sat down and started singing. After some moments of quiet tension, something or someone moved or made a gesture that provoked the police, who attacked the students with truncheons. The Velvet Revolution had begun. Ironically, the violent end of the demonstration of 17

November, later named "the massacre," was the only act of violence committed during the entire revolution.

The police attack on the students, among whom were also many nonstudents, including a number of prominent dissidents and their family members, proved to be the needed spark for the opposition to act. The report of the death of one student, Martin Šmíd, fostered the indignation of the populace, though the report was later proven false. Šmíd remained very much alive (see Petr Uhl, chapter eleven). Following the 17 November demonstration, events transpired at a breakneck pace, ultimately leading to the complete capitulation of Czechoslovakia's Communist government.

Students quickly organized meetings to discuss and disseminate the details of the demonstration and the police action. Dissident participants in the demonstration spread word about police brutality to other dissidents, including Václav Havel, who was at his country cottage at the time. The opposition, including chartists and other prominent dissidents, quickly joined forces with the students, meeting in several Prague theaters to plan strategy and formulate demands to the government.[53] Havel's headquarters during the early days of the revolution was a dressing room in the basement of the landmark Magic Lantern theater, where Havel and his inner circle of fellow activists planned strategy enshrouded by cigarette smoke and surrounded by mirrors and tutus.

Within a couple of days, the opposition coalesced into one group under the name *Občanské forum* [Civic Forum] with Václav Havel its de facto leader. Civic Forum made four initial demands: the resignation of Communist leaders who prepared the Warsaw Pact invasion of 1968; the resignation of those responsible for the police action on 17 November, Minister of the Interior František Kincl and Prague party secretary Miroslav Štěpán; the establishment of a commission to investigate the government's actions on 17 November; and the immediate release of all prisoners of conscience.[54]

In Slovakia, religious dissidents and intellectuals formed Public Against Violence (PAV) on 20 November. Alexander Dubček played a role in the leadership of PAV which was to assume a function very similar to that of Civic Forum.

In the following two weeks, Civic Forum would operate almost around the clock. Plenums had to be planned and mass demonstrations on Wenceslas Square and in the Letná soccer stadium had to be organized and timed appropriately for maximum effectiveness. The leadership also spent hours privately and in plenary sessions discussing how to build the kind of government and society they desired, should the revolution succeed.

The demonstrations were an effective public relations tool for Civic Forum and a means of testing the public's will. The demonstrations not only provided opportunities for Civic Forum's leaders to address the masses on a personal level but gave them the opportunity to create moments of emotional impact which would keep the public encouraged and themselves inspired in order to persevere. Alexander Dubček joined Havel more than once on a balcony overlooking Wenceslas Square to the crowd's chants of "Dubček-Havel," at once merging the symbolism and emotional weight of the failed Prague Spring with the euphoria of current events. Prague's layout and structure made it a veritable revolutionary's paradise, for "the core of the intellectual and cultural communities, the country's major university, the politicians, and a major concentration of industry are all packed into a single urban space."[55] The institutions of government administration, the Office of the President in Prague Castle and the Federal Assembly building, are located in rather close proximity to Wenceslas Square. The chanting of the crowds of 200,000 or more gathered on the square could no doubt be heard in government offices, grating on the nerves of threatened government officials and creating for them a premonition of their own demise. The demonstrations played a vital role in keeping the momentum of the revolution going while feeding the headlines of domestic and international newspapers and television networks.

After a week of plenums and press conferences, massive demonstrations, and negotiations between Civic Forum and the government, carried out initially through "the Bridge" (Michael Kocáb, chapter four), the Politburo and the entire Secretariat of the Communist Party Central Committee resigned on 24 November. The government appointed a new Politburo and party Central Committee, yet the unpopular Štěpán retained his office. The next day Civic Forum announced its dissatisfaction with the new government appointees and called for a general strike to take place on Monday, 27 November. The strike was largely symbolic, scheduled to last only two hours beginning at noon and timed in order to "encourage worker participation and to avoid disrupting production."[56]

Prime Minister Ladislav Adamec finally accepted a meeting with a Civic Forum delegation led by Havel, which took place on Sunday, 26 November. Both sides announced the results of the negotiations on 28 November. The government agreed to meet three of Civic Forum's demands, including the release of prisoners of conscience and the establishment of a parliamentary delegation to investigate the police action of 17 November. On 29 November, the Federal Assembly repealed Article Four of the constitution, thereby removing the legal basis for the leading role of the Communist Party. However, in response to the government's announcement on 3 December of the composition of the new cabinet which included five non-Communists and fifteen Communists, Civic Forum called for a second general strike.

A second general strike proved to be unnecessary; by Thursday, 6 December, Adamec had resigned. Civic Forum pressed its demands with the government to accept its candidates in a new cabinet. On 10 December, Gustáv Husák swore in the new cabinet then resigned as president. The Federal Assembly elected Dubček as chair, and on the following day, 29 December, with Dubček presiding, elected Václav Havel as president of the republic. Free elections would be held in June 1990.

In a matter of a few weeks, the revolution catapulted former dissidents and political prisoners into leadership positions of the Czechoslovak Socialist Republic. Ján Čarnogurský—released from prison in the government's amnesty only two weeks earlier—assumed the post of first vice-premier. Václav Klaus, who would later be the prime minister, assumed the post of minister of finance. Jiří Dienstbier became foreign minister. One of Dienstbier's first acts in office was to cut the barbed-wire fence on Czechoslovakia's border with Austria, joined in the ceremony by Austrian foreign minister Alois Möck.

Having claimed their prize, the leaders of Civic Forum now faced the daunting and overwhelming tasks ahead: preparing for the elections in the coming June and formulating its role in building a democratic government and civil society. In private conversation in April 1998, Eda Kriseová shared her philosophy on her own role in the historic events of 1989: "I believe that if you tear something down, you have the responsibility to replace it with something better."[57] This statement, in a sense, can be taken as a summary of the aims of Civic Forum, the Havel presidency, and the story of developing democracy in the two successor states to Czechoslovakia, i.e., the Czech Republic and Slovakia, in the years following 1989.[58]

In the following chapters, eleven individuals provide their own personal perspective on the events described in this introductory essay. Each of these persons, both as actor in and eyewitness to momentous events, made history. Their perseverance through the long years of dissidence and their contributions in public service to the establishment of democracy in the post-Communist era, have earned for them their own place in history, both collectively and as individuals. In consenting to be interviewed and in permitting his or her story to be first recorded, then published, thereby adding to the historical record, each individual once again commits an act of public service.

2

Ivan Havel

We were proud of the fact that it was velvet.
—Ivan Havel, 1998

Ivan Havel *is co-director of the Center for Theoretical Study and adjunct professor of philosophy at Charles University in Prague. He graduated from the Technical University in Prague in 1966 and earned his Ph.D. in computer science from the University of California in Berkeley (1969-1971). His research interests cover a broad range of topics including theoretical computer science, artificial intelligence, and related philosophical issues. He has authored numerous articles and reviews in scientific journals, as well as three books, including collections of short fiction and essays. He is the editor in chief of the scientific journal* Vesmír [The Universe]. *The interview, conducted in English, took place at the Center for Theoretical Studies in Prague.*

Members of our family have been citizens of Prague for several generations. Some older generations were millers. My grandfather was a very able entrepreneur. He built a large building in the center of Prague, a large palace which is called Lucerna, which was actually a cultural house with the largest ballroom of that time in Prague. My father, his son, afterwards continued his work in caring for the property and he himself actually developed a quarter in Prague which is called Barrandov, and especially a restaurant, Barrandov Terraces, which is a large and relatively famous garden restaurant.

So, I and my brother were from a relatively well-established family. We were born in the late thirties. I was born in 1938 and my brother in 1936. And from my mother's branch of the family there were interesting people. My grandfather was sort of a Renaissance man. He was a scientist and diplomat and writer, journalist. He wrote several books. He spoke several languages fluently. And actually he was very important for me, because as a child, I was very attracted by his talks and explanations, and I wanted him to explain to me everything all the time. So during the war, we survived without too much hurt. Our house in Prague was partly destroyed by an air raid. So at that time we had to spend a couple of years, or three years, in our country house, which was in Moravia. And this was actually a very nice time in my life. I was a kid and I just played, no problems, just playing. This was the early stage of my life.

Then after the Communists came, I was not able to get into high school, or university, but I managed. Actually my mother managed to get me through to the evening school, the evening gymnasium, which means high school. Then later I had to go into the military service for two years. I managed to get into the technical university, again in evening school, evening courses, which I finished in 1966.

The reasons why I couldn't—and actually my brother was in the same situation—study in the normal way, was because our family was considered to be a bourgeois family, and under the Communist regime we had a very bad mark because of that. And of course the property was nationalized already in 1948. Even our country house was confiscated and we were expelled from Prague. But by the help of good people we somehow survived living in Prague.

In the sixties the situation was slightly better. And when I finished my university studies, I started a full-time program, the Czech equivalent of the Ph.D., which was called Candidate of Science. But I interrupted my studies in 1969 after the Soviet invasion, by a possibility which was actually started in early 1968 before the invasion, to go to the States for study, and I realized this was a good opportunity. I studied computer science for three years at the University of California in Berkeley. I should mention that my studies here were in the faculty of engineering, and my specialization was in automaton theory, which is something in cybernetics and computer science. In the States I studied computer science, theoretical computer science. I returned in 1971.

Then for eight years I worked in the Academy of Sciences, and my main field of interest was artificial intelligence and automaton theory, theoretical computer science. It lasted eight years, and after that the situation became much worse. It was the time of Charter 77. My brother was a leading person in these dissident activities. I myself was involved in some *samizdat* publications. And I organized an unofficial seminar, a philosophical seminar, in my flat. So I necessarily got into trouble with the police and with the Communists. Then I changed jobs twice and I finished as a freelance programmer. In fact it was a good time, because paradoxically, I was the owner of my time. I could decide what to do.

The logic behind this was that the Communists didn't want me to meet too many people. They didn't want me to work in a normal environment, where I would supposedly influence other people. We, more people were actually happy because of that. Some people. My advantage was that I had a profession in computer science, so I could work as a programmer. Some other people who didn't have an education in some field usually ended up, or who were philosophers, or who were writers who couldn't find a way how to work, at least partly, in their profession, usually took a job as a stoker which was a very common profession for dissidents. This was the eighties.

In 1982 I was arrested for four days in the famous case of the truck smuggling some *samizdat* literature. And I was charged with subversion. I was not prosecuted, and the charge was actually a threat to me and my family. And, actually, it lasted until 1989. After the Velvet Revolution, the charge against me was dropped.

After November [1989], I spent half a year in Civic Forum. It was my short story with politics. And at the same time, I started to look for some way to work in some intellectual way in my field, or in some related fields. I entered the university, and with two other friends, started to set up an institution which is called the Center for Theoretical Study, which is this interdisciplinary advanced research institution, which is now a joint institution of Charles University of Prague and the Academy of Sciences. I'm also the editor in chief of a journal *Vesmír* [*Universe*]. And I teach at the university, only one class, which is called Natural and Artificial Thought. This is perhaps, briefly, my life story.

When you returned from the States, were you able to maintain contact with people in your field in the United States?

Yes, but it was not too extensive contact. The point is that at that time there was no e-mail which would make it extremely easy. And we were all the time suspicious, and perhaps correctly suspicious, of letters being read and telephones being tapped, and all of that. But I had some correspondence as far as my time allowed. I was in some program committees of some international meetings. Sometimes I was even allowed to go to the meeting in the early seventies. Later it was more and more difficult. At those meetings we organized meetings here for our colleagues. But, you see, this was computer science, theoretical computer science, a field which was relatively ideologically pure, that means not touched by ideologies, so that we could have certain contacts.

Of course there was a rule in the academy. I was in the Academy of Sciences at that time. It was a rule that any encounter with a foreigner—whether it is on the street with a tourist who would ask directions or something—we were supposed to write a report about that and file it somewhere. Some people just ignored that rule, as I did. Other people took it seriously and preferred not to meet foreign scholars, because they didn't like to make the reports.

Can you talk about the seminars that you conducted?

It started in 1977 or '78. It was every other week on Mondays. We called it "Mondays" sometimes, sometimes a "salon." And it started with a discussion among two or three philosophers and myself about the lack of opportunities for people to meet and discuss. And we meant it completely intellectually. We didn't mean to mingle with politics in this way. And so we started to do it. . . . The majority of the topics were philosophy, science, the relationship of science to philosophy. There were some history lectures, some theological. It very much depended on the people who were available who were willing to come. For a couple of years, it was relatively without problems, but later, especially after Charter 77, the harassment started. The police started to be interested in these meetings. So several times they stayed in the downstairs of our house and everybody who came in was asked to identify themselves, and they made a list of people who were going there, which caused some people to stop coming.

I was trying in this way to help with contacts among people who were on the side of the dissent, dissidents, and who were purposefully cut off from interaction with other people by the police. Contacts between them with people in the so-called "shadow zone," that means, people who were perhaps not Communists but still working in their fields having their jobs, being without direct problems with the police. And especially because we avoided political topics or lectures for a certain time, those people felt that it was without problems to go there.

Now, of course, we know much more. We know that the police were following who was there much more, and they purposefully led some people in the illusion that they did not know about them, so that they had a reserve of them when they needed them, to press[ure] them, or to be informers. Some attendees at these seminars were harassed, some of them not. Some of them were asked for cooperation. Some of them refused and had problems. Some of them didn't refuse. And so it was a mixture of fates for the people who were going there. In fact I plan sometimes, when I have time, to go and look into my files, my police files, which might be very interesting, and it would help, because I have bad memory. I do not remember when what was.

It may help my memory very much, because sometimes the reports were probably very detailed, at least who was where when, and so on. Okay, so what more about those seminars? In fact, my attitude was always, all my life, I wanted to learn. I wanted to know as much as I could. And, so, there were often lectures which I didn't understand completely. And I just wanted to acquire knowledge. Although I didn't concentrate with the selection of topics in a particular direction, the topics were quite diverse, and there was very much breadth. In fact, in a sense, we continue now here in the Center for Theoretical Study in the same way to try to establish contacts among people from various fields.

Did any foreigners come to give lectures for the seminar?

About twice. Very seldom. And always there was a lot of problems with that. But in a sense, we purposely made an undecided division of labor among various seminars. So, most of the foreigners were going to Tomin's[1] seminar for a certain time before he left. And all the time to Hejdánek's seminar. The idea was to use the opportunity of foreign scholars coming here. Those scholars were, or the visits of such scholars, mostly philosophers, were organized by the Jan Hus Foundation. And so they had support to come here. And so they could be as tourists; they went to the seminar, they talked there, and then left. And some of them had problems, which you probably know.

How were you involved in Charter 77?

I was not directly involved. There was a sort of agreement that, in our family, that one in the family is enough. And also in the beginning, until 1979, I was still in the academy. And my decision was, as was many other people's decision—unless there is a real reason—not to abandon my profession. Because it was not a humanitarian field, it was not a writer's profession, or a cultural activity. It was pure science, and so we thought that that could be continued. And also it was not at all one which would support a government or support a Communist system. It was a pure science which has no immediate consequences. And so I actually stayed there until 1979, and then my problems started.

Of course, they were mostly my friends, and so I met them there. In my seminars there were always several chartists present. And to be a signer of the charter was almost like having a yellow star on your jacket. Because other people knew who was who. And some people stopped coming, because they knew that some chartists were coming. You see, there were various attitudes. And so I met them a lot, socially and otherwise, and so I was considered to be, perhaps, almost a member. From the perspective of the police, there was not too much difference.

Can you talk about your involvement in samizdat?

I was not so involved as a writer, of course. This was perhaps later. I will mention later the group around Radim Palouš. But I was more or less involved in the technical things, because it was an edition which was called *Edice Expedice* [*Edition Expedition*], which was started by my brother in 1976. And my brother and Dana Horáková, his friend, started originally just to copy, to have a typist who would copy other *samizdat*, mainly *Edice Petlice*, Vaculík's *samizdat*, and to bind it and to distribute it, about twelve copies among friends.

I remember, my brother came to me and said "you are addicted to books, so would you like to be a subscriber," and so I said yes. So I was a passive subscriber from the beginning. But then Dana Horáková left the country, and there was nobody. She was doing the dirty work, the organization, and bringing the manuscripts to the binder. My brother was just sometimes choosing the titles and at that time he was signing every copy by claiming "I made my personal copy of this book for my use and my friends' use," which was mistakenly believed to be a way how to avoid some legal restrictions.

Then when Dana left, I think in 1978, or late '77, I took on myself the difficult work; difficult in the sense that it is not intellectual. But you have to keep the papers, to have several typists, to go to them, to bring them paper, bring them the manuscript, to explain to them how to do that, then to take it back, to make corrections or ask somebody to make corrections, then to take it again, and distribute it under the table, and see that these twelve copies are sorted. This was done usually by Olga, my sister-in-law. And then to take it to the binder, again in danger of being harassed by the police. Everything had to be done secretly. Then bring back, then decide how much actually the expenses were, because we paid the typist, and we paid the binder, and sometimes we had to support certain authors who had problems. And to keep track of that.

And as I mentioned, my memory is not the best, so I had to write down everything. Now, when I wrote it, I had to write it in a code, a special coding system. Because if the police would find it, they would find all of these people involved. So, this was my work, and later my second wife started to help me a lot in that. She even learned to bind books, so she bound some of the volumes. And she brought it to be copied and so on.

It was a lot of work, but fortunately, there were a lot of friends who helped. And very seldom, would somebody say "I have no time," or "I do not want to do that." Of course, I didn't ask those people whom we knew could be endangered very much by contact with us, or who would refuse, because they would be afraid for their families or something. It was a sort of collective cooperation of many people. I continued that until the revolution. There were still some volumes which remained unfinished.

Could you talk about your involvement in the Velvet Revolution?

There was this Palach Week. And there were other occasions—various anniversaries, and Škroupov Square [*Škroupovo náměstí*], where surprisingly, the police allowed the meeting. I don't know what the chronological order was. Somehow everybody expected that something might soon happen. Nobody knew when. And actually, the evening before November 17th, November 16th, I met my friend, my school friend, and later, fellow student Jan Škoda. He had at the same time an official post in a minor department in the so-called Socialist Party, which was not the Communist Party, and which was more involved with more humanitarian things. And so, we talked, and he was saying that he guessed that it would take two years, but something would happen. He was certain that something would happen, some radical change. Unless there is some flood or some natural disaster, it would take two years. And the next day.

And also, I attended a meeting of students. I remember Vašek Malý[2] was there also. Young students were starting to organize something. Actually they wanted to organize the November 17th manifestation or some sort of event. And I and my wife attended that event which was in the afternoon, Friday, November 17th. It was a large rally in the place where the university has certain buildings in Prague, in the center. And there were some talks. I remember Professor Kacetov—who used to be the rector of the university in the fifties, but then had a problem, political problems later in the seventies and he was semiofficially still working, a famous mathematician—was there. He worked in his field but at the same time made some attempts to organize a different type of seminar. It was a seminar under the roof of the university, an official seminar, but he allowed questionable people to talk there, philosophers or so. And so it was an island of freedom, intellectual freedom, under the roof of the university. So it was a different way of organizing these things. And he gave the main speech there, then some other people. And then the students moved to Vyšehrad hill, where it was supposed to end. But there was, as I remember, such an elated atmosphere. There was not visible, at least from my point of view, any interruption by the police, even though there were rumors that they were waiting somewhere or other.

The meeting of students was supposed to end at the hill. There is a monastery there, not monastery, a cemetery. But the atmosphere was so happy, and the students were in such a good mood, because there was no interference up to that time. They didn't want to disperse. They wanted to continue. And somebody said "let's go to Wenceslas Square," and immediately everybody went. Now there are disputes, whether this was a provocation, or whether this was a spontaneous wish. Definitely everybody wanted to go. Then they went close to the National Theater and through the National Alley, or National Boulevard [*Národní třída*], to Wenceslas Square.

And then at a certain place, which is actually not far from here, the police stopped them. And we were going not in the very front, but not far from the front, and so we saw the police lines. The students stopped and sat down on the street, and waited for what would happen. A long time. They sang songs, and some time later there started to be a certain tension and some small disturbances between the students and the police. And I and my wife happened to be somewhat close to that, and so, we had a certain conflict with the police. They arrested us, and my wife even was hit by a *pendrek* [club]. And she had to go to the hospital the next day.

We were arrested, but they just asked [us] to stand next to the police bus. And, fortunately, I looked a little bit older than the students and I had a briefcase. And my wife told the police "Look, he has scientific papers in his briefcase." I really had, by chance. They were afraid that they might get into problems, because by mistake, instead of a student, they arrested somebody else by coincidence, so they released us. It was not like the recent interruption of police with this Global Street rally last month. They didn't do that. They arrested people who were just observers, and not the active ones. But after that, we left the place. And as it happened, the most serious conflicts, attacks by the police were after we left. So we didn't see any blood. We saw only occasional conflicts.

We went to Benda's place, where we telephoned and reported to Radio Free Europe, or what it was, I don't know. But it was immediately reported and many other people were going to call, so that the reports were combining together. So that was all. We left Prague for the weekend for our country house. And then we listened to the radio. Nothing too much was on the radio on Saturday. Only reports about something, but on Sunday there was a report about the supposedly dead student. You know, probably, the story which appears to be a provocation, but nobody knew that then. And we immediately felt that it was more than enough, that something would happen, because it was really visible that the will of the people was on the borderline to do something. And this was, apparently, enough to change it completely. This was a bifurcation point.

And, so we came back on Sunday, early afternoon. And my brother, who was sharing the flat with us, was just leaving. And there was a couple of dissidents there, and they just were discussing something, and I just overheard that there was a meeting in the Činoherní Club which is a small theater near Wenceslas Square. So I decided to go there.

And there the atmosphere was enormously interesting. I was sitting, I think, in the third or fourth row, and the main people were on the stage. I say main people because some of them were dissidents, but even my friend whom I mentioned, Mr. Škoda, who was in the Socialist Party, was sitting there. And some of them were somewhat nervous just to appear on the stage. And it was, of course, quite an interesting mixture.

Fortunately, there are photographs and the historians can analyze who is who and why they were there. So, there my brother read the proclamation of Civic Forum, as a unified activity of all independent movements, just to do something, not to leave things as they were. But Civic Forum history is already written by some people.

Monday started with a press conference in our flat, which was prepared much earlier, because my brother got some prize from Sweden, so newsmen were coming because of that. But at the same time it was an opportunity, actually, for the first press conference. And at the press conference. . . .You see there was a room packed with newspaper men and journalists and TV cameras, everything, and in the middle somebody came and said something is happening on Wenceslas Square. People are gathering. You could see how the journalists left the room quietly and the TV cameras disappeared, and everybody went to the streets.

First, there was for a short time a place in Manes, which is an art gallery. And then the very early stages of the activity, it moved to the gallery U Velčicky, which is not far from Wenceslas Square. And there was some art exhibition there, but the rooms of the exhibition were given to the activities. So for a couple of days we stayed there. And then it was quickly no longer possible to be there, because there were so many activities, and so many journalists, and so many visitors, and people offering help, that we were not able to do anything reasonable there.

There were two main activities of Civic Forum in the first week of existence. The first activity was to prepare afternoon rallies on Wenceslas Square. Every day there was a gathering of people in Wenceslas Square, so we had to prepare the program for that. My brother happened always to like to be a director of his plays or something, so he directed, he made the program of who will talk when, and when will be a cultural activity, some song, and so on. So this was one main activity, to organize these public rallies. And the other was to prepare visits or negotiations with the government. And so this was more closed. It was not so much publicized, and they did it in a separate room, because it was very sensitive. This was the first week, two weeks of Civic Forum, which was a hectic time.

And I think one of the best reports of that, from the second or the third week, was written by Timothy Garton Ash, this *Magic Lantern*. He even captures the atmosphere, that was there, and how things were so hectic and people moving about. Anyway, then I stayed. I had time, because I was a freelance programmer. I didn't have to work and have to report anywhere. I stayed in Civic Forum, and slowly I became some sort of *Postherr*, "postman, courier," there, not really a leading role, but one of several people in a group, how was it called, I think they called it spokesman or something like that.

The point is, that the most important politicians of Civic Forum were leaving for official posts, to the government. My brother became the president. A group of people went with him to organize his life as the president. And now I'm thinking about the turn of 1989 to 1990. Another became the mayor of Prague. And another became the director of radio. Another became the director of TV. You see all the important posts were sucking people from Civic Forum. So just a few people remained. And a lot of volunteers wanted to do something, but it was not easy to organize. And we elected a rigid, "official" organization—to have working secretaries, a clear division of labor, or so. More or less everybody wanted to do everything. So it was, but it worked, and enthusiasm helps to balance organizational problems.

And, so I know that the last chairman, or leader, I don't know what was the title, of Civic Forum was Jan Urban. Before that I remember Vojtěch Sedláček, and Petr Pithart, who left to the Czech government, and some others. Well, it's written somewhere the names. When I start to say names, I would always omit somebody important.

And, for example, I should not omit my wife, who stayed there a year, not half a year. I left Civic Forum, and she stayed there. And in fall 1990, I went—when I decided to continue my profession—again to Berkeley, because I had friends there. So was my three months in Berkeley in the fall of 1990. And during that time, my wife was one of the leading persons in Civic Forum, until the Klaus[3] takeover. And Martin Palouš was there also until the Klaus takeover started.

You didn't have any desires to go directly into politics yourself?

No, I never had such desires. And, actually, my period in Civic Forum . . . I was very happy that I was there, but mostly to observe the situation, to have direct experience of how it looks in something like that. But of course it was not regular politics. It was a very revolutionary situation, where the decisions were more or less made in a very often nondemocratic way. Somebody had an idea and immediately realized it without discussing it with the others. And then sometimes we spent hours and hours with the discussion of some issue and we lost time. It was almost a unanimous consent, that we cannot make a revolution in a democratic, I mean, on a micro level; micro-decisions cannot be made by some group of people discussing. There were times, there were these advisory boards, and the main board, as it was called. . . . It was the Civic Forum Coordination Center, and it was the board, leading board or something . . . I do not know even the Czech words now.

There were about twenty people, or thirty people, I do not know. And they gathered every day, trying to somewhat simulate democratic decisions. But it didn't work too much, because the next day the situation was completely different and somebody had to decide without discussion. It was interesting to observe, a happening, a very interesting happening, and we were close to it. But I didn't have the intention. Politics is something where an intellectual wouldn't know too much what to do. I know there are some counterexamples, but it requires [one] to be, to react very fast in situations where one is inclined to weigh various possibilities, to think about that. You are not supposed to think too much. You are supposed to act immediately. At the same time when you are supposed to make open speeches, you should talk in the way which is understandable to ordinary people. And you have to repeat all the same sentences all over, again and again, which for an intellectual is painful. Because one would like to put in newer and newer ideas. And also, intellectuals want to sit and read and write and think, and so it's not possible in active politics.

Some people give a lot of credit to Reagan for the changes in Eastern Europe. Others think Gorbachev was more influential. In East Germany, for example, some of Gorbachev's speeches were not even printed in the press. How was that handled here?

You see, I am not a political scientist to tell you something exactly. My feeling is that what was important here was not direct actions by those two important people, but their existence. The fact that they are there, and so it was a gate, moral and political support, to know that there is Reagan saying such and such things, and that there is a Gorbachev saying such and such things. Probably for people with left inclinations, and you see, there was this huge amount of former Communists who were harassed after 1968, and in the last twenty years were actually in dissent, and were friends with dissidents. They probably didn't like Reagan as much as Gorbachev, because he was their man. And Mlynář, Zdeněk Mlynář, was the father of the kind. . . . He was the fellow student of Gorbachev. They were probably more influenced by the fact that Gorbachev was saying such and such things. People on the right who were used to having information from free Europe, Radio Free Europe, and Voice of America, or so, would confess that they were more influenced by Reagan's actions. There is no, no truth in politics, you see. You will find various opinions and it's very difficult to sort it. So, I think it depends on concrete people.

But, in fact, what was important, was that the influence in both directions was the same, had the same outcome, so that people could cooperate. An interesting point is the first occurrences of differences between people on the left and people on the right in Civic Forum. The great advantage, and maybe, in my opinion, 80 or 90 percent of the success of the activities of Civic Forum were consequences of the fact that in Charter 77 and in dissident movements, in

VONS and others, there was a mixture of people with various ideologies. There were former Communists. There were famous Trotskyists, Peter Uhl. There were religious people. Atheists. There were rightists, conservatives. And they were friends and they trusted each other. And as a consequence, they were on a first name basis, which is more rare here than let's say first name in the States. We call it *tykání*.[4] So that means they could make a coherent group in the very beginning.

Now of course, a little digression, there are disputes about the extent Civic Forum was actually organized by hidden forces from the Communists, who wanted to manipulate people. It didn't look that way in Civic Forum at all. What was visible was real enthusiasm on all sides and cooperation, and trying to force the government out, and strong feeling which was the consequence of the fact that Charter 77 became not a political movement but an ethical movement. There was the strong attempt not to commit excesses, the velvetness of the Velvet Revolution, which is now objected to by many people. Many people say it was too velvet. But at that time we were proud of the fact that it was velvet. And we were proud that it was so fast. And I think that the smoothness and fastness is rare. Either you can have it fast and bloody, or slow and smooth, but not this combination.

Anyway, I remember the first time when we wrote a sort of proclamation, not the first proclamation of the establishment of Civic Forum, but the text, the program, what we actually wanted, or some text of this form. There was a trend to say that we do not want a totalitarian system any more, a Communist totalitarian system, as it was here for the last twenty years. And now somebody said "why twenty years? Why not forty years?" And now some people were struck by that, because, you see, for many people the period before '68 was somewhat okay, especially '68 was okay, and so they considered now November '89 as just a return to '68 and forget what was before. There were mistakes or so, but let's just forget it. Let's return to 1968 and start again where we were stopped by force that time. And so they only wanted to talk about returning twenty years back. But democrats said, "Why twenty years? We should return forty years, back to 1948."

And so this was the first of a certain divergence. Of course, those people from '68 couldn't argue in favor of the '50s, because everybody knew what happened then. And so they yielded, and so actually, now we always talk about forty years of the totalitarian system. But there was really a short period when we were talking about twenty years of the totalitarian system.

Another problem, I think, was among the politicians of the type who didn't like the revolutionary atmosphere. They wanted to start real serious political activity, to set up parties, to give them programs. They were more or less people who were studying political science, or so. And they started to form small parties actually. And some of them wanted to stay under the roof of Civic Forum. Some of them wanted to go out of Civic Forum. But, in the first days, this problem was not very advanced. The problem was only that these people wanted to talk, to discuss, to have sessions, where they would analyze the situation. And therefore they were slow. Those people—like my brother at that time—did not want to theorize too much, but to make "theater," to move with people, and to do something, negotiations or so, and not to think too much about whether we should be more conservative or liberal or Friedman. So there was a certain tension among them. And this still now is the difference in the viewpoints of people like Doležal or Madler, and actually Benda. And, I think, Benda was the first who wanted to go out of Civic Forum and form his own party. And a special other case is the Civic Democratic Alliance which was the first one. It was before the revolution, not officially, but they already had their program. And so this is the first of the democratic parties here. But they went into the first elections under the roof of Civic Forum. And it was, I think, a good decision, because the first election was a referendum in a sense. Either Civic Forum or the *status quo*, that means Communists. And now some people claim Civic Forum was vague and wild, and that there were too many opinions, and that it was not clear what they wanted. This is perhaps correct, but it's not an objection. It would be an objection in a stable democracy, but in a revolutionary stage?

How would you evaluate the last ten years? Have things turned out the way you imagined, or have there been disappointments?

If I'm disappointed, I'm mostly disappointed by the disappointment of others. I do not want to say the disappointment of others is incorrect, it is correct. But I would not be so much disappointed by the reasons for this disappointment as the disappointment itself. I don't know whether it's clear.

You see, we were going very fast into a transition, which is not "a" transition, but a multiple of transitions. You have to change the economy on various scales. You have to change politics on various scales. You have to change public organization, or municipal activity in multiple scales. You have to change people's minds, their behavior. You have to release the freedom of the press, the freedom of movement. And now all those changes cannot be done at the same time. Some of them are fast. The freedom of the press was done in one day. Freedom of travel was done in a few days. It was just canceling the exit permits which were obligatory, so whoever had passports could go. Immediately. To issue a new passport took maybe some days, some weeks maybe. But to change the economy, it cannot be done overnight. And now the fact that there were various speeds for these changes caused the transition period to seem not logical—it was neither totalitarian, nor democratic, nor something else. It has no name. It was just a mess. And what we enthusiasts, we optimists, thought is that the mess would last two years at most. And it lasted ten years, and still exists. Now it has changed its forms. But the form now is the unreliability of the private sector on a large scale.

And now people would like already to live in the same way as in the established Western democracies, forgetting that those democracies have hundreds of years behind them, and we have just ten years. Okay, so these are the economic problems with cheating on the large scale, cheating on the small scale. I do not know the details and why the standard of living is going down. I do not see it too much with my eyes, but I read in the papers that the effective income is going down. But I see more and more restaurants, more and more shops. And I see Czech people in the shops and restaurants, not only tourists. And I see new buildings being painted and reconstructed. Well, it's true, probably, that there is much more expensive rents, so this might be the main reason of disappointment for many people, because they either have to lose all their salary in paying the rent for an apartment or to move to some less prestigious place, which is very painful.

And I remember, actually, how the threat of the Communists in the '50s, to move our and many other families out of Prague, was so much considered to be a serious threat. So now people have to change and move from Prague, because they cannot pay the rent in Prague. In this country people are not used to moving so much during their lifetime. I have been living in my apartment since birth, and actually my family lived there since 1905. So, it's not the habit to move every year to another flat.

Anyway, then another source of disappointment is, are our politicians. The reasonable intellectual friends slowly left politics and it's normal. As I mentioned, it's not for them. They can observe, but from a distance. And the new people are somewhat, I do not understand them quite well, and I do not meet them so much. I know them personally, but there is not too much opportunity to spend some time with them, and understand their motivations, their intentions. And it often looks like small children who argue about any stupid, petty detail.

I understand the procedure in Parliament for when a law is going to be passed, that there is reasonable time spent studying the law, or that there are committees and subcommittees which should look at the consequences, side effects, all of that stuff. I take intellectually, that it is an important way to correct a law, to polish it, and to make it final. And the fact that there are various parties, various opinions, causes disputations which may be productive, that there is not a simpleminded, simple line. But what happens is that much, much more important than whether the law is correctly written, is which party was proposing it. And if it is a party other than my party, it's a bad law, and I should vote against it. And if I vote for a law which was proposed by another party, I have problems with my party. And without explanation, just because I voted in a different way than my colleagues in the same party. Then I do not know why there is a freedom of vote in Parliament. So, maybe it's a naive view of politics, but people are naive in the majority. So, they think that the main business of politicians is to read papers and find the errors of other politicians and make a fuss about that.

And then when one finds that the other one had some financial problem, immediately publicize that, and he, what does the other one do? Instead of doing anything else, he is looking for financial problems of this guy.

You see, the problem is that as time elapses, people always remember first better things than worse things, so they remember better things in the totalitarian system. They remember how they didn't have to care about their future so much, because they had certain reliable positions, and they had permanent jobs and permanent futures, most of them. Those dissidents are such a minority that it's not important. And, so they actually do not see how different it is; that they can read various opinions, in one paper one opinion, in another paper another one; that they can go abroad wherever they want. That even the police on the street are nicer. I do not know whether the policemen, where they are recruited, but there was a period of an enormous number of jokes about policemen. And the jokes were about their stupidity. And there are not so much jokes about the stupidity of policemen now. Maybe either the police are not so stupid or people are interested in other things. I do not know.

I think it would be very wise to put on TV some documentaries from that time. Even if the documentaries were made in order to praise the government and to show what was nice. They couldn't avoid putting into the scene, let's say, a window of a shop. Empty. No goods in the shops. Long lines waiting for bread, butter, meat. There were days in the week when there was no meat. And for hours and hours you were supposed to stand in a line for something among people who were upset by standing in the line for something. And therefore, they didn't create a nice atmosphere there. And you are losing your time in this way.

Your car has broken, and you had to bribe someone. First find out who would be willing to repair it in less than one month. Find out how. Find out how much you should pay him in order to do that. And then to make sure that he did it correctly. That he didn't put another wrong part into your car. So, all of that. And stealing on a large scale, there was probably a lot, but nobody knew about that so much. So I do not want to say that everything is better. But I want to say why I am disappointed by the disappointment more than the reason for the disappointment.

3

Věra Jirousová

I didn't always know that art was so political.
　　　　　　　　　　　　　—Věra Jirousová, 1998

Věra Jirousová, *art historian, was an active participant in the musical and artistic underground during the Communist era of Czechoslovakia. Since 1989, she has worked in public relations for the National Gallery of Modern Art in Prague. She continues to write articles and reviews on artistic and other cultural events in the Czech Republic. The interview, conducted in Czech, took place at the National Gallery of Modern Art in Prague's Veletržní Palace.*

I think that I was one of the children who was still brought up in the street, and I did not realize that until my children were not. Since my youth, everything went on outside and we were not at home in the apartments. We were always outside, because I was in the outskirts of Prague, between Palmovka and Balabenka. It was very much a working-class, common environment there, and my father was an electrician and he thought that I would be one too. I graduated from an electrical engineering high school, and when I was eighteen, I decided to study art history, because that was much more interesting to me than all the mathematical disciplines. I think that it was so very, very beautiful because I was always independent.

　　I felt, for instance, terribly sorry for my children, and that was also why I later left Prague for seven years, so that they could also be outside and on their own. I didn't like to always give them to someone, so that they would be, from as early as three years old, in kindergartens, then in schools, and have over them some institutionalized supervision all the time. I did not like that. I think that it is much better if a person learns to be self-reliant in a situation. So, I think that as a child I was half the time playing and running around like all children run around everywhere, and half the time I was reading. That is also something that is quite often not possible to do in Prague anymore; it is not possible downtown and in the suburbs, where there are large apartment complexes. It is not as interesting as it used to be in the forties and the fifties. Prague suburbs used to be extremely interesting.

How did you find yourself in conflict with the former regime?

That is hard for me. I think that I perceived the conflict very early on, because I was in a pioneer[1] summer camp, and in a children's radio group. Already in about the fourth grade I was asked to leave, because in the evenings I would tell the other children in the summer camp scary stories. Those were not quite like fairy tales and it turned out that my imagination was too rich for the pioneer thing. But I was rather glad that they threw me out. At that time I still only perceived the constant tight jacket, like something tight. And when I was eighteen, when I graduated, I didn't want to feel obligated to the regime for anything, things like "we make it possible for you to study." So I said that I didn't ever want to study. And I finished. Then, not until a year later, I decided that I was going to do what I was interested in most, and that it was not going to be something to do with the regime, but was going to be my own thing, something I was interested in.

And the real conflict was, when a person is working—or when one starts to study art history. I was generally interested both in the old and the contemporary art. I never separated the two. I never wanted to specialize too soon. Not until the end of my studies did I choose to devote myself to the twentieth century and contemporary art, because in contemporary art, there was the closest contact with—a possibility to talk to the people that I was interested in, in the situation of the artist in society. And, of course, all the high-quality exhibitions were quite often prohibited. In fact, all during the sixties and during my studies I was growing up in this environment where there was constant discrimination against free art. They always allowed one thing and then again prohibited another thing, and we were used to dealing with that.

During the sixties we kept turning more and more to conceptual art, to the expression of an idea, as opposed to continuing in the trend of aesthetics. I was always more interested in that which I was not familiar with, which was new, and which was itself, expression, for instance, the whole world of conceptual art, nongallery space, action art. Now, for example, there is a big retrospective, an exhibition that was in Los Angeles and is now in Vienna. So I went to look at all the history of action art, which is extremely important in art in the second half of this century: the pressure that always—in opposition to aesthetics—a new idea would be expressed, something new that grows out of the relationships between society and the artists. All of this we were actually trying to implement with the people who were here, and naturally, it lead into the area of rock music.

I actually worked with the band Plastic People, because the circle simply gathered at an exhibition. Now, when an exhibition was prohibited, so what? We could go, we could do it outside, the way we had learned to do things, so we would not be dependent on the conditions.

For instance, all the action art in the Křižovnická school happened at a table in a pub. Art was happening there, because it was not allowed in a gallery. Galleries were prohibited. So from this circle I actually learned to preserve a measure of freedom for myself, the possibility of creative work in any environment, which was certainly terribly important.

Then there is also the fact that women are not very patient. I certainly am not very patient, for example, when something keeps happening in a pub for two years and one finds out that the majority of it is plans and it starts getting utopian.

So one day I took my things from the table and told them that I was going to do something. A lot of the people had decided to emigrate. I was too optimistic. I thought that the change would come in maybe five years, that the regime had a kind of a sinusoid development and that while we were studying, it was all right, and in five years it would get better again. But it was to be twenty years. That was a rather bad estimation in my case.

Actually, sometime around the beginning of the seventies, even when my son was born, I kept telling myself that I didn't want to just become a part of what was leaving and could not be realized anymore. And we kept looking for some opportunities to do things, so that there would be something real, and so that it would be art for a larger audience, for the public. And gallery space was closed. My husband at the time, Ivan Jirous, decided to take risks to the degree of doing something within the sphere of his concerts. And the concert scene—the stage was a certain environment—was a part of graphic art action. And that was how a person, without even knowing it, found oneself in the underground.

I think that you probably know some of the stories about having concerts outside Prague and how, for instance, we all met because of music, because whoever has ears and is from Bohemia—Bohemians are very musical—listened to the LP issued in the fall in New York or somewhere abroad. We knew it here right away. We had it all here, all the music, because everyone who got a hold of a thing like that immediately passed it on to his or her friends. So the concerts had a large circle of people who attended regularly, and we came really for the music.

There were also Saturday night dances with popular brass music. There people fought and got drunk a thousand times more often, while in this circle people got wild, but everybody was there for the music. When there was, for instance, the famous concert of DG 307, the first one, the police came to surround the place because they had learned about it. Maybe ten buses of policemen came. And no one had even had a beer by that time, because everyone had agreed that first there would be the concert, and then during the break that would be the first beer, so that it would simply be the concert. We needed the people not to disturb [things] by going to get a beer. So the police were quite surprised that they found a large group of people and everyone was still, that no one even had any percentage on their breath.

Some people even, who were not able to adjust—I didn't think that there was anything wrong with such a lack of adaptability—may not have been able to work anywhere, because they were not able to conform to the Communist environment. And in order for them to be allowed to attend the concerts with no problems, they would show Ivan Jirous their ID, that they had found some work by now and that they could go to the concert. Because people who did not work were "parasites" and the police used to immediately take them away somewhere. I don't know, they were then "supervised" because of that, and had to apply and were required to look for a job.

Then, actually, they started to tighten up the whole circle—there were two very significant circles in Prague. One was the circle of the Jazz Section [*jazzová sekce*] and the other was the underground circle. The underground circle was somewhat more elaborately interconnected and wilder. It worked more with common people. I thought that the jazz circle was great and they worked a little more with students and the middle class. While the underground circle was the working young people. The majority were young people who worked, whose only expressions of freedom came through music, through this kind of creativity.

When they arrested the Plastic People, we simply decided that we had to do something that would be a real politically significant thing. Because it was not possible—I thought it was unacceptable to prosecute young musicians. Even under that regime, when someone, an intellectual, had a conflict with the regime, it was possible to express it. But with the musicians, someone else needed to do it, to stand up for them.

So I think this was actually how the whole circle from which Charter 77 later developed met at the trial of the Plastic People. Musicians came as well as professors. Everyone had children and their children all listened to rock and roll at home. So it was simple. When someone wanted to stand up for them, for the Plastic People, they were standing up for their own children, too.

That was in fact, how it was possible that a real, broader kind of a base was established. And it was the people who were too aesthetic, who didn't want to join up with someone who was a former Communist—their focus was simply too narrow—who would only fight and risk their skins only for art and nothing else, not just for political ideas. And it seemed important to me that in this case, that everyone was concerned, because it was about children, or the children who were growing up.

Can you describe the trial of the Plastic People?

In school during lectures, I could write very fast. So during the trials, where I was admitted because I was still Ivan Jirous's wife in '75. . . . We then got divorced, because we had not been living together for five years. Every time he got arrested, it was clear that it was not quite possible to live with him. I have a different sense of responsibility and a different kind of approach, but I always defended many of his characteristics, a kind of determination for freedom and creativity, and especially when he was arrested. So I attended the trials and would always tell them that I was an unmarried sister of Ivan Jirous, as my name was Jirousová. And I would take detailed notes so that we could then write up a report. And they thought that I had some kind of a recorder but those were not allowed in court. No, I just took very quick notes, and from those notes we reconstructed the whole trial. The trial was shameful, because at all the trials I had been to, which were always recorded somewhere as misdemeanors, they actually did not allow the defendants to present their arguments. The evidence was always very doubtful and rather made up by some witnesses. And the witnesses, all those that would testify for the defense, including some bartenders, were not called. So that was easy. That wasn't any just trial, was it?

And then I was also giving an interview for Reuters, and the secret police were on guard all day, because they had learned about it through the agencies—they had learned that Jirous's wife was giving an interview for Reuters. But they followed Juliana Jirousová all day, then picked her up in a street somewhere, pushed her in their Volga, and took her away. And she had no idea what was happening, because it was me giving the interview. So it took them at least a year before they found out that in the underground there were completely different relationships among people from the regular, the kind in common civic society.

How was the underground music scene affected by the arrests of the Plastic People?

Their concerts stopped. But there were others who played, for instance DG 307. After Zajíček was released, they also had concerts at Chomutov. And Artificial Material [*Umělá hmota*] also played. It had been a diverse scene and everyone would organize a concert somewhere outside of Prague, close to Prague so that they could get there by bus. And when they arrested the Plastic People, they arrested one of the most important bands from this circle, but the others went on playing. There was no reason to do otherwise. We just had to keep under better cover. I think that we had developed very elaborate ways of "conspiracy," because there was not a single poster anywhere, and everyone knew that there couldn't be any written information passed on, not even over the telephone. Everything had to be passed on only orally and through friends, but it worked perfectly.

Someone has even observed that the underground circle that was in the political charter was in a way an absolutely efficient interference shield, because the people were so unpredictable and uncontrolled. Anyone could do something quite unpredictable at any moment. The people, the common establishment, do this and then that during the day, and it is like when the hunter is able to follow its prey, because it does the same things every day. While the underground was quite an uncontrollable force—anyone could just up and do something at anytime, and that was really very difficult, hard to coordinate. One had to rely on the others to tell their friends and to know that they couldn't tell anyone else. Of course, something always leaked out, because there were many people who were planted. But the really important things never leaked.

That was a certain kind of luck, and it shielded, made it more difficult for the system of surveillance, but they learned quickly. I didn't underestimate the police system at all. They were able to figure out a lot of things. But this was simply impenetrable for anyone. It worked only through a system of relationships, only through a system of sympathies and not in any predictable way.

Can you say something about the charter from your perspective?

For me it was very important that the leading personages of the charter were all people that I deeply respected. Whether it was Professor Patočka or Professor Hejdánek, they were, I don't know, Václav Havel, Jiří Němec, I probably won't remember all of them, and now, or I won't use names at this occasion. Then the whole circle of *Tvář* [*Face*].[2] Actually, many circles of people participated with whom I had a kind of a personal relationship. There was Ludvík Vaculík, for instance, among writers. These were people who, during the many years, as one observed, had stood up to the regime. So this was very important to me. And also important was the fact that it was a legal means. I really would have, as I already had a young son at the time, excluded all the ways that would have been illegal. It seemed to me, that one should insist on the level of human rights. And that it was not an equal fight, but that I could simply go on modestly telling the truth and stand up to the regime. While if I had let them push me—the underground in the arts is different from the underground in politics. The underground in the arts is actually a given, it comes gradually, while the underground in politics is illegal. That is then the area of, I don't know, terrorism and some such, and that was always very foreign to me.

In this respect, I think that in the sixties, the students from the Communist countries had a completely different approach from students from the Western democracies. Over there, they were maoists too easily and they screened off the whole real regime of Mao, the Communist regime of Mao. So for me that was an important legal means. Then I consider it very significant that, for instance, the philosopher Hejdánek was at the time—it was he who came up with the idea that there actually existed the Helsinki Accord, that it had not only been signed but also on November 13, 1976, was issued as a legal regulation. So we had it here written down, a written document of the legal system which we could build on. And that seemed extremely important to me, because I think that, in fact, my approach as a woman was also very practical, that one was forced—all the caring and arranging of things, when one was taking care of a young child—it made it necessary to be practical. And practical at all levels, even at this one.

Apart from this, all the texts were always brilliantly formulated. I got a lot of satisfaction from the fact that, for example, the circle, I don't know, of Petr Uhl and the leftist movement, that Professor Patočka's texts, which were important to me—that they expressed even their ideas or their approach. That seemed to me to be a certain satisfaction, because otherwise I would have felt a bigger distance from this whole leftist approach. It was my early environment. My father was one of those who simply trusted the regime and after the war he thought, rather optimistically, that a better social structure was going to be established here. It was for him a certainty. I think that as an electrician and a person that actually believed in progress and things like that, he thought that he was supporting something socially and politically very progressive. And then he was, of course, very disappointed. That's why I have always kept a distance from these ways, from what they actually still practice here today—what is still on the agenda of the Communist or leftist parties, including the Social-Democratic Party. So I've always felt a distance from that. It was simply important for me that it was an orientation that I was able to support, because the leftist orientation, for me it had already—my parents' generation had actually already gone through that experience and I didn't need to go through it again.

Did you attend the seminars at the underground university in the seventies?

No, I attended Professor Patočka's lectures, and then I would go to the seminar that incorporated the Nietzsche seminar of Zdeněk Neubauer, Honza Sokol. And Jiří Němec later incorporated, in fact, included the whole large circle, the mathematics circle of intellectuals, and Ivan Havel and Jiří Fiala. There were a lot of people. Actually, it evolved into a kind of wider interdisciplinary team. I went to these lectures relatively often. For me it was a kind of natural continuation after school. At that time in the Faculty of Arts we really had just a minimum of philosophy. One or two semesters of lectures in philosophy can't be considered even an introduction. It was just a kind of first step.

Were there any lectures on art at the underground university?

Not much. And it was because I was not ready, at the time, to formulate my views on art. I was doing more writing, and more writing of poems, and it was not that I was not familiar with the contemporary scene, I was very familiar with it, but, in fact, between twenty and thirty, I was not yet at all able to independently formulate.

There were maybe two lectures on art, but they were really bad. I won't even say who it was, but I was just miserable and said to myself that I had never heard so many mistakes together at one time, so much incorrect information. Because the circle of mathematicians and philosophers was actually a circle with a very demanding way of thinking and they did not understand at all what art was or what kinds of issues there were. They considered it quite incomprehensible. And that was because it was not formulated. It was when someone talked about their personal ideas and compilations and all. It was really something incomprehensible.

But maybe ten years later, a lot later, in fact, I am now actually able to define the issues, the kind of real expression of ways of thinking, that has, for instance, been important since the beginning of this century, in postwar art. And also the whole, the confrontation of bourgeois art with the new public art, with the new public space, so the big transformation. In the sixties we didn't understand that yet. It was only perceivable. There were only occasional traces of that.

I considered voice to be important. I considered action art important, and not until the seventies, when there was a real minimum of any information, so I followed various trends. For instance, the American conceptions of art, European—the actual connection of the American and European scenes—before the large format and the transformation in the role of the artist, the transformation, in fact, in the artistic expression, that it was work, a kind of work like any other. When someone talks about the surface of it, about the exhibitions and this artist or that, it is only talking about a net that is not anchored. I simply always need to have the thing anchored, the social sphere, all the various possible ways that actually constitute the art scene. And in the seventies I was separated from all that the most. I wasn't allowed to go anywhere. I didn't have a passport, and I always just happened to come across a few journals somewhere, from which I tried to put together information. I was not able to define it at that time.

In the nineties, so the first five years, as much as I could I went to exhibitions and traveled abroad, to see everything with my own eyes. And then I had a chance to see the work of the people of my generation. For instance, when I saw the document, the ninth document in the castle done by Jean Hood, I suddenly realized that it was in fact the precisely formulated way of thinking of my generation, that it was a great work, even teamwork. What an exhibition! It was an extremely positive thing, really, a terribly positive thing, which was going to make it possible for people to come and be affected by it, and in turn, to look in it for what they themselves were interested in. Even the expression of feelings, and all these things—you then realize that it is really a great work that can be done by someone who has been able to devote twenty intensive years to it, to their field. And that's something we were not able to do here. So that was for me a kind of meeting with what had actually passed by.

What activities were you involved in during the eighties?

Toward the end of the seventies and at the turn of the seventies and eighties, I think the situation in the charter was the most critical. Many people had emigrated, and most of my friends that had small children had left. And I myself, I didn't want to leave, because once I make a decision, I don't like to then change my decisions later. If I had wanted to, if I had decided to work in my field, it would have been quite possible for me in '68. I had two offers: from the Gallery of Eastern European Art in Düsseldorf and the Museum of Modern Art in Tel Aviv.

Those were two great opportunities for me and I decided, because of my dissertation, to let them be and to finish my dissertation on the graphic and poetic works of Bohuslav Rejnek. He was at the time already an elderly man. He died in '71, a year later. It was very important for me to complete the dissertation, and to do it at such a pace that would be acceptable for the man. By the way, he was one of the most important poets who stood completely in a kind of opposition to the whole bourgeois culture and with long experience of the whole nineteenth century. He was born in 1892 and was the first to translate Trakl.[3] The whole experience was for me, simply, contact with something that one usually knows about only from books. But to also know a real person who has actually lived through it, that was for me an important part of the poetic experience.

So that is what I decided at the time. And then later, I didn't want to be thinking one year about emigrating and the next year about not emigrating. That's what a lot of people were doing, always changing their minds. I didn't want that. So during the crisis period at the turn of the seventies and eighties, I often went to visit my friends in the country. And in the end I decided to leave Prague, because my son was very ill, he was twelve, then I had a daughter. And when I saw how things were looking for me here in Prague—I didn't have a job, only interrogations, and on top of that I had a baby—so I said to myself it was impossible. Emigrate with two children? That would have been nonsense.

So I decided to try to live in a way that would actually be good for my children. I said to myself that poems and real milk, those were rather important things I thought I should insist on. So I went to the Czech-Moravian Highlands. We got a house there, and then a year later I even got a cow. It was a little farm with chickens, a dog, a lot of cats, and the cow. I milked it and I sold the milk, and that way I earned every month as much as if I worked as a cleaning lady in Prague. I was too small and not strong enough to be a cleaning lady. I can take care of one cow, but not a big farm.

And cleaning? That was always a disaster for me. I would work for maybe three months and then be seriously ill, because of the heavy buckets and too much work. It was not at all something that I could physically manage. Well, and apart from that, I thought, my children would be able to run around freely. Tobias could ride his bike and Sara could play in the yard. That was something that I could not have had for my children at all in Prague.

So in the eighties I was in Kostelní Vydři at the very southern edge of the Highlands, where there is a Carmelite monastery. The last Carmelite monk, who was allowed to live there until his death, died in the spring of '90. And new monks came again to this monastery in 1989. So it is again a true Carmelite monastery. So I was glad. It was the kind of place where I wanted to stay. I thought that it would become my home, because there was a certain, kind of underground, circle, and they could understand me from one angle but not at all from another angle. That's because they are not used to a woman with a job, even really that a woman takes care of the children and so on.

And then, when I had an opportunity to go back to my profession in '90, I did. And I think that for my second husband it was a very strange thing, that I seemed a different person. Before, I always adapted myself to the circumstances, because I thought that was the only thing possible. But at the moment when I am allowed to work, then I try to adapt everything else so that I could work. The children, of course, can always fit into that, but there is not time anymore for the very relaxed and uncoordinated way of life in the underground. One has deadlines. I was a half hour late today, but that is, that can happen to me because I still have a little more to do than I can manage. On the whole, I think, that when a poet takes care of two children by herself almost all her life—and my son is now a student and my daughter is fourteen—I still have enough responsibilities for two.

In '89 I was still living in the country. We were really very poor. It was rather funny, because every month—we were living on about a thousand crowns—I would have a debt in the local store, two hundred for butter, bread, and so on. And I would pay that when we got paid, and by the end of the month there would again be a debt of two hundred. And we always joked with the storekeeper there, that it was a debt I had on the state. The two hundred was always so much that I couldn't pay it.

Well, that was how it was, for one earns really little that way. You sell ten liters of cow milk—that was about eight hundred. That was terribly little, eight hundred and eighty, very little money.

When did you move back to Prague?

At first I commuted for as long as half a year, all the time back and forth, back and forth. And now I was thinking hard, because it was a decision that was to be not only about me but also about my children. Actually, Tobias—he was already eighteen at the time and had finished high school—wanted to go to the city, because in the country he didn't have very many friends. So for him the city was important. My daughter would have just gone to first grade in '90, and in the country environment, she also didn't really have anyone to spend time with. And I, a job there? That was nonsense. That doesn't even exist in Kostelní Vydři. There is a museum there, but the local museum is at four grades lower than the level I was interested in. I really couldn't work there. And the artists I work with and write about—their exhibitions would even today be for three people in the town who would understand it. Maybe three. And it would not work that way. There the middle level needs to be filled in, so that people would get used to it. I don't know. Waco, for instance, is certainly a different artistic level than New York, but it is possible to find there the very, sort of the middle, a very good basis, because it's been established there, the structure. And that is what would be needed to get established in Kostelní Vydři. But that is hard to do in such a very tiny town, and especially by someone like me. That would have to be done by someone local.

I was still at the time a dissident. And I decided to go back to where I finished in '71, when they closed down art, to go back to an art magazine. And in the summer I started in the magazine *Atelier*, where I was for about a year and a half, and then I transferred to a very good magazine *Vytvarné umění* [*Plastic Arts*] which seemed to me to represent something that was really important, a retrospective of the last twenty years, getting familiar with the contemporary world scene of art. And this magazine—unfortunately, I worked there for two years—was in very bad shape economically. And then it changed into collected volumes. Later they could do only collected volumes. I wouldn't be able to support my children with that, so I went to the Ministry of Culture to find out why we couldn't work abroad. And today I know very well why we can't work abroad. At the ministry, when some problems come up, they don't know how to resolve them. They are only able to sweep them under the table.

I watched that for two years, how the majority of the real problems were swept under the table rather than being solved. And then they suspended the chairman of Veletržní Palace here, Jiří Ševčík, who had clearly been a key integrating personality throughout the eighties of all the art, all the artistic circles here, and who was competent and had devoted ten years of his life to the idea of the Veletržní Palace. So when the ministry and Tigrid[4] let Mr. Zlatohlavek, the executive director who is still in the office today, fire Ševčík, I said I wasn't going to assist in this, in these ways. And in response to that Tigrid told me that there was a free press, to go and learn it.

So I went into the free press, so that I could have influence in this thing. And I tried that. I think that at *Lidové noviny* [*People's Newspaper*], where I worked for two years in a rather professional manner, people would even tell me that, considering I had never been abroad, I didn't have a narrow view. I had a wide perspective on things, on the fact that there were in the current scene several generations together with various experiences, of whom the older ones spent most of their lives not being able to realize their ambitions as fully as in a free society. I always tried to take all this into account, but also not to see only the Czech world, to see that we are a part of the context of Central European, European, and world art. But there are few people who like to hear that, because it is better to be a big artist in Bohemia than a small artist in Europe.

I left when they changed the whole editorial board at *Lidové noviny*, last year. I left because the new team of younger people had all transferred there and didn't have much interest in my work. So I decided, when again I didn't have anything, to put together my book.[5] I had two or three months free. And I found the old stories and they were all unfinished. I never had the time to finish it all. So instead of finishing them up—that would have taken at least a year, or half a year for sure. I haven't yet had that much time. I cut it up and made a kind of a book from it, from what was dense and what seemed important to me, that dreams were more significant than reality, but both were regarded as equal, so that the surrealism would be gone from it. Dreams are not a road to somewhere, somewhere away, but they are a way, one of the layers of what, where we live. So I thought that I wanted to say this through the book, and I did it. That was more important than finishing it.

And then I was offered a position here at the press department. I could work here because they put on good exhibitions, and I wrote about them. I evaluated them in a positive way. And the important thing was for people to come and see the exhibitions and to have all the opportunities to form their own opinion. I don't want to be a critic. I want to be someone who will make the people come and see the exhibitions, whether by what I write or by whatever I do. I don't think criticism is that important. I think it is more important for people to make, to develop a relationship and create their own opinion. So I came to work here.

How would you evaluate the last ten years?

That was something extremely important for me, really exciting, because when I lived in the Highlands, the only communication channel with the world for me was the Austrian ORF, Austrian television. And you actually could see the fall of the Iron Curtain directly, how it gradually collapsed, starting with the refugees who came to Prague. And it was like layers gradually collapsing, and that seemed quite wonderful to me. Then I thought, as one thinks in territorial terms, about the whole area, that this was one kind of a movement. And the Soviet Union? The transformation? God knows what might happen.

I looked at it as these two movements that were and, I think, still are very dangerous today. The way the whole area actually keeps changing with the various civil wars. That it is terribly, terribly dangerous, because when you give up on the most advanced technology, you fall into a lower historical level where you have constant territorial civil wars, that are in turn interconnected with the whole world. Everyone well knows that wars are not about the existence of some groups, some conflicts. They are about one territory not being well enough protected, legally and in all other ways, against trade with old guns, old weapons. I see the wars as a movement on a map of economics. The very poor countries, the neglected countries, where they don't have a political administration, fall into being divided and economically exploited by this class, this profiteering society, that actually profits by the continued trading with the technology, that is, all levels of the large technological society. When someone cannot politically protect the country in an effective, democratic way, it then falls into this sphere in which it is hard to offer much help. When I look at the Balkans today, I know that it is for me a country that wasn't able to protect itself from being destroyed in this way by traders with weapons. The conflict—everyone knows that it is very easy to initiate them and it is very hard to end them.

That was the last generation, for instance in the Balkans, the last generation that still had the clan experience with war. Their fathers killed one another. If it didn't happen now, there would have been a whole generation that would have been without this hatred and without this revenge. But that, in my opinion, was also one of the initiated wars, and it was initiated at the time when an opportunity came up to sell weapons there.

From this perspective, it seems to me, for instance, that even here—where we have always been on the bridge, and the bridge is at times very thin between the East and the West—it was really tense, whether we would be accepted into NATO or not. Unfortunately, there has been the separation of Czechoslovakia into the two states. Everyone considers the separation a drawback, but we were not economically so well-off to be able to support Slovakia to such a degree that it would be interesting for them to stay with us. They are going through their own historical experience that separates them from us again by a certain deep,

deep abyss. These are big things that probably won't get quite resolved in the very near future. I'm talking about—this is women's politics, but I see things differently. It may be that until the whole area of Eastern Europe quiets down and is interconnected with some really effective structures, Slovakia and we will in fact remain separated.

And from this perspective, I also consider my work as work that is, after all, a part of a very important field. All this interconnecting and meeting of cultures that has actually been happening in art since the sixties and that can now finally formulate, that all these movements, they have been happening, I don't know, since Gauguin in Tahiti and since the interest of the artists in Paris in Nigerian masks. In fact this way of meeting, whether it is through the plastic arts or through music, it is a very positive trend in every society and also on the international scene, where, I believe, there are things happening—so that I could support them and consider them good, because I am also a part of it.

I didn't always know that art was so political. I insisted that I was a lyrical poet and it is *they* who make it political. When they told me that I was politically active, I said, no, no I wasn't politically active, and I was separated from politics and I felt separated from politics. And now since the nineties, I have known that I am a part of a certainly very important political trend and that I couldn't have known it like this until now.

4

Michael Kocáb

We wanted the Communists to depart forever from our history and our lives.

—Michael Kocáb, 1998

Michael Kocáb, *jazz musician and entrepreneur, acted as one part of "The Bridge," the liaison between Civic Forum and the Communist government in 1989, and as an MP was instrumental in negotiating the withdrawal of Soviet troops from the country. Since 1989, he has built a media empire in musical recording and video, continues to write music for theater and film, and tours with his band Prague's Choice. The interview, conducted in Czech, took place at Prague's Hotel Diplomat.*

I was born in Prague into a family of an evangelical parish priest and a psychologist. In '54—all through the sixties, eighties, always about every ten years—we moved, so we lived, successively, at first in Zruč nad Sázavou until I was six. Then for ten years through grade school and junior high school—[those] I attended in Karlovy Vary, and then during high school I lived with my parents in Mladá Boleslav. I graduated from high school and I then went to Prague to the conservatory to study composition and the organ. [I studied] the organ with Professor Robek and composition with Professor Hunín, which later came in handy, these two professions, when I was executing the withdrawal of the Soviet army. It came in handy that I could play the organ and write music.

And after the conservatory, which I attended for six years, or thereabout, I played music and made a living as a musician. I played at first with jazz bands, for example with Jiří Ctivýn or the *Pražský džezband* [Prague Jazz Band] with Milan Svoboda. Then I started my own band *Pražský výběr* [Prague's Choice], which was and still is today very popular. After a short jazz-rock period it has transformed itself into a rock band, and up until today we play rock music. Right

51

now we are rehearsing another repertoire and we are going on a concert tour which starts in about a week. The concert in Prague will be on October 28th [1998], which is the date when the republic was established, or the anniversary.

In '82 we were banned. There was a campaign by the secret police against us, during which they prohibited our activities. They literally got into one concert in Hradec Králové and canceled everything there. And this police campaign and the following persecution actually resulted in a five-year break, during which we were not allowed to practice our profession. We were not allowed to play with the band and were subjected to various kinds of political persecution. I was [persecuted] the most. They even took away my social security and health insurance, which was something that not even the Communists were allowed to do, because everyone was granted social and health insurance by law. Nevertheless, they tried it on me as a certain kind of psychological pressure.

In '86, or since '85, I again began to make a living—then already as a composer of film music—and by '89 I had written music for around three hundred films. And also for a variety of audiovisual fairs; I wrote the music for a pavilion, the Czech pavilion, but also the Canadian pavilion at EXPO '86 in Vancouver. [I worked] for several EXPOs and wrote music for various pavilions and amusement parks. And I was present, most of the time, at these expositions abroad. I did something in Dijon in France, in Tunis, and so on. I also wrote theater music, and I composed a kind of ballet opera *Odysseus* which has run since about '87, I think, continuously, for over ten years now, in the National Theater. So it has been very successful. I also cooperated on the script and the directing. Apart from that I also codirected a full-length film *Pražákům, těm je hej* [*Those Praguers Sure Have It Good*], where I also played a part, [and] which is about my band.

In '89, I established with a friend of mine, Horáček, an initiative *Mosty* [Bridges], or *Most* [The Bridge], in which we in a way encouraged the Communist government of the time to enter into a dialogue with the opposition, or, in other words, with Charter 77, with Václav Havel in the lead. I got this idea when, after one live performance of my band, as we were accepting some prizes at the *Děčínská kotva* [Děčín Anchor], I said that every nation had the kind of government it deserved, which is a general truth, but it caught the attention of the prime minister at the time, Adamec. And he asked me what kind of interesting thing I meant by it. Then I acquainted him with the meaning of that sentence. I used this brief contact with him, and in the first document of The Bridge—which I started with Michal Horáček, a well-known songwriter and a poet and writer. So it was Adamec, the prime minister at the time, to whom I addressed the first document *Ve společných rukách* [*In Common Hands*]. And he responded to it very quickly. And it happened quite, or to a certain degree, by chance, that we came at the right moment to the right person, and immediately we got, somehow, to the center of what was happening. And since that time— and that was just two, three months before the revolution—or since sometime in September, maybe even since August '89, we were already preparing a kind of meeting between Adamec and Charter 77.

It was not so much an effort to create a roundtable, because at the time we did not like the idea of a roundtable very much. A roundtable, the way they were trying it out in [East] Germany and in Poland, led to and had a tendency to bring together, a tiny little bit, the parties that actually met at the roundtable. And a roundtable means that the people understand one another in some things, that they interconnect. We wanted bilateral negotiations. Something like negotiations of two enemy parties, such as when you put up a white flag during a war and now the two sides come together and have to negotiate.

We were very careful not to make our initiative come out as an attempt at bringing together the positions of the two sides. We wanted the Communists to depart forever from our history and our lives. And we did not want, under any conditions, some interweaving like in '68, some "socialism with a human face," some bringing together of the ideas. For us, the idea of socialism was so definitely and totally historically finished and over with, that it was essentially a matter of persuading Adamec and the government to start an organized retreat. We thought that if they prolonged their aggressivity—which was directed by Štěpán[1] and which was already apparent at the time in the displays of state power by the Ministry of the Interior in the town square—then it was clear that they were going to be driven out sooner or later by force, and that, unnecessarily, there would be bloodshed. Their positions seemed to us already lost at that time, but it could have still been very complicated. And we also wanted to take advantage of the mildness of the Czech character that always gives up sooner than, or about five minutes earlier than is completely necessary. And it seemed to us that it was Adamec who might have understood that.

And, as it turned out in the end, he did. In the materials of The Bridge, it was clearly declared that we were not interested in bringing together positions— that was stated explicitly—but only in negotiation, in the peaceful transfer of power. We acquainted Havel as well as Adamec with this initiative, and both sides—Havel agreed with the idea that a meeting could happen. Adamec did too, but he was afraid. He thought it would be more acceptable to negotiate, not to negotiate directly with Havel but with some members of Civic Forum. At that time they thought it could be, for example, Křižan, and others. Well, right into this first kind of "sounding out" contact, which was actually already opened, came November 17. And that was why we succeeded, in a flash, two, three, four days after November 17 in immediately beginning effective negotiations, because we did not need to open the contacts. Those were already established, not, I repeat again, not just friendly contacts, but the channel had actually been built. So it was possible to contact Adamec directly, through his consultant, a certain Oskar Krejčí, but later also through Marián Čalfa[2] and other people.

And Adamec was ready, and had somehow got used to the idea that the negotiations were going to happen. And we became, in fact, The Bridge initiative became, the mediator of all the negotiations that there were between Civic Forum and the Communist government after the revolution. That was lucky, tremendously lucky, because this role was sought by *Obroda* [Renewal]. Renewal was former Communists from '68, who in the meantime had been, of course, also persecuted in various ways, and they were preparing for this historic event. They wanted to seize the initiative, so that they could institute again a better '68 and a better middle way. I was very afraid of exactly this, and that's why I did not let the initiative get out of my hands.

A part of Renewal's idea was even that the president or the prime minister would have been Dubček, a former Communist, who would have continued from about where he had finished in '68. But that was the thing that we actually needed the least. Dubček, as a longtime collaborator, or, in fact, a member of the leadership of the Czechoslovak Communist Party, and a collaborator with, or a certain long-distance colleague of, the Soviet government during various periods, was a decent, kind man, but nevertheless fascinated by the power of the Soviet Union. And so he would not have been able, would not have been willing to take certain steps. He was afraid that a big brother in Moscow would hit back too hard. And Dubček had already experienced '68, the invasion of the Soviet army, and therefore he would have been easily crippled in the force of his actions.

But Havel not so. Therefore, from the very beginning, in the negotiations with the government, I argued for the idea that the next president should be Havel. And I let Adamec know that. And Adamec told Gorbachev even before it was decided in Civic Forum itself. There were two currents. On the one hand there were the Renewal people, the '68 people, the former Communists. And then normal people, who did not have anything to do with Communists. And between them it was being debated whether it should, most likely, be Dubček. But I was already—at the government level with Adamec, but he passed it on to Moscow—pushing Havel. And so, paradoxically, the "enemies'" side accepted that it would be Havel, which meant that it would actually be a genuine political takeover. They accepted this before Civic Forum itself which did not even know that it was possible to reach this far. However, not to be unfair, that was a difference, a discrepancy, of about two, three days, because Civic Forum was immediately adopting and taking up positions for itself—behaving like a typical army, like an invasion army, and as soon as it got a hold of something somewhere, it was already voicing further requests. So things were moving very quickly. I don't want to take credit for this all myself. Nevertheless, I had definitely nominated Havel for this position well ahead of time. Then I still had to get it approved in Civic Forum so that Havel would become a presidential delegate, which I brought up several times. That is on record. They rejected it twice, and it was approved the third time. And so this was then one of my roles in The Bridge.

I also played a role directly in Civic Forum, because The Bridge was not a nonpartisan mediator but—the Bridge, my initiative, was a part of Civic Forum. And there I was actually given the task, or I became, in fact, a member of the Coordinating Center of Civic Forum, and also of the so-called Crisis Headquarters of the Coordinating Center, where there were about five people. There was Havel, Vondra, Křižan, Jičínský, Pithart, and me, and that was about all, roughly six people, yes, and Malý, six or seven people, and I was in charge of the security issues. That meant that I immediately set out—and at that time I brought Klaus, the future prime minister, with me as a second man, basically. It also stayed that way. He was at the time quite unimportant.

And we set out for the Western Military District to see General Zachariáš who was, in fact, in charge of that part of the army that would have been taking action against the demonstrators. We set out, and we essentially persuaded General Zachariáš and explained the situation to him and made him promise us not to take action against the demonstrators. If Václavík, who was indecisive, at the time had made a decision, then Vacek, who was then the chief of staff, would likely have issued an order, and then Zachariáš would have acted on the order. And that would have meant that, most likely, tanks would have started out from Tábor, the Western Military District, which was positioned against West Germany. And at that time army vehicles would have started out, or tanks, or I don't know what they would have set on Prague, and probably the air force, too. We somehow succeeded in stopping this initiative in time, because I knew about it, somehow I learned about it, and apparently in time, so it worked out that Zachariáš understood the situation and was assured by us that we did not want to go ahead with—there were certain alarming rumors that we wanted to use violence against Czech soldiers, which was rubbish. There was never anything like that. They simply got that from the Russians. So that was another of my initiatives, very important and essential. General Zachariáš then passed the information on to the Chief of Staff Vacek. And I then went to see Vacek—he later became the minister of defense—and we negotiated with this understanding. And we were actually already preparing a meeting with Havel, and so it happened that, actually, this important part of the army had already become more or less loyal to the demonstrators or to the leadership of Civic Forum, or, at least, it had decided not to stand in the way of this popular initiative, the initiative of the Civic Forum.

After that I initiated and participated in the writing of a certain document, a proclamation, an appeal to the Supreme Soviet of the Soviet Union and Gorbachev, which we put together with a certain editing team. Jičínský, I think, was there, Malý, Havel, me—or Horáček, I don't remember anymore. And Michal Horáček and I took it to the Soviet embassy and gave it at that time to the Consul Filip, who sent it to Moscow to Gorbachev. We asked him as the president at the time, or the chief. He was the chairman of USSR, right, Gorbachev—CCCPSU, the Central Committee of the Communist Party of the Soviet Union. So we asked him to begin negotiations with the aim of withdrawing the Soviet armed forces from our territory. We simply asked for a reconstitution of the sovereignty of our state. And that could not have been done in any other way than by their actually evacuating, by withdrawing their army from our territory. So that was the very first initiative, that was about, roughly, about fifteen days after the revolution, after the beginning of the revolution, that means still in November '89.

Even the Russians were asking whether we were not going to use force against the Soviets on our territory. We assured them that we were not planning that, that nobody here wanted to use force at all, that the times of bloody revolutions had been over for a long time. And it even seemed a little humorous to us. They still lived in the dogmatic captivity of the experience from the year '18, their own Bolshevik Revolution from that time, and thought that all takeovers of state power were necessarily accompanied by lampposts full of hanged men, that simply, blood had to flow. That means that they had not read Czech history carefully, but that they knew their own history well. It was then easy to assure them that we were not planning anything like that, that nobody would even want that. In Civic Forum this idea was quite unambiguously rejected and the demonstrators didn't have such tendencies either. That was quite an unnecessary concern.

And then I participated in a series, in mediating a series, of other meetings with all kinds of representatives of the former regime. And it even went so far that later I was contacted by the Russian side with its representatives from the Central Committee of the Communist Party of the Soviet Union, which meant the Russian Politburo, and also the KGB, with a request to arrange talks with Civic Forum. I, however, acted rather autonomously. When I saw that it was a request for the kind of contact that could have threatened, and I'd say, to have crushed the determination of the leaders of Civic Forum to move resolutely forward, then I did not arrange it at all. I simply took responsibility, and today I consider that a big credit, that I simply did not pass the contact on any further. I simply lost it somewhere, as if I had forgotten about it. It was clear to me that as soon as the KGB started threatening our revolutionaries, our revolutionaries would get very scared and would begin—especially, again, it was those people who were close to Havel and were former Communists—to completely shake with fear. They had always shaken with fear of the Soviets.

Not me. For me the Soviets had, luckily, always been so far away, and I was not so much affected by repression by the Soviet Union, so that I did not get scared that much. That was my big advantage. And so that was one contact that was supposed to have happened during the time when there was a general strike. I intentionally forgot about it, and then I did not actually inform Civic Forum or Havel until afterwards, when those people from Moscow, the ones from the KGB and the CCCPSU, had gotten frustrated and already gone back to Moscow upset because we did not respond to their effort to make an agreement. It was clear to me that they couldn't have offered anything good, only some threats. And, further, we had decided at the very beginning, for a certain—we did not call it that at the time, but in retrospect we named it "Operation Wedge" [*Klín*], that's a relatively fitting name. We ignored all contact efforts from the side of the Central Committee of the KSČ, the Czechoslovak Communist Party, that means from the side of Jakeš's[3] people. We responded only to the government and the ministers and did not respond to the comrades from the Central Committee of the Czechoslovak Communist Party, by which we actually created tension in their camp.

They at one point even wanted to arrest Adamec, because they were mad that we talked with Adamec but not with them, not with Jakeš, with Vojtík, with Belet, and with those people. By that we executed a perfect Operation Wedge without even realizing it. And they began to argue full-scale among themselves and never got to making any move, because they were not able to unify themselves. And each of them started thinking about how to save his own skin. And so that was then another of my activities.

Then in December of '89, I became, with the first group, a member of the Parliament. At that time we were specifically appointed to the Federal Assembly and I actually sat in chair number one after Štrougal,[4] who was at the time, under the Communists, the prime minister. During the takeover, he became just a member of Parliament. So I inherited this chair from Štrougal. I became, in fact, the first member of our parliament with the identification card number "one," and so it was as if it were actually mine. I was from Civic Forum. I was seated in the first row directly in front of the speaker's platform, and that was an excellent position, because I could observe quite perfectly the thought processes and the emotional processes of the former Communist MPs. We were still just a small group of people from Civic Forum, all the rest were still Bolsheviks. And when they spoke, they were not feeling too good anymore. I had them very close, so it was quite interesting.

Already in December I had made a motion for the Parliament to form a committee on, and to immediately start discussing, initiating, the issue of the withdrawal of the Soviet army. At first I wanted to offer this initiative to the Foreign Affairs Committee of the Parliament, because I thought that it would be better if the suggestion were actually brought up by the Foreign Committee and not by a single MP. And so I went to the leaders of the Foreign Committee, of which I was a member, but it turned out exactly like in the fairy tale about the little hen, who needed water for her rooster, and everybody passed on the suggestion of the withdrawal of the Soviet army to someone else like a hot potato and no one wanted to seize it, to take it up, because everyone was afraid. So the Foreign Committee told me through its secretary, who was also a holdover Communist, that it was a great topic but that the Foreign Committee was too insignificant for it, too small of an authority to ask for something like that, something like the withdrawal of the Soviet army, and to suggest it to the main council of the Parliament, where Jičínský was, one of the former '68 Communists. The main council of the Parliament appreciated my initiative regarding the withdrawal of the Soviet army.

So then I took my suggestion to Dubček. Dubček appreciated the certain resoluteness of the suggestion but said that it was too risky an issue, that we depended on the Soviet Union for our energy needs, which meant, especially, oil supplies, natural gas supplies, and other raw materials, and I don't know what all else, and that he didn't think it very appropriate for him in particular, since he has always been regarded very ambivalently in the Soviet Union, to be the one to demand the withdrawal of the Soviet army, when it was under him when the Soviet army actually came into the country. Which was not a logical argument. It should have been exactly he who should have demanded it, and it would have been a big topic, and he could have partly rehabilitated himself. Otherwise, Dubček had a good reputation. He said that it actually would be good if it were suggested, inconspicuously, by a single MP. Which I did not feel too eager about, when I realized that such a political issue "number one" was being avoided by everyone, and that they in fact did not think politically at all, because that was the most essential topic, and it was supported unambiguously by the entire society.

So I said to myself, all right, if you don't want to, I'll do it myself, and I made the motion myself, and that's how the whole process started. Then the Parliament responded by suggesting that a committee should be put together for monitoring the actual withdrawal, and I then became the chairman of that committee. And then, after I had made the motion, it became a big deal, a big show, and all the other MPs realized what a mistake they had made by not seizing upon this initiative themselves. But it had already been done, and since then I was in fact in charge of this issue until the withdrawal was completed.

Once I went even directly to Moscow where these things, these circumstances were being discussed in the Supreme Soviet in the Kremlin. There I met Shevardnadze[5] and even Gorbachev and so on. I remember a piquant story when one member of our committee, who was very envious of me and my initiative, so he said that he also wanted to participate in the press conference and that he was going to make an important address. He was an MP. I could not have told him no. So he got ready for it—you may not have heard this before—and there was maybe a thousand journalists from around the world, the BBC, and CNN, and so on, because those were important steps. So he got up and proudly announced: "We have just returned from a short meeting with Mr. Brezhnev and Mr. Brezhnev has decided to support the withdrawal." He meant Gorbachev, but said Brezhnev, by which he made a complete fool of himself, so that I won't mention his name, and forever lost his respectability. Everybody laughed like crazy.

It was around June 30th or June 29th, I don't remember exactly, that the last soldier left the country. We celebrated it also by putting on a concert of Prague's Choice, and that was how we, one way we celebrated it. Mr. Zappa also participated in that concert. And about half a year later, I resigned as an MP, as a chief, then as a member of the high council of the Parliament, because I was high up in the parliamentary hierarchy. I resigned, because I had said that I would actually leave after I finished this work of mine with the withdrawal of the Russian army.

In the meantime, however, there were parliamentary elections when I again became an MP. That was during the time when the withdrawal was in process, and in those elections I got—and that was what my rather strong political confidence was based on—52 percent of preferential votes. That was probably more than Clinton would have had when he was elected president. So I had 52 percent of preferential votes directly for my name, which was amazing.[6] And then, when I resigned from Parliament, I worked and am still working today as an external advisor of the president [Havel] of the republic. That was all of my political activities. It is still quite an important position, because the president of the republic—even though the constitution does not grant him that much authority—but

Havel has a lot of it because he is Havel. So I still work, cooperate with the president today, and I am very interested in that.

What is your perspective on the last ten years? Have there been disappointments for you personally?

Essentially, the view that I have, a certain, let's say, a political view, that's what I'm going to tell you now. Because the personal view is, on the one hand, interrelated with that. It can be sharper, but it is not by far as, let's say, as revealing a thing. I think that if one takes it personally, as a regular little person, it is easy to complain about all kinds of things. Everybody feels that we are not quite content with anything and have a tendency to draw vague conclusions and generalize mistakes. And when you do a certain little political analysis of what has in fact happened in the last ten years, the situation is much more positive.

So what is it that has happened? We have completely regained our sovereignty in all areas. We have become fully economically independent from the Soviet Union and from the countries of the former Soviet Union, and that is a thing that the Slovaks have not been able to do. They are still dependent on the Soviet Union, economically in part and militarily completely. They have an army whose equipment is compatible with the Soviet army and that is a certain disadvantage and that puts them still a little bit under Russian influence. And even if today Russia is not capable of exercising this influence, one cannot exclude the possibility that it will be capable of it in the near future. They have reached a significant political and economic crisis, and if the situation gets put, probably, under control, maybe, well, it is not quite clear, but there is a certain danger that the situation could be placed under the control of the army, that is, sooner or later. They are going to try to resolve it politically, but, according to my opinion, that will simply be impossible. Russia is in such a situation that a political resolution probably won't be enough. The military resolution won't mean force, that is, those times have already passed, those games. That is over forever, but they can somehow try again to strengthen their security structure and they can try again to somehow reestablish order among citizens with some more force, more force than Yeltsin.[7] Under Yeltsin there has been only a burst of uncontrollable chaos. At that moment it would have been very disadvantageous for us to remain militarily and economically tied with Russia in any way. And we are not. So that is a very, very positive thing.

Further, we have succeeded, at least in part, in resolving the issue of state ownership. In this country that has succeeded rather well, but, unfortunately, with excesses, with a significant level, or with a significant increase, in economic criminality. Nevertheless, a large part, or a major part, of state property has been transferred into the hands of private entities. That has been achieved. That is important. It proceeded in a rather smooth development without crises. The entities that currently own the property are not quite, to a certain degree, so solvent. Also, the property is still scattered among a large number of owners. It is still owned by various funds that consist of even more thousands, tens of thousands of people.

So it is not state ownership anymore, but it is group ownership and the groups are tremendously large. Which means that the ownership motivation has still not been fully activated. But, nevertheless, nationalization is already actually nonexistent today and everything has been denationalized, and again property in the country has become privately owned. Which means that the foundation has been laid for the regular functioning of a market economy, even if with excesses. But the excesses, that is something that is poisoning our young democracy—economic criminality in the degree that it has somehow established itself here. It has discouraged foreign investors a little, even though, I'd say, the situation is not all that bad. But how are foreign investors supposed to orient themselves? They, from the outside, have a feeling that here the situation is a little bit unclear, and so, it is risky to invest money here, or at least a little risky, and that results in the fact that there is a lack of the kind of medium-small capital, and it is hard for us to restructure the economy. That means that at this time it is necessary to regain their trust, as it were, in our companies, in our banks, in our economy, and so on. And then the situation should stabilize.

One thing we have strongly succeeded in is our foreign political orientation and our foreign policy. Thanks to Havel, before that Dienstbier, and thanks to, I'd say, a rather positive foreign politics, or policy, we have become one of the first applicants for membership in NATO and even in the European Union. And if that happens, the transformation of our society will be essentially complete, and after that, I think, nothing can quite threaten us.[8]

There are, unfortunately, certain bad developments in the area, for instance, of productivity. We do not produce well, or there is a rather significant decline in a high percentage of industry. Unemployment is growing, which would not be quite so bad, but it is not being quite balanced by an increase in production, or, let's say, in the supply of new goods. The restructuring has not been quite successful and many companies and even such large, such concerns, they could be called, are hesitating and are not able to somehow establish themselves in foreign markets, are not able to produce goods that would succeed in competition. So there is in this area a little crisis and decline, and we need to get through it somehow.

We have some problems that come out of a certain dissatisfaction of the citizens that things have not moved as quickly as they had hoped—that we would turn this corner faster and would be well-off.

They don't realize that it is their own fault, that they still don't want to work hard, and that leads then to a certain mild increase in race intolerance. It is not racism in the full meaning of the word, but, nevertheless, the people, they are in a way, somewhat stressed and that is apparent everywhere where there are somehow various kinds of social conflicts. For instance, with the Roma,[9] but also with other citizens of differently colored skin, students, and so on. If we were more content, somehow happier, it would probably not be this way, because Czechs do not have a racist disposition. I don't believe that. It had never been very apparent here. It is a certain almost unexpected increase. I believe that with time we will succeed in overcoming that, but it comes out of, as I have said, out of a certain dissatisfaction. People are behaving irritably even among themselves. It does not have to be a race issue. But when there is then a conflict with the Roma, well, it foams up and explodes. So those are certain negative effects of the development.

Prague is, in Prague you can see, if you've been here before, you can see a relative movement forward. Here the small businesses, the medium and small-scale businesses have done rather well, and Prague is being renovated and looks rather nice, but all the other towns not so. Pardubice, okay, a lot of towns, it probably depends a little on how enlightened the leadership of the given town or village is. So there are a lot of towns that have quite woken up and become really nice and are doing well. But there are also a lot of towns where things are simply not going so well. We have some excellent products, like the Volks-wagen, with help of the Germans, that work well, or Škodovka. There things work perfectly. And we have areas of decline, unfortunately, rather significant, Tatra, Aliaz.

Unfortunately, our aviation industry, which had always been excellent, is in decline, and here we need help, help from America or, most likely America, which is interested in cooperating with us in the area of aviation industry. So it would be good if Boeing and all those, who in fact are already here, would step on it so that our aviation industry would be saved. It was able to produce good planes but a certain substantial investment is needed, but also know-how. Money is not enough, but mainly know-how, because, nevertheless, during all the years under the Soviet Union we have somehow lost contact a little bit.

In the area of law we have major problems. The legal system has maybe been constituted rather well, but law enforcement does not work. Courts are slow. Cases are not discussed until months, even years later. In the area of criminal law, let's say, it maybe somehow works all right, but in the area of business law, it is a complete disaster. And so any kinds of debts and things like that, and conflicts among businesses, those are not being successfully resolved at all. As I said already, the enforcement is so ineffective that a lot of people take advantage, and it happens that, essentially, it looks as if people could get away with not paying taxes, not making payments on their debt, and various financial disagreements, because the legal regulations still do not work. So that is the area of the law.

We also have problems in health care. I wouldn't want to go into this be-cause I am no expert in it, but we are still not successful in establishing the health system and implementing it in an effective way. There is a problem, a little bit, with the increase in bribes, in that certain patterns still survive from the Communist era when one could achieve more in any area with a little bribe. Which means that the health system, even though it has been worked out some-where, has not been introduced, has not been implemented. Implementation of systemic solutions is hard for us, and so, then, a few crowns make things seem better.

So these are some of the . . . but there are also a lot of pluses as well. The standard of living, I think, is relatively decent. People grumble, complain, but in comparison with other countries, I think, we are still relatively well-off. So, that's about it. That's how things are.

I have it good, you know. I, actually, in the areas that I have ever been involved in, I have always done well. I have been successful in music, in politics, and in business as well. For example, we have a company that is called Bon Ton, which is the largest company, quite a giant, in the area of multimedia. We produce CDs, films, videocassettes. We own movie theaters. We even have a branch abroad, and so on. We built it from scratch and today we have a turnover of a billion, and it is in the area of culture. We also have many American entities that are co-owners of the company. We have film studios, video studios. In the music sphere I am also quite, so to speak, well established and we have a famous band Prague's Choice, and in politics, that I have already talked about. So I can't complain much. But, I am not a good example. If everybody had it so good, like me, well, the world would be paradise.

What the world will have to deal with is the thing I talked about, in this country, too, and that is intolerance among people. Racial intolerance—and religious—is something that is constantly poisoning the world. That is the problem in Ireland. That is the source of all the tension in the Middle East, in the Arab countries, and so on. Wherever you look, you can see this problem. So if there is something that will have to be dealt with in the next century, it is exactly the intolerance, which is quite unnecessary. That is one of the easily removable things. Because it is not objectively anchored in anything but demagogic and dogmatic opinion and in a certain pride, and in a feeling that my opinion is somehow better than the opinion of someone else. That is simply not based in anything. Racial intolerance is something that could just magically disappear. There would not be any visible tear. Oil no, oil can't disappear. Atomic plants can't just disappear either. Surface mines can't just disappear. Freon can't just disappear. There would be chaos without freon. That can only be lowered. Airplanes can't just disappear, they will always pollute the air. These are things that people more or less depend on and no matter how much they may be destroying the planet, we need them. But racial intolerance? That we don't need for anything. If that disappears, then it simply won't exist. Maybe some attack from space by some other civilization would help with that, so that humanity would realize how it depends on itself and that it needs to pull together.

So that is what I think that we will have to resolve in the future. And after we resolve that, there still will be generational intolerance. Nothing can be done with that. That will exist as long as humanity exists. But that is a smaller problem, because, luckily, there are the bonds between parents and children, and those can somehow resolve the worst problems. But racial and class intolerance, that is something with which humanity will always struggle. That can't be liquidated. Also the classes, according to property, according to education—that will always be here. That should also be dealt with, but it can't be overcome. I know that. But the racial, that could be done. So I would start there. So that all people, whether you are green, purple, blue, or I don't know what, that should not matter. Everyone is tremendously alike, and when you look at a human skeleton—it is enough to visit any museum—and at human capabilities. When you compare those with the capabilities of other species, it is clear that people are all so much alike, like two eggs. So that's what I would say to the world.

5

Eda Kriseová

Writing was my own psychotherapy.
—Eda Kriseová, 1998

Eda Kriseová, one of the Czech Republic's leading female novelists, is the author of numerous short stories based on her experiences as a staff assistant in an institution for the mentally ill during the Communist era of Czechoslovakia. She is the author of the first official biography of Václav Havel and of some children's books, and has received critical acclaim for her recent novels Kočičí životy [Cats' Lives] *(1997), and* Perchta z Rožmberka aneb Bílá Paní [Perchta of Rožmberk or the White Woman] *(2001). Ms. Kriesová resides in Prague and continues to write and give lectures on writing at a variety of venues. The interview, conducted in English, took place in Berlin.*

I was born into a family of an architect and a sculptor. And it was a sort of artistic milieu I grew up in. I was the oldest of three children. And I spent my childhood in old Prague, in one of the oldest parts of Prague in Jilská St. [St. Giles Street] in a studio which was on the sixth floor and from where we could see almost the whole of Prague. We could see forty-eight Prague towers. The studio had a window like a glass wall. So it was a very special place where I grew up. I was living there with my parents. And my grandmother and grandfather were living in the Jewish part of the city. And from their flat, we could see the medieval Jewish cemetery which was also a decoration of my childhood. And, from today's point of view, I have lost my childhood completely, because now these places are packed by tourists. So I don't feel at home there anymore. It was very different when I was small. And it disappeared completely. The atmosphere disappeared. Also I would say that the aura of this place, that means, a sort of shining of this place disappeared, because there is no time for regeneration.

65

For instance, I was thinking about it when I was in Algeria a long time ago, in Republic M'Zaab. This is in the middle of the Sahara Desert. There are seven holy towns there. And one of these towns, for example, which is called Benizgen, is closed to tourists from seven in the evening until seven in the morning. If you go there, you can walk through, but you are forbidden to eat, to drink, to smoke, and you are forbidden, of course, to sleep there. I was thinking that would be good for Prague, if the city would have time to breathe, to regenerate. It came to my mind when I came to the Jewish town by night—I used to come always when I was feeling miserable, or when something bad happened to me. It was like a part of my flat. It was like my house. The houses were all familiar like the furniture in my flat. And I knew all these smells, nice and bad, and all these colors. And I knew it in every light. And I went there at night, and I'm thinking, maybe I will be there alone. And I saw a group of tourists, and they were on a night trip. And so I ran away, and I said now it's finished. It's finished forever. So this is my childhood.

Well I don't blame tourists. It's badly organized, first of all. I know that we are living on it, that we are living on Prague. Prague brings a great part of the income. But it's a little bit misused, I would say, not by tourists, but by the Czechs, who are misusing it for their own benefit. And I feel it terribly badly of course, because this is my childhood. But otherwise I am not patriotic. I can live in another place, and I can feel at home anywhere. I mean I need some nature, I need some atmosphere. But even in Berlin I can feel at home. There are places in Berlin where I really feel at home. There are even places in America. I have some places in Washington, I have some places in New York, where I feel at home. So you know this is not patriotism. This is just a remark.

Can you say something about your education?

I had a normal education like all Czech children. I wanted to be a journalist, because in fact I wanted to travel. It was not possible for us to travel. And I was thinking, if I would be a correspondent. My first idea when I was sixteen was to be a sports correspondent in China, because I had always felt that the Far East was for me. I also was studying Chinese for four years. I was able to translate with a dictionary, which is quite a high level. I knew something like 3,000 characters. But then I left it, because I found that I would have to devote my whole life only to Chinese. I was thinking it was not worth it. I had other topics of interest. So I gave it up and I forgot it. Then something like four years ago I was in Taiwan. I could find which was the exit and which was the entrance, which was the men's toilet and which was the women's. It was quite useful. But, of course, I was not able to speak. And there was, of course, nobody speaking any other language but Chinese. It was a great problem.

I wanted to be, first of all, as I remember, a Far East correspondent, a sports correspondent. Sports, because I didn't want to have anything to do with politics. Because nobody in my family was a member of any party. Not even my grandparents. Politics was considered to be something not for intellectuals. The intellectual level was quite high on both sides of the family. So politics was considered something to be too much of today, and too much misused by different characters. My people were looking for something more substantial, I would say. I have some political experience. I had it for two and a half years. And I would say it's true. Anyway I like literature much more than politics. That's all, I would say. So, I passed the entrance exams to Charles University to study journalism. But I was not admitted because I was from a family where nobody was in the Communist Party, and they were intellectuals. So I had this "I" [Intelligentsia] in my papers. I started to work in a weekly paper, and then I started a distance-study, and then I was admitted. I was admitted when some people left, or when they were kicked out, or they didn't have enough students in the third year, or something. So after two years, I was admitted as a regular student.

So I became a journalist in the sixties when it was somehow the best time in comparison, quite a good time for being a journalist. Because from '63 the system started to be more and more open, and more criticism was tolerated. I was in the magazine which was called *Young World*, a weekly magazine for young people. I was working there as a reporter. And I was a really passionate reporter. And I was very critical, because I was young. I very quickly became a popular reporter. There was a survey, and the readers were asked, "who is the most popular of the staff at *Young World?*" And I won. And so I said to myself—it was in '68—well this is the time to leave, because, we call it, this is an eye peeking through the blinds. It's always better when you have somebody you can learn from.

And Ludvík Vaculík invited me to be a reporter at *Listy* [*(Literary) Pages*], which was a great honor for me. Ludvík Vaculík was a great person. And I knew that there was something I could learn from him. It was risky, because *Listy* was the so-called most counterrevolutionary paper which was published at that time. And with any change, it was the first paper that would be closed. I knew it very well.

At that time I had a small baby, and my husband Josef was studying at the film faculty, and I promised him I was going to earn the family money. And, then I decided I'm going to risk it. And he told me, you just go like nothing happened, like you would normally go. In this country the situation is always risky. So I went. And after a couple of months, in April '69, the paper was closed and all these people who were working there were banned. Their names were put on the list of people who are banned from publishing anything in papers, in magazines, even books. I realized that to leave for *Listy* was a good decision. I couldn't have followed the political change of Normalization at all, I mean, I would leave any newspaper. That means total lies about everything. I mean, I didn't have any hesitation. At least I was shut down. I couldn't be a journalist in the time of Normalization. This was something I couldn't stomach.

So I finished this job, which was very painful. It was so painful, because I was really popular, and I was successful. I felt like I was on top of the world. And I was traveling a lot from '65 to '69. And I was working in different countries, on civil projects, with Service Civile International, and with American

Quakers. I had a great life at this time. Then it ended. The border was closed. I lost my job, this beloved job, and I had no money at all. My husband was studying and we had a baby. It was really such a bloody situation. And there was no perspective at all. It looked like it would last until the end of my life, of our lives.

The beginning of the seventies, this was the worst time of my life, a dark tunnel without any light. And then I had a couple of jobs which had nothing to do with journalism. And then I had a second child. And in the meantime, in summer '69, we often went to a village in south Bohemia, where there was a big mental hospital. It was in an old monastery. And there were 460 patients. I was so desperate at that time that I was really afraid that I might go crazy.

One day I plucked up my courage and I went to the chief doctor, and I told him, look, can I come voluntarily and help the nurses with the patients, because I just felt like I had to do something useful. Then I was going there every day. And I was helping the nurses and talked with the patients. The chief doctor was very pleased, because there were two nurses to every 70 patients. They were feeding them and cleaning them, and they were not able to talk to them. They had no time, so I was the one who was talking to them. They were mainly chronic schizophrenics. So they were there for twenty, thirty years. The families had already forgotten them completely. And they were very pleased to meet me, a lady from Prague.

And at that time I started to write my first short stories, and they were about these people. And I realized after a couple of years, these people helped me much more than I helped them. Because they were free. They were in a house where there were bars everywhere and all the doors were locked. There was a much more free atmosphere than outside in the world of Normalization. And so I felt free there. These people could say whatever they wanted, because they had papers on hand. And I also realized much later that from a big prison in which the whole country was changed, I went into this small prison, where I felt more free than in the big prison.

And sometimes it seemed to me—and this is one of the topics of my short stories from that hospital—that these people who are inside were much more normal and free than the people who were outside. People who were outside were more mentally ill, because they were lying every moment. This was a time of pathological lies. If you would say something is white, then the authorities would say it's black, and then everybody would say "yes, you are right, it's black." I couldn't live in such an atmosphere. So it means that it brought me a great relief to be able to live partly in this mental hospital. I was afraid that I was going mad, and I went to the right place. And it helped me.

And I was writing. Writing was my own psychotherapy. Then when I had three books, well, manuscripts, Ludvík Vaculík came to me again, and he told me that he had founded an underground publishing house *Edice Petlice*, and he asked me to give him my manuscripts. And I gave them to him, and since then I had real troubles with the state police. And then I started to publish abroad, in exile publishing houses in Czech, and these books were smuggled to Prague, or to my home country. I had a Swiss publisher, who bought all the rights, and my books were published in different languages. And, of course, we were not able to live on my royalties. The main income for a couple of years was from my guidebooks on Prague. It was quite well-paid work. I had a friend whose mother language was German, a Jew. She was an Auschwitz survivor. And we were working together. We were writing the books directly in German, and we were smuggling it to this German publishing house, Merian, one of the biggest publishing houses for guides in Germany. We were working hard for a couple of months, and I was living on the royalty for one or two years. And I was able to write my own stories. That helped me a lot to survive. This job was found for me by Jiří Gruša,[1] who was banned from citizenship at the beginning of '80 and had to live in Germany. He gave me part of the jobs he got in Germany. And then after the change, he was our ambassador to Bonn for six years. Now he is in Vienna. So, this is the way, how I survived, until '89.

Can you talk about the revolutionary period, about how you became involved with Civic Forum?

Well it was all so natural. First of all, they [the authorities] oppressed you. They didn't let you publish. Even my two children's books were published in London. They were forbidden to be published and they were completely innocent, of course. I mean, they do not have so much to do with politics. But in this totalitarian regime, everything that is connected to life which is really livable is against the regime. Life is against the regime, you know. And if you are only a living person, you are coming naturally into conflict. Any other life is not possible for you.

I think life is something so precious that you are not allowed to let it be limited, to follow any limitations. I mean voluntarily. Of course, you can be put in prison, or worse things could happen. But still you may feel free. And I think to live life and not to be satisfied with it is a great sin. You have to make the space wider and wider. It guides you to the edge. But it doesn't mean that you are a hero. This is a normal life. I don't know if you or anybody in America or anybody in the West could understand. But this is what makes your life valuable, what gives sense to your life. Otherwise it's just . . . it's too poor. It's not worth it. So you tend naturally to drift along this free stream. There is a common oppression. You are more and more pushed into this ghetto of people who are against the regime. This is not an intention. This is an expression of life, because life is against any oppression.

At the end of the seventies, we started to publish an underground literary review which was monthly. And it was always, it was again the same people: Vaculík and Klíma,[2] and Gruša was there in that time also, and Saša Kliment, Rabeš, Pecka.[3] This was a sort of making sense of our life, that you had to come every month to our gathering, and that you had to bring something like a poem, a short story, or essay. And this was a duty. I mean nobody would say, "I don't have anything." You had a duty to bring some of your texts, or to bring somebody's text. It was, again, a free expression of life. Of course it was published in a couple of copies, maybe fifty, one hundred. I don't know who reproduced them, or how many there were. But it was something we were looking for, which brought something like discipline into our lives. And Havel was there at the beginning too, then he was in prison. This was his long prison sentence, four and one-half years. He was released in '84, and he joined us again.

We were also smuggling, not only periodicals, but manuscripts and petitions, etc., through secret channels which went out and back. It was a sort of society which was very close together, because everybody has to rely on the other. All of us were in danger of being exiled or put in prison for these activities. And it was a nice time, I must say. I remember it with pleasure. I don't regret it. I don't know if you have read Ludvík Vaculík's *Český snář* [*The Czech Dream Book*], his novel. He is describing one year of his life, also of our life, 1979. My younger daughter read it again a couple of months ago. And she told me: "This looks like you had a completely different life from the whole world. And it's so romantic, and it's so nineteenth century. And how is it possible that this nineteenth century survived here until '89?" But I must say that this life in the ghetto had some very nice sides, like this friendship, and that we would do everything for each other. And that's it. There I was often meeting Václav Havel, and we had some actions together and on which we were cooperating more and more. And then I was on National Street on the seventeenth of November, because both of my daughters went there, and I was so frightened that I went also. But I lost them, of course, in this mess. And then a couple of days after that I learned that Havel had founded Civic Forum. I called him and I told him "I am at your disposal." And he said, "Will you come immediately?" And I came in half an hour.

And when he was elected president, he asked me and some people from Civic Forum to follow him to the castle and to be his so-called advisors, I mean, this is a stupid term. It's better to say coworkers or helpers. Of course, he could not be there alone. It was an old president's office there. We inherited all the Communist bureaucrats. We were about ten [persons] with him in the beginning. It was a sort of Kafka situation, because we came to this castle, this biggest castle in the world which is used. And it was full of secret police. It was full of soldiers with weapons. And it was full of people, who were sort of enemies, of course. And we were sitting in one room, in one room the whole first week.

And I must say, I am not a person who has fear. When I was younger I had fears, but then I started yoga, and this was the second goal I achieved. The first goal was that I was able to concentrate. It was very important when the children were small. When they went to bed, for instance, and I was not able to concentrate immediately, I was losing time. So the first thing I learned was to concentrate at the very moment. And then the second thing I learned from yoga was to lose fear. It's a very good thing, because you don't lose energy.

But at that time in the castle, the whole first week we were sitting in one room. Imagine in this huge castle! And I went to the toilet which was along a long corridor far away, I was thinking, well, maybe I will not come back.

But, anyway, it was a wonderful time in our lives. It was like a miracle. And we were full of euphoria and full of optimism. And we were thinking, you can move the world. It was beautiful. I'm very happy I was there. It was a great experience, I would say, especially for a writer, because you see how power somehow corrupts people. Not only money, but power is a hard drug. And this is something I hadn't experienced before. It's very interesting, sometimes very painful, but very interesting.

After half a year, I became director of the Department for Complaints and Amnesties. We found that this very big department in this president's office didn't work at all. There were thousands of letters coming, about ten thousand letters a month. And there were people coming in person. Because after forty or fifty years of a totalitarian system, people were thinking that Havel will change everything. He was the only authority. The institutions didn't work. There was no legislative authority. Everybody thought, of course, because people are very egoistic, egocentric, they thought well "now it is my turn, now I'm going to solve my problems." And they had, of course, in a great majority of cases, false expectations. They were thinking Havel is a magician. He has a magic telephone. He will phone somewhere and life will be changed for this person.

So I was the one who was in between this "great magician" and reality. And sometimes it was very difficult. I was working twenty hours a day. I had to change the whole office, because it didn't function. People were getting terrible, formal, and arrogant replies from the old bureaucrats. It was damaging the image of the new president.

And there were people coming in person. They also felt free to demonstrate under the balcony with different demands. Prince Schwarzenberg,[4] who was the chancellor, often called me and said, "Go downstairs, there is another demonstration there. Do something with it." And there were many mad people who were coming, especially when there was a full moon. And then I had to go there and to talk to these people and to persuade them to go to the mental hospital, or just to get rid of them, in a good way, I mean, in a nice way. It was exhausting, but on the other hand, it was, again, a wonderful experience for a writer. And I had all this past experience in the mental hospital I could use. Because you had to be like a priest, a psychiatrist, and a lawyer, and then somebody who has some charisma, you know.

I was so full of energy at that time that I managed to change almost all this office. And it started to work. But I was, I must say, always thinking of leaving. I wanted to be a writer finally.

In '92, in summer, our president resigned. That was before the split of the republic. He resigned, and all of us left with him. None of us came back. He was reelected president of the Czech Republic and started a new office with people who wanted to be bureaucrats, who didn't have any other task, or any other interests, or ambitions.

Because we, all of us who were there before, almost all of us were creative people. And so we were very happy when we were released. And this was our common agreement. The president said, "Now, I'm going to have bureaucrats."

And we said, "Thank you, we are not going to be bureaucrats," and our taking off was friendly. So I am a freelance writer, and of course, I'm complaining, because things are not going so well as I thought. They are not going according to my expectations. And always when I'm depressed, I always say to myself, I can travel, I can publish, and I don't have any more troubles with the state police, which is already wonderful.

What do you think are the biggest obstacles facing the Czech Republic today?

I'm thinking, what were the mistakes? I think there were many mistakes, but on the other hand, I know there was no ideal power which could organize the whole transformation. What was the Czech opposition? One thousand, two thousand people?

In Poland the opposition was much better organized and much broader, and Solidarity, and even they didn't manage until recently. In our republic, there was a couple of hundred intellectuals, who would resist, who were somehow organized as an opposition and who were active. In Poland there was a mass movement. Workers took part in it.

Now people are asking me, why was nothing done with members of the Communist Party, with the people who were rich and who were wealthy at that time of totalitarianism, and who became even richer? They were well organized, quickly changed their coats and became capitalists. How could you recognize the old bureaucratic mafia and say, "this money is dirty and this is not dirty, and you were a member of the Communist Party, you are forbidden to buy this or that?" It had to be started, the whole process. And who should be the judge? The courts, the legislature, were in the same hands as before. You didn't have so many people of good morals and qualifications. For instance, all the good lawyers became commercial. And the others who were more stupid or less encouraged, they stayed in the legislature. And where do you get people of morals? People had false expectations. They think some wonderful people will emerge from nowhere, who would create paradise for everybody. But who are they? Where are they? I haven't seen them.

Of course, there were holes in the legislation. Smart people went through these holes. They used their opportunity very well. But who would be a policeman, if you are not able until now to organize a functioning police? People are so easily corrupted, even the police. This is a matter of character, first of all, a matter of how these people were brought up. These people were brought up with the mentality that they can steal everything. That everything that is not yours or another person's can be stolen, because it's common. They don't have any feeling of private property, of rights, of limits between individuals. Decency. I'm surprised that I didn't know anything about people's character some time ago. Of course, I was reading Dostoevsky, but it was nineteenth century. Now I'm reading Dostoevsky again and I say, "Oh, they are just the same." And of course I'm disappointed at how they are. They are thinking only about today. They don't think about the future. They are very materialistic. They want everything.

They are never happy, but want more and more. They basically have no character, no self-honor, no decency. They have no shame. That's all. They don't feel like citizens. The state does not belong to them. The state is still their enemy.

The Western respect for individuality, for rights—each individual has a right to be happy—combined with complexes, no proper education, selfishness, bad manners, and no character, this is a disaster. This sounds like a complaint. But this is reality. And when I'm speaking with the people in the village where we go for summer, this is incredible. They have forgotten about all Communist crimes, if it didn't happen to them personally. They only want and want and want. And don't want, of course, to work.

Is there anything that can be done to counter that?

If I am optimistic, then I would say, it needs time, and that the generation of my children, for instance, will hopefully be different. Take the generation of my parents, for example. They were real European people who, for instance, both of them, spoke three European languages, and they were reading poetry in the original. My father would say "translation, what's that?" It was somehow of no value for him. My father studied in Berlin. And my mother studied in Paris. And they had grants from the state. They were not rich. They were sent to study abroad, because they were smart. They were real Europeans.

And I am very grateful that my children are going to be again Europeans, if there is time. The world is different. My younger daughter said, "Well, I will live partly in France and partly in my home country, because I have to go where I will find work." She feels at home in Europe. She doesn't feel at home in America. She was too young when she went to America, and it was a very hard time for her there. This is something I am glad about.

When I am thinking of the Czechs, the nation, this is a mixture of Germans and Slavs with some Celtic background. My only hope is that they will be invited into the European Community and they will adapt. I don't think the Czechs are able to exist separately. They always functioned well in the big empires or unions. They could be smart, they could be intelligent. They were revolutionaries, but they were not able to rule themselves. They were always working very well together with the others. The best quality of their character is the ability to adapt—in better conditions and also in worse. So I hope they will not spoil everything enough not to be admitted into the EU. And that as soon as they will be admitted into the EU, they will adapt themselves. So, in fact, this is my only hope, this is my very sincere faith. They may slip again back into Russia's arms, and then I don't want to live here anymore.

Was there any particular philosophy that kept you going, or any kind of motto that you've tried to follow to lead you through the dark times?

It's very difficult now. Just do what you need to do, what is absolutely necessary, what makes sense for your life. That's why I was writing without having any chance to publish. I was writing for myself, in order not to go mad. If I don't feel like doing something, I won't do it. Nobody would press[ure] me to do anything that I don't want to do. I think I'm more and more sensitive to that which goes against my nature.

6

Daniel Kummerman

I was born an enemy of the state.
—Daniel Kummerman, 1998

Daniel Kummerman, *journalist, spent most of his adult years under the Communist regime of Czechoslovakia trying to get an education while also participating actively in the underground. Before signing Charter 77, he worked as a computer programmer, then afterwards as a window washer. He was an active participant in Civic Forum until the 1992 elections and was a reporter and writer at the newspaper* Právo.[1] *In 1999, Kummerman left his post at the newspaper to accept an appointment as ambassador of the Czech Republic to Israel. The interview, conducted in English, took place at the office of* Právo *in Prague.*

I was born in Prague, but I grew up in a small city bordering Prague. It was a kind of city where you are just staying, most of the time only to sleep overnight, but you live mostly in Prague. So, it means I spent more or less all my life in Prague. And, about the history? My father was a Czech Jew and my mother was a Viennese Czech, and so I was baptized when I was born, but at the age of something like twenty-one I converted to Judaism.

Well, I was lucky that given this background I probably was branded an "enemy of the state" from the very beginning. I was born an enemy of the state. But fortunately, I was seventeen in '68, and I finished my high school in '69, and therefore I managed to get to the university quite easily, because, basically, in '69 it was still in the shadow of '68, which means that the party and the process of so-called Normalization wasn't really strong yet. So in this way I was quite lucky, and I managed to finish. I majored in English. I graduated in '76. And in '77, Charter 77 came, so I lost my job as a computer programmer. For four years I was a storekeeper, nine years window cleaner, and since 1990, I've been a journalist.

How did you become involved with Charter 77?

Basically, I think I was kind of predetermined. I mean, actually, it's a kind of theory of mine, that most of the signers, if you follow their personal history, were sort of pushed into it by their circumstances. This means, like among the original signers, there were quite a few people who I knew from school or from other circles, which means that I was kind of involved in it, in those circles, for one. Secondly, there was something like—I don't know how to describe it—an inner need to declare certain standpoints and views. And, so because I knew the signers, it was quite easy. Because for some people, it was difficult even to reach those circles, to know the people who signed. I should say also that, actually, it wasn't that easy. I signed it in winter '77, when the charter appeared. And I had a so-called secret signature, which means it was not published. And I openly re-signed for publication in summer '78. So it was in two stages.

How did you feel growing up as an "enemy of the state"?

It was very simple, because, for one, we were quite poor. Even in a Communist society, the whole society is quite poor, but we were much poorer in a way, technically. And they let you know it. I mean, in every school there was always some Communist teacher who didn't like you, openly disliked you. I will explain why. My father was a Jew who was quite rich before the war, who spent the war in Palestine, and was with the British army for a while. And my mother had two sisters abroad, which was something which was a big minus in the Communist years. So all these things accumulated. Just one example: In '64 I was in the eighth grade of the elementary school. And many decisions were being made about where to go on, whether to high school or some kind of apprenticeship, or whatever. And some teachers told me that actually I didn't stand any chance of going to high school with my background. Of course, the process of liberalizing the regime was going on, so by '66, when I finished high school, eventually, it was much different, and I did manage to get to high school. So, I mean, there were small signs to tell you.

Did you ever think about leaving the country?

All the time. I mean, we spent hours and hours discussing it at home, because I majored in English and my wife was—neither one of us had this kind of handicap like being cut away from language. I mean, we both studied in the English language society, which means we knew what we would be going into. But somehow, I would say, the problem is, I would see a reason in emigrating somewhere for a certain purpose, a positive purpose, but being driven out of the country just like that, somehow we couldn't put up with that. So, basically, many times even, we were saying we would give up and go, and we never did. We never made the final decision. But yes, we thought about it a lot.

Also, another thing was, the children were quite small then. The real question would come when they were at the end of high school, if they were not allowed to study, which would happen if the regime went on. They would probably have a lot of problems. That would be a good reason to go away. But that didn't happen. By the time they finished high school, the regime was gone already.

After you had signed the charter, were you engaged in any other charter activities?

There was a lot of small business. But then in 1982 I took over one operation. It was tied to Jan Kavan. Jan Kavan was a guy who was very active in '68 and who then stayed in England and who was running something called the Palach Press Agency in London. Basically, he organized contact with people inside the country, with the opposition inside the country. So, smuggling things in and smuggling things out, publishing charter materials in the Western world, etc. In '81, the police caught one van of this operation, and basically, one stage of the operation was finished that way. And after that, some two months later, I sort of took over that, and it was running on a smaller scale until 1989. So, that was my major involvement with this thing where people were coming in bringing some stuff or just messages, and I was also sending things out.

Were you ever arrested?

Not arrested, detained. There was this system of forty-eight-hour detention. So, five times. Five times for forty-eight hours. That's it. I guess one reason why I got involved in this smuggling operation was that I spoke English, which was necessary, because it was an operation where mostly foreign people were involved. And secondly, I had quite a low profile. Before I started, I was involved a little bit with the opposition, but not really. I mean, not like one of those people who are in the sunshine. I mean, those who were known, those who were quoted, and those who were visited by the Westerners. Actually, that's why I got involved with this operation. I wasn't much known.

Did having a low profile help your work?

I guess so. Because as far as I know, I mean, I don't know how much I can believe it, but when somebody was interrogated, the rule was usually you would go and talk to the people about whom you were interrogated. So, I understand from this that the police didn't take me very seriously. I mean, one of the reasons was I wrote my thesis on comics, and of course they didn't take comics seriously. I remember that when they interrogated somebody, they spoke about a guy, the "Mickey Mouse guy," you know that's how they called me. They didn't take me seriously, the better for me, you know.

How were you involved with Civic Forum in 1989?

I was there. One major involvement the first day was translating into English or from English. I was involved there, then I got caught very much in, how do you say, a revival of the Scout movement. Because Czech scouting was underground. The window-cleaning group where I was, was mostly Scout people. They were involved with underground scouting. So, I was involved with that. We published *Scout* magazine. Both my children were in secret troops and all that. That was a major involvement.

And then, a few months later I started journalism. I was almost forty, and I was learning a completely new business. I had been involved with *samizdat* before, but underground publishing is different. In *samizdat* you don't write for people, you just write for a limited circle, and the fact that you write something is value in its own right. But normal journalism, you have to learn to sell it in a way to the public. So, I was learning the trade and it took most of my time. A few months later, Civic Forum became like a normal political institution, so either stay in politics, or take some other possibility. So, I decided for journalism. Therefore, I left open politics.

On the one hand, I am enthralled by politics. I'm opinionated and all this, so I would like to have my views realized through politics. On the other hand, if I look at it rationally, I can't speak publicly. I'm not this kind of presentable person. It's also a kind of trade, and I don't think I would be a good professional. I can be self-critical enough to evaluate myself and realize that I would probably, that I wouldn't manage, so I would be a failure in politics.

Did you write for samizdat, *and if so, what topics interested you?*

Yes, since about the mid-eighties. For instance, foreign politics. One of the advantages of the opposition is that once you declare yourself as having some kind of views, having some kind of position, you didn't have to care about things like hiding. There was an American library in Prague, for instance, at the embassy. And I could go there anytime I wanted, because, all right, I was already an enemy, so what worse could happen, could have happened. Therefore, I read English media or followed English media all the time. So, basically, I can say I had some kind of expertise in foreign politics. There were certain regions which I followed quite closely like the Middle East. This was one thing. And I wrote quite a lot about America. There was a magazine which was called *Society of Friends of the USA*, so I wrote most of my original materials in that magazine.

I was quite critical about America. If I had to define myself, I would probably be, in America I would be one of those liberals, a Boston liberal or something like that. But, at the same time, unlike those people, I believe that the American system, the democratic system, has some kind of self-cleansing or self-cleaning mechanisms, and therefore, I think that something down there, something is healthy in America. So I would be critical like that. I wouldn't say that America is the devil or death or anything like that.

Are you a practicing Jew?

It's a question of time. I mean, yes, I'm trying to get involved or have some involvement in it all the time. Yes. But not really. Not enough, as I should have. One problem is that there are very few people left, you know—emigration and the Holocaust all together. In Prague there is something like fourteen hundred people. It would be a long explanation probably, but basically, already for two hundred, the last two hundred years, the level of anti-Semitism in the Czech lands was very low. And therefore, Jews became very assimilated in these regions, much more than in America today, I guess. And, therefore, we have very many people who are either not practicing Jews really, but are more interested, or there was intermarriage with them, or we have a lot of people who are Jewish but don't care enough. And then, we of course have a few Orthodox people, so there is a mixture, a kind of cross section through the whole spectrum. And this whole spectrum put together, that's a big problem, to make it interesting for everybody. So that's a kind of problem there.

How would you evaluate the last ten years? Have there been disappointments?

I would say yes, there was a disappointment, a big disappointment in a way, but disappointment given by too much expectations. I was very skeptical in the beginning. I thought, all right after all this experience, we are in for many many very difficult years. And, somehow, when suddenly it all changed, was changing quickly, well, actually, I also fell for the idea that we are, that this nation is basically democratic. In fact, Czechoslovakia was the only functioning democracy between the wars in this region, really functioning. I thought that, I did believe for some time that we are maybe in for some economically bad years, but that democracy somehow was deep in the genes of this nation and that the very moment we get rid of the Communist regime we will be more or less democratic.

And there I was quite disappointed, because I found out that most people not only don't know what democracy is about but they don't even care what it is about. On the other hand, economically we are not doing that bad so far. So, yes, a major disappointment was that I somehow believed that the spiritual progress would be much quicker, that we'll be a functioning democracy and actually like a civil society and all these things. That doesn't really work yet.

So I returned to my old skepticism. It will take a whole generation before we have people understand that democracy is not where Communists shut up but where Communists can speak. That's about it.

Did you have a personal philosophy that kept you going though the tough years?

First of all, I would say deep down, this message, that the world won't be destroyed. Somehow I do believe that the world is supposed to survive, and that, even if we are going through a lot of troubles, I do believe that there is some meaning to the world, and therefore, I'm probably part of the meaning. That's why I try to define my position within it. That's one. Again I spoke about this predetermination. I feel, if you make a kind of investigation among the charter signers, you would find that many of them had plenty of problems at school. Like, when there was too much injustice at school, you would speak up. I mean, somehow you have to stand up against something which is offensive to you.

Looking a generation back, they let the Communists win so easily. They just took over. That's it. People didn't really fight back. I mean it was probably too pathetic. But to be able to look into the eyes of your children and say that you did something. I mean, of course, it sounds a bit silly, a bit ridiculous, but it's about the only way you can describe, that somehow you mustn't shut up when some kind of nasty system wants you to shut up.

I don't know how I would have reacted if it was like in the fifties, when it was, when your neck really was at stake. I mean, I don't know if I would speak up then. I'm not that sure about myself. Basically, it's when the only risk was really your career, and also this even limited possibility of travel and all that, so that really, surely was worthwhile risking. I mean also, as I said before, by that way you were buying yourself some kind of freedom. All those people who tried to make some kind of career, who had to think all the time, where they can slip, a kind of slip of the tongue, whether they made a mistake here, a mistake there. I mean they got caught somewhere. It was all quite unpleasant, a life full of strain. I mean, of course, I was under strain. I was an endangered species in a way, but on the other hand, not much worse could have happened. So it was kind of a free life. I mean, you could meet whom you wanted. You could do what you wanted. We had a lot of foreigners staying with us. All right, I mean, the other people would be worried even to talk to foreigners in the street, because somebody might see them. We could have them as guests in our house. Who cares? This is even some kind of positive sign of that.

Since you're writing for Právo, *what types of topics are you interested in?*

I'm on the foreign desk, which means that I write about certain regions—the Middle East, Southeast Asia, places like South Africa, Canada. You know, within this department the world is divided, so I have certain regions. And the other line which I do is I write home opinion pieces. We don't have the system of *op-ed* in your terms. You see, it's not common to mix these two things in Western papers, but, basically, here, if we want to build a functioning democracy, the only way to do it is also to compare yourself with other functioning democracies in the world. And, therefore, a person from the foreign desk is much closer to understanding how the system works than somebody who is on the home desk who knows it only theoretically. And also, somehow, once you get involved in influencing home politics, it's difficult to leave it out. I mean, somebody talks nonsense and you want to write about this nonsense, then I have to do it this way. And I also write in both languages [English and Czech] now. I've been writing for *Prague Post*[2] and these other media, because I can produce English text that can be used separately.

So therefore, this is the good thing, on the one hand, because of the past I have. I understand what the Western world, the English-speaking world, is concerned with. On the other hand, unlike foreigners who work at the *Prague Post*, I have the local experience, the local subconscious. I can combine the two, so that's also useful. You have a lot of people here who have been here several years, five, six years, and they understand what's going on. But, they don't know the subconscious of the Czech nation, how it's abused and it's used. So these are the things that unless you live here for twenty years, you can't really feel.

What is keeping the nation from really developing into a democracy?

It's not that stable. One major problem in this country is that so far we haven't had a change from one side of the political spectrum to the other. Poland, Hungary, they had this right-wing government, then a left-wing government, then again a right-wing government. I mean, this kind of normal change. So far we have had only seven, eight years, either a colorless government or a right-wing government, and therefore, the left side of the political spectrum is still demonized in this country in a way. Most people don't understand that there can be a non-Communist left, for instance. It is normal that in the democratic world the system remains and only the political, the top echelons change, and they don't really destroy the system. They just change certain stresses and certain attitudes, and then the other group comes in. This is normal. So we don't have the experience of normal working politics. That's one thing.

And second, it is the deep understanding that democracy is a positive value on which you have to work. It's not only how many years it goes in that direction that's important, but it's also like having a civil society, like having concern with what's going on in your vicinity. And it's also like this famous slogan that even if you don't agree with certain views, you will fight for them to be expressed. These things that come naturally in working democracies don't work here, or they don't exist here. I would say, part of the forces of the system here still works on the negation of what was here before rather than on positive values. I mean, even though it looks pretty democratic, the thing is, it's not really based on a solid attitude. So this is a deeper change of attitude and that will probably take development. Most of the people are afraid, the older generation. It would be really difficult to change it, break it in themselves. They will never be really that deeply democratic. Though I guess it is the younger generation who has this experience at the moment. That's it. Our president, the founder of the republic, Masaryk[3] spoke about democracy, that democracy needs some fifty years to be fully established. And we had only twenty years between the wars. Therefore, we need maybe thirty more years. Maybe. Or, if we get involved in democratic Europe, maybe it will be even less than that. But, basically, it takes time, and we, so far, have had only seven, eight years. So, we can't even expect much more than we have. Let's say this government that we have had so far didn't help at all. Basically, if you have a government whose ideology is that anything goes as long as it helps the economy, that doesn't help society for sure. I mean, we now have a kind of idolization of wealth as compared to morality. And, so that's another problem, but it's now characteristic of this country. But again, it's only seven, eight years so far. And still even then, all that's still much better than it was before.

7

Dana Němcová

I am not a party person, and I never will be.
                                            —Dana Němcová, 1998

Dana Němcová *is deputy director of the Advice Center for Refugees, a Prague-based nongovernmental organization that provides advice and legal help to asylum seekers. Němcová has been a member of the Helsinki Committee of Czechoslovakia, and after 1993 the Czech Republic, since its inception in 1988. Němcová actively supported and participated in the musical underground in association with the Plastic People of the Universe and later in their defense. As a VONS member, she was arrested along with Václav Havel and others in 1979, for which she received a suspended sentence. In 1989, she was one of three speakers for Charter 77. The interview, conducted in Czech, took place at the Advice Center for Refugees in Prague.*

I was born in northern Bohemia, which means that I have a certain experience with Czechoslovakia before the war and with living together with the German minority. In '38 we moved away from there, and during the war we lived in eastern Bohemia. Then we went back to Chomutov, where my father, as a school inspector, was introducing a system of Czech education. And as an eleven-year-old girl, I was traumatized by the removal of the Germans,[1] because it seemed to me that it was not an adequate way of solving things, neither of the past nor the present.

Those were people who for me were civilians, and innocent, and the ones who were in charge [of the removal] were not at all those who, like my parents, had left the territory at the time when it actually became a part of Germany. It was a rather ugly situation, such as usually follows all takeovers, and I have, in fact, experienced several of these takeovers. The next one in '48 was a certain development for the better, and then again a turn for much worse in '68.

As far as my education goes, I studied psychology and philosophy at the Faculty of Arts of Charles University, but I worked only part-time when I could. I had seven children, whose upbringing I enjoyed the most and regarded as most meaningful. When the children were older and I started working in my field, then I again couldn't work because of my attitudes toward the regime. I had friends in the underground, in the band Plastic People of the Universe. I was involved in their defense in '76—so then I lost my job definitively—and in January my name was publicly announced among the first group of signatories of Charter 77. In '79 I was arrested as a member of the Committee for the Defense of the Unjustly Prosecuted (VONS). In '89 I was a speaker for Charter 77.

I also began that year with a few weeks in prison related to "Palach Week" and the fact that we brought flowers to his memorial. And it was a dramatic year. Immediately after that I, of course, took part in founding Civic Forum and later was elected as a member of the Federal Assembly of our Parliament. I was a member of the [Parliamentary] Board, a vice chairman of the Committee for Cultural and Social Affairs. I was never a member of any party, and even now I am not an organized member. My position is in what is called "civil society," and in this sense I am also involved in the present.

When I left Parliament in '92, I began working for refugees, which is still my profession today. I work at the Advice Center for Refugees of the Czech Helsinki Committee. I have been a member of the Helsinki Committee ever since its establishment in 1988, while it was still illegal. And after Ms. Olga Havlová died in '96, I was elected chair of the board of the *Výbor dobré vůle*[2] [Committee for Good Will]. There I try, according to her vision, to help those who have problems because of a certain handicap. So, I've always been interested in people who were in some kind of trouble, who were in some way handicapped, harmed, persecuted, and who I tried to at least somehow counsel, listen to, and help. That's the story of my life.

Was there some moment before your involvement in the defense of the Plastic People of the Universe when you found yourself in conflict with the former regime?

Well, a rather symptomatic thing is—as I've talked about my constant identification with someone who was persecuted—that I was baptized in the Catholic Church in the fifties, when the majority of this church was in fact in prison, and it was of course having serious difficulties. And my husband was, of course, also involved in the area of layman's activities, so we were actually under surveillance during the whole time.

In the fifties there was brutal violence against a majority of the people, because there was really a fundamental change of systems and the destruction of all classes that could have been resistant to the socialist model, that meant all those who had something, private owners, businessmen, tradesmen, and so on. Prisons were filled with people, whether political opponents or potential enemies. There were fixed trials. And for me as an eighteen-year-old girl, the fact that, for instance, people were willing to sign petitions requesting the death of Dr. Horáková;[3] that was something that I simply could not digest. Such an injustice and such madness of a mass of people always affects me in an extremely strong and repulsive way.

In the fifties there was a certain mixture of the mistaken revolutionary enthusiasm on the one side—there were people who believed in the socialist, Communist ideal and there were executioners of the most brutal injustice with which they liquidated all types of opponents. Then there was a certain thaw really, and the sixties were marked by the fact that—it was visible in editions of books, for instance—publication was allowed of books that were important for the people's certain deeper orientation, deeper thought.

A certain thaw, for instance, a dialogue of Christians with Marxists, a mutual dialogue of Christian churches, was happening at the Faculty of Evangelical Theology. And because the Evangelical Church as a minority church was less persecuted, it provided space for the dialogue. That was a very important, in fact, open platform, where philosophical and religious issues were discussed, and it was also a certain political [platform]. And then the year '68 with big expectations.

However, it was clear that after the occupation, there would no longer be Communists who believed, but that it was really going to be the things connected with occupation. That meant a pure pragmatism and the execution of power. And those, of course, were very hard and ugly years. And as far as the repression of young people, for instance, the audience at the concerts of underground music, when I saw that really the innocent young people, who only looked different and traveled from all over the country to [hear] their favorite bands and then were beaten, were, it can be said, persecuted. During one of the concerts, or, I should say, before a planned [concert] in Rudolfov near Budějovice in '73, an emergency unit came, and it really was a massacre. So that, of course, confirmed my solidarity with this resistant group of young people who simply wanted to listen to their music and support their musicians.

But because it actually was a large circle, a suspicion sprung up that it was an organized group and that it was a certain political activity. The whole situation was made political, and that's how, in fact, the necessity then developed for the artificially constructed trials of the musicians in '76. All this was publicly revealed, opposed, Helsinki documents were signed, and we actually used this and officially supported the [need] for protection of human rights. So all our activities were then started within the framework of the charter and the Committee for the Defense of the Unjustly Prosecuted. Of course the charter was a certain umbrella, under which a whole series of unofficial activities could be hidden. So it could actually be said, that at the turn of the seventies and eighties, there was a culmination in the repression of the open opponents—although I should rather say, supporters, in the positive sense, of human rights and values which were officially guaranteed by the government, but of course were in fact not granted or provided. And then during the eighties, the level of persecution was, so to speak, less predictable. At times they struck hard. At other times things worked out well, and the wave of interconnection among certain positions of opinions and of the things that Civic Forum actually later grew out of, that gradually increased until the year '89.

Can you describe in some practical terms exactly why the Committee for the Unjustly Prosecuted convened and what its activities were?

The need for founding such an organization became clear to us in connection with the concrete confrontation with cases, with people, and with families of those who were sentenced according to articles related to their political beliefs or their dissemination of some *samizdat* texts or their religious beliefs. Those were people who had been in prison—and, for instance in the fifties, their neighbors and even their relatives were of course afraid to keep in touch with such a family. And we thought it was necessary to counsel the family, to support it morally in some way, and to publicize the cases. Because those were cases clearly in conflict with what the state was officially proclaiming. It was persecution for reasons of beliefs, whether political, religious or, simply—of course, racial factors were also present. And so we in fact worked with the prosecution, with official documents.

We always tried to establish contact with an attorney. I must say that in this respect, of course secretly and with risk, Dr. Motejl,[4] who is today the minister of justice and who defended many cases, helped us a lot. So when I went to see him during his office hours or sometime toward the evening, he would let me look at the documents, at [the arguments of] the prosecution, [and] we were then able to support our documents, which we published for the individual cases we followed, with real facts. So we did not distort them. We only reflected and evaluated the measure of injustice that was being perpetrated on the person. And besides that, we also tried to support the family a little bit in some practical ways.

For that we had opportunities and means from abroad, from emigrants. Professor Janouch[5] collected a certain amount from which we could support a little, for instance, a family that was suffering for the fact that the breadwinner was in prison and the wife was persecuted, because her husband had been arrested, when it involved a family with children and so on.

Can you describe from your own perspective what Civic Forum was, how it emerged?

I think that this history has still been rather short, on the one hand, and on the other [it is] distant, because since that time many demands, a lot of work has rolled over us. But the first impression of Civic Forum was that they were people who really wanted to get together and really introduce the principles of democracy, dialogue, and, simply, a completely different social system. Of course, if you then looked at individual cases and how things developed, you would find many problems, too, but the first enthusiasm, that was indisputable. Of course, there was also a lot of amateurism.

Nobody had formulated in their mind the idea of a shadow government. So when we then entered Parliament and into real political decisions, we knew better what we did not want. That went very fast and it was a wonderful feeling, when, for instance, there was a vote about abolishing the leading role of the Communist Party in the state, which was something they had guarded as their strongest idol.

And that was at the time when it was still the co-opted Parliament, which meant that there were still some of the former MPs from Communist times. But since they were used to always obediently raising their hand, they raised it even in this case. I watched that with a lot of satisfaction.

We then tried to adjust the legal regulations according to what we knew, what we were aware of. For instance, at that time the East-West Parliamentary Practice Project, financed by the Ford Foundation, was very helpful to us. It gave us an opportunity to meet experienced MPs from Western democracies and to learn about constitutions, and how specific regulations in the social sphere work, how to make up a budget, and so on. All that was, I think, very good for us, and I think it was a great mistake that the next Parliament, since '93, actually considered itself so wise that in fact this project ended. That was a big mistake, because we had really learned a lot.

It may be necessary to add that the initial euphoria, the enthusiasm of the whole society, the goodwill—that's something that lasts a certain limited time period. Then things have to go back into their tracks, and that's another story.

How long were you in Parliament?

Two and a half years.

And what made you decide you should leave it?

I am not a party person, and I never will be.

How do you reflect back on the last ten years in terms of progress that has been made?

I think that the change has been fundamental. I am happy that I have lived to see this time. Progress, what is progress? Things are completely different. And that is good. For that I am happy. And if people expected changes from one day to another, then I think that the expectations—for their practical lives—were not realistic. We must expect a much longer time and exert a lot more effort to get to the place where, for instance, a society, which had gone through a certain continuous democratic development since World War II, is [today]. And at the same time, I don't idealize the situation in which all the Western democracies are nowadays.

Problems exist. Today we have different tools for solving the problems. People have a right to their own opinions, their views. After all, they vote. The fact that they are used to sloppy work, that they are still prone to a certain demagoguery, that is a fact that we will still carry with us for some time. But we can't blame anyone else but ourselves. And we also reap the fruit ourselves. So I am an optimist. I am patient. I know that things need more time to mature.

I think that we really need more respect for the third sphere. All the institutions of civic society have not yet taken a deep root here. But it is becoming clear, that in the state administration, for instance, in the social sphere or even in the area of care for refugees and counseling refugees, they can be very useful, and [that] they create a completely new climate for those to whom these services are provided. So this is what I am now interested in: simply that people won't get discouraged, won't behave selfishly, egotistically, making a profit at any cost.

The new age has opened up many opportunities, and people feel that if they have enough money, they will be able to enjoy all the opportunities that they didn't have before. And some of them don't care at all how they get the money. Others resent the fact that some have the money while they themselves don't have the money and so on and so on. I think that's all normal, that we simply have to go through this stage, and I am an optimist.

What is the biggest issue facing the Czech Republic in terms of stability and development of a stable democracy?

I think that there is a whole series of steps ahead of us that we still have to take. We have talked from the very beginning about being a part of Europe. That still needs to be demonstrated in a whole series of legal regulations that would be comparable to European law. We need to, of course, really do something about the corruption, which is a certain syndrome of the illness of the Eastern world—that everything can be bought, everything can be obtained by a bribe. Our policemen, or our journalists keep writing about some mafias, but mafias would not be thinkable, if they were not linked to the state administration, the state apparatus. I see it—the really poor refugees here, while they may not fulfill the contents of the Geneva Convention, they really are poor and nobody is helping them. While those involved in criminal activities have permanent residency and all the advantages provided by the same police or by a part, maybe a different part of the Ministry of the Interior, than the one that is always talking about threats to the country—they are just, unnecessarily, creating xenophobic moods. That is very frightening to me.

We have to do something exactly so that we could become more open, so that we would be more tolerant toward foreigners, especially toward the Roma ethnic group that lives here with us, that in fact belongs among us, which is a huge task, though. I think that the whole society, not only the individual branches of the executive and legal systems, but all individual people have to start working on themselves and understand, somehow, that we won't get further if we hold on to our old stereotypes formed from the various *kitschy* TV series, whether of Eastern production in the past or Western production in the present.

History has been, essentially, always on the same note and each of us, I think, has been justly assigned the same task. Simply, either we are people or we are not people. And my—if it should be a philosophy—then it would be a certain "personalism" and if something more, then it would be a common Christian faith.

8

Martin Palouš

Our position was the emphasis on politics from below.
—Martin Palouš, 1998

Martin Palouš *received his Doctorate of Natural Sciences in chemistry at Char-les University in 1973 and went on to study philosophy and social sciences (1977). He was one of the first signers of Charter 77 and served as charter speaker in 1986. A founding member of Civic Forum, Palouš was elected to the Federal Assembly in 1990. From there he joined the Ministry of Foreign Affairs of Czechoslovakia as an advisor and then as deputy minister of foreign affairs (1990-1992). Palouš joined Ivan Havel at the Center for Theoretical Study in Prague in 1993 and became a member of the Faculty of Social Sciences at Charles University in 1994. He is a past chair of the Helsinki Committee for the Czech Republic. He has lectured extensively in the United States and is the au-thor of several publications on topics in philosophy and political science. Palouš presented his credentials to President George W. Bush on 10 October 2001 as ambassador to the United States from the Czech Republic. The interview, con-ducted in English, took place at the Center for Theoretical Study in Prague.*

I was born in 1950. I was eighteen years old, or seventeen and a half in '68, which was obviously a quite important threshold for me, or the first big, political experience, I would say. In the three years '67, '68, '69, we were given the chance to travel, and—whatever you want to think about the content and strate-gies of the Prague Spring—it was certainly a very interesting opening of a closed society, and a society which has had a chance to breathe freely for a cou-ple of months, to be closed again.

In '68 I was just finishing high school, and I entered Charles University. I studied natural sciences first and then philosophy and social science. I ended my studies in 1973-74. Then, already, it was the process of Normalization, which means this type of totalitarian regime which was not that cruel as it used to be before. I mean, in the fifties. But it used different methods of oppression. And I could see among my fellow students, my colleagues, the ways they started to compromise again, and to join all these façade organizations such as the Socialist Union of Youth, etc. Just so that their careers could go forward smoothly. For some reason, I don't want to say that for moral superiority, whatever, I couldn't do that. So, I had sort of a problem finding a good job when I finished my education. So in '74, actually for the first time, I worked as a stoker for a year, then I went into the army. I spent a year in the army. In the fall of '76, I came back and started to work as a teacher of programmers for a small Czech IBM—it's not IBM obviously—it was *Kancelářský stroj* [business machines], not computers.

And then, in the fall of '76, obviously, things were already on the way. This was the trial of the Plastic People of the Universe, and I started to think about forms of resistance against this morally corrupt and unbearable spiritual and political situation.

Actually there is one thing I should add. Philosophy, or this type of thing, was very well established in my family. My father was a university professor. He also had a lot of troubles after '68. But still, he was teaching at the university. And Jan Patočka, a Czech philosopher, who was to play an important role in the Charter 77 movement, was a family friend. So I was exposed to his lectures since I was ten years old.

And after '67, '68, when I started to study philosophy, I was following Jan Patočka as my philosophy teacher. I belonged to the last generation of his students. And he was at the university, then he retired, and he went around, and I think he founded the origins of what later was called the "flying university," or "independent university," which was already established in these seminars. And so Jan Patočka started to be politically active. By the way, you can trace these ideas back in his thoughts back in the seventies. And so, I think I was inspired by this example and maybe some other impulses, when I was approached in December of '76, and I was deciding whether to sign Charter 77 or not. I was young and didn't feel that I had that much to lose. So I said yes, and I belonged to the first group of signatories of Charter 77, which obviously put me into the ranks of dissidents at that moment.

So a consequence was that I had this normal experience with the police and this type of harassment so that I lost my job. I was fired. And then for twelve years—this means between '77 and '89—I did all sorts of jobs, stoker and many others. I was sort of cut off from any contacts or connections with official life. I couldn't be at the university. I couldn't do anything. I couldn't have a passport. This type of stuff. But I was very much active in the movement, if you want to say, in what Václav Benda called later the "parallel-polis," which was this type of independent circles.

Obviously we all lost a lot of things, opportunities to follow our careers. But we got something as a reverse compensation for these losses. What we got was friendships with interesting people. And this type of personal links. I met Václav

Havel for the first time, just to name the most known person in this group, but not only Václav Havel but others. So, my second round of education took place in those circles. Because I did this work as a stoker—we all did this type of work—I had quite a lot of time to do other things. So we had a close circle of friends. I studied old Greek, or ancient Greek, and we read Homer and also Virgil in Latin and all these types of classical texts. And we could discuss them. We really did a lot of independent things in this context. So, life went on. On the one hand, there was this spiritual, intellectual level in it, but it also had its political aspect. Charter 77 was a parallel-polis, which means that we, on the one hand, couldn't or didn't want to participate in political life in the proper sense.

Charter 77 was not political, oppositional. It was a group of people who didn't want to take part in the established system of lies and routines. Obviously, politically we could use, or were reflecting or following international processes, the Helsinki process. Or we used the international documents or arguments from this sphere to support our cause of human rights. But I think the course of human rights in this context was something much broader. It was not only a catalog of rights, or a type of entitlements. It was this active attitude, commitment to something like the common good or transparency in the situation which is called society, or this type of society which existed under Communism.

In that context my title came in '86, because the rule or tradition was that there was the position or institution of "spokesperson" of Charter 77. The original spokespersons were Václav Havel, Jan Patočka, and Jiří Hájek from the Ministry of Foreign Affairs in '68. But then other people were coming just to take this role. And I finally got this role myself, too, so I was a spokesperson for Charter 77 with Anna Šabatová and Jan Stern in '86. And then also, '86 was already quite close to '89, so the situation in the second half of the eighties— Gorbachev was in power and perestroika was on the way, and an all new politic. Maybe it was the very beginning, but I think we might have seen a lot of signals which were already in the air. To sum up this experience: '68; '86 I was spokesperson; '87, '88, '89 were already these years of transition, which means, in the beginning of that year it was not that clear, what would happen.

I took part in the Velvet Revolution in my own way, because my former activities happened to be in the middle of all these things. After January '90, I found myself suddenly in Parliament. I spent six months as a member of Parliament. And I also, for instance, organized the first trip of Václav Havel to the United States. My first visit to the States was when I stayed there with Ivan Havel. It was really the first visit in January, and then I went again to prepare the president's trip. We started in New York, went to Washington and to Canada, and ended in Reykjavik. And then the presidential party came to Reykjavik, and we went backwards with them, which means Canada, then Washington, New York, then back to Prague. It was 1990, in February. It was when Václav Havel had his first address to the joint session of the U.S. Congress. It has been published.

I was in Parliament. Then I found that I would rather devote my time to academic things. I planned to go to Leuven, to Belgium, to study in the archives.

I already had arrangements for that, but in the beginning of July, I was asked by Jiří Dienstbier to join him at the Foreign Ministry. So I felt that, because my stay in Leuven was planned to start in January of the next year, I could do it for the next couple of months. So I started to work at the ministry as an advisor. But in October of that year, the Deputy Foreign Minister Dobrovský was promoted. He became the minister of defense. And then I was asked if I would be willing to work as the deputy foreign minister. So I spent the next two years, between October 1990 and October 1992, as the deputy foreign minister. So I had quite a good chance to participate in the foreign policy debates in this period.

Then, obviously, I was active in the losing side of Civic Forum, which was in the process of fragmentation. Václav Klaus says, "oh yes, there is only one rule." And all others who didn't agree with him happened to be on the other side. It was OH, *Občanské hnutí*, or the Civic Movement. We lost the elections in June of 1992. I still worked at the ministry. Dienstbier obviously resigned. And I stayed for another three months. It was the time when the state was in the process of divorce.[1] And so, then I resigned sending a statement to Minister Moravčí that I didn't want to participate in that process. So I left the ministry. And from that moment I am the chair of the Czech Helsinki Committee, which is, I would say, the leading human rights organization.

I spent a year '93-'94 at Northwestern University. I was teaching there as a visiting professor, and now I'm at Charles University at the School of Social Sciences, and here [Center for Theoretical Studies], so now I'm partly in academia. I very often teach various groups of American students. We still have a program with Northwestern, the one we are now finishing with George Mason [university], and many others. But I teach at Charles University and I am involved with the business of civil society. So that's basically my story.

Did the authorities try to censor Gorbachev's speeches or information about perestroika?

I'm not an expert, but just from my point of view, or as I saw the situation, yes, obviously. Because Gorbachev's policy definitely did not correspond to or was not in conformity with the doctrines dominant here. There was one big question especially. There was a document which was adopted by the Central Committee of the Communist Party in '69—*Lessons from the Years of Crisis*. And in this document, I think, all principles and policies of the Husák regime were defined and stated. And the question was whether the party was still to stick to this document, just to keep the *Lessons of the Years of Crisis* as a kind of dogma or the main principles of their policies. Still I think that in '88, when the spirit of change was somewhat around, Gorbachev was visiting Prague, and we were curious about what would happen. Still the Communists were very reluctant. They didn't want to retreat an inch from their position. So I think they were very much aware of the growing discrepancy or tension between their position and the Soviet position.

But what I would like to say in this context is that our position, and maybe our fundamentalist human rights position, was the emphasis on our politics from below. We didn't want to admit that our strategies were dependent on the maneuvering or moves in Moscow. We felt that, actually, we were doing that, just promoting a consistent stance which was the respect for human rights. And obviously the situation was changing, so sometimes it was more favorable to our cause, sometimes the times of crisis and repressions came. But obviously in late eighties, the dynamism was already, or it was clear that something was going to happen.

Did the chartists begin planning for a shadow government? Was there any thought that the current regime might actually disappear?

Not at all, I would say. But it is a broader question. It might be interesting. First of all, the original diversity, or the original political pluralism in the charter was better expressed in the institution of three spokespersons. It was generally believed that each spokesperson should more or less represent—there was not any formal system of political representation—one of the three main streams within the charter. One stream being the former Communists. Maybe those who still believed in the reformability of socialism, eventually in "socialism with a human face." These people, obviously, were, more than the others, inspired by Gorbachev, and they from time to time were even ready to think about, to start to strategize, how they should react to this or that signal coming from Moscow.

Then there was a group of Christians. People who had a strong moral, or somewhat otherworldly motivation for their deeds. And there was a third, maybe loose group of liberal intellectuals. People who—Václav Havel maybe was one of them. It's sometimes difficult to use these classifications. But these three main streams existed.

And there was a fourth sort of entity—the underground. I don't know whether you have heard this term in this context. But there was a group of young people, who, just because of their age maybe, or experience, had—not programmatically, because there was no program behind them—antiestablishment attitudes. They were, I would say, anticareerists. They had no problems with being losers in that sense. So they were not quite clearly represented, because they were not representing any, I would say, specific position. But they were there.

So this was the original version. But what came, and that's why I am telling this story, was a kind of generational discussion in the beginning of the eighties, because the original group of signatories already, after several years of existence in this type of opposition in the parallel-polis, developed certain routines. What connected them was their common experience of being "against," to protect the walls of the parallel-polis against all enemies. And they were just dropped together by this feeling of a basic sense of solidarity.

And then, I would say around '84 or '85, even before the signals from Moscow started to come, a younger generation started to appear. People who signed the charter only in the beginning of the eighties felt themselves to be newcomers. And these people, well, maybe they are younger, they have younger souls, so they were more political, more radical, because the original version of Charter 77 activities had, I would say, a very anti- or apolitical attitude. This was Patočka's moral stance. This was the joint awareness that our program is the protection of human rights and no other political programs. The newcomers couldn't understand that, because it meant that the chartists only signed their documents and petitions and sent their letters to the government, and there were no responses, obviously, no positive responses coming from this side. So this younger generation was looking for other methods, a more dynamic style.

By the way, the generation of people who still runs *Respekt*[2] is, I think, this second generation. This is quite an interesting theme, this first and second generation of dissidents. And obviously in this atmosphere a new phenomenon started to first appear, then almost to mushroom—an independent peace movement which started with the John Lennon celebrations in Prague. There is this wall,[3] and then the first small marches over the Charles Bridge in Prague. The chartists were not used to appearing in public in that way. Their only public appearance was in the courtrooms, or outside the courtrooms, when they were coming to demonstrate their solidarity with those who were arrested or on trial. But these young people started to do new things. And obviously the original version of Charter 77 was a very specifically Czech, very philosophical attitude, I would say.

The second generation was much closer, for instance, to the strategies of those who followed very similar goals in East Germany. So you suddenly had in '85, well this, and the case of *Jazzová sekce* [Jazz Section]. It was another interesting group, which was not, we say, made up of professional dissidents or which didn't grow directly from Charter 77. But these new phenomena in this space of parallel-polis—and they started to appear in the eighties with the international changes—well, created a better, or created an environment in which these initiatives could appear. But they were not, definitely, sort of directly articulated, conscious responses to what happened in Moscow.

Charter 77 offered a kind of mirror to the regime. Not only raising certain questions, but making it possible to see what kind of situation existed with the regime: Were they ready to use all sorts of repressive means, or were they ready to practice more tolerance? And still the situation had its ups and downs. If you remember, it was in the beginning of December '88, when there was the first demonstration which was allowed. Václav Havel appeared for the first time as a speaker on a public square. And then came all of a sudden the repression, another wave of aggressions; and Václav Havel again in prison for a much less, lesser I think, crime than he committed by being quite outspoken on this square in Žižkov in December. So it was clearer at that moment that on both sides, in the government and the opposition, there were different perspectives, different strategies, obviously different aspirations.

Where do you place yourself among the various groups of chartists?

It's very difficult, because obviously, as I mentioned, I was a part of this first group. So in that respect, I have to say I was an old-timer. I belonged to the young old-timers, or relatively young old-timers. I was one of the youngest spokespersons and I was quite close to all the people of the second generation. I also took an active part in the polemics between the first and second generation. I would rather see myself as a bridge between these two than to put myself into the first or the second.

Can you describe your involvement in the Velvet Revolution?

I was involved in the Velvet Revolution from the very beginning, so I was part of the developing structure. I took part in all the planning sessions, and obviously, some of these activities were more relevant in the political context. Some of these activities were more organized just for the sake of organization. But, yes, I was part of it.

With your experience in Parliament, did you not feel that you would like a political career?

Obviously, all these things were quite an interesting experience for me, but I simply wanted to go to Leuven to study. Everything was very new for us. I traveled abroad for the first time after twenty years, in January 1990. I had no plan of what I was going to be. And I really wanted to leave active politics. The proof is that I didn't participate in the elections in 1990. Obviously I could have easily been elected, but I was not on the list. But then I agreed to go to the Foreign Ministry, and I ended up there for another two years.

How would you evaluate these last several years since the Velvet Revolution?

Obviously, I think, in general, revolution is the situation in which you finally understand that your tomorrow will be different from your yesterday. It is a kind of discontinuity in time. In that respect, this was a new situation. A new situation means that you are put into unpredicted, and unpredictable maybe, situations. Obviously, there were changes. We were more optimistic, more self-confident, in January of 1990. And the moment of my sobering obviously came in '91-'92 when I saw, actually already in 1990, when I saw the second revolution and Václav Klaus just going to power. It was in the fall of 1990. What we tried to do after the change, after the elections—because it was maybe the first period, the end of the first period of this revolutionary, or positive, transformation—was the first free elections.

And I wanted to go to Leuven, but I ended up in the Foreign Ministry. But at the same time I was still involved with Civic Forum. And I was not in Parliament. I stayed in the headquarters. And we had the task, or thought we had the task, of organizing this body which grew very spontaneously into a structure. And we did it with clear rules and a system. And we were doing that in the summer of 1990, not knowing that Václav Klaus was already preparing his, quote, coup d'état. What happened was that as a part of the institutionalization of *Občanské Forum* [Civic Forum] it was decided that there would be an election of a chair and/or president, and I remained then to be the candidate standing against Václav Klaus. It was in October 1990. And I was supported by the leadership of Civic Forum.

I think that I had 67, almost 70 votes, and he had 125 or something. So it was two to one, so I still had some supporters. But, obviously, it was not my frustration because I was not elected, because of that slide, but the political style, the consequence, or the context of this victory was the sort of first negative signal. I guess the process of sobering started. And then obviously, when the political scene started to be, some people say now, standardized, or just transformed to standard political parties. There were already some signals that the situation would be bringing us into a new situation. I don't want to say that we or I knew everything before it happened. But it's a process of learning, and I think that heuristically an extremely interesting situation, to be a part of such a process.

Do you see a future for yourself in politics?

I am not an apolitical academic and I'm not going to be, but I am really not a person who would say here that's the only alternative or final goal of my life. So if I wanted to do that, obviously the best thing would be to join some or one of these big parties and then to try to make a career there. I didn't do that. I'm saying, that for my own way, I think I have political projects based on human rights, civil society, and this type of new politics, whatever it is. I'm ready to think about it, I'm ready to write about it, theorize it, do it, but, well, what will happen will happen. I don't know, but there are no strategies in this realm in the foreseeable future.

Since you mentioned human rights, and you are a member of the Helsinki Committee, what are the biggest racial issues facing the Czech Republic?

First of all, obviously, the question is, what is our racism. In our case, I would say that it is not what I would label a classical racism. Because classical racism is a sort of feeling of superiority of your own, let's say white, race over the others, less developed. It might have even a very sophisticated, almost cultivated expression in all forms of Eurocentrism. You can believe that *this* is the civilization and that the others have to be educated in another way. But I think our racism is rather based on the Czech feeling of smallness; not superiority but a complex of inferiority, rather fear, lack of openness, the feeling that we have to struggle not to allow foreigners or disturbers of the peace to enter our territories.

Maybe I'm wrong, but I think the American racism in the nineteenth century or even during the Civil Rights struggle in the sixties was maybe unjustified, but still based on this sort of feeling of a superior race over those who are inferior. So our racism is, I think, slightly different. And I think that it's a rather negative concept than a sort of positive attitude. It's a lack of civility rather than deep conviction, a deep belief in something. It's a weakness of the rule of law, it's the weakness of the lack of communication in the society, the absence of intermediary bodies, the absence of all structures, which according to Alexis de Tocqueville, create, represent the *sine qua non* of a democratic society. So, I think that the human rights struggle, the cause of human rights, is exactly now these institutions or instruments we have that bridge all these gaps which exist in our society by some sort of positive programs, just to try to open as many channels of communication in society as possible, to help those who feel that they cannot easily talk to the others. Because if they are left in this situation, then they can easily be persuaded by apostles of racism or simplistic solutions. So, I think our racism is rather a consequence of the poor state of civil society, of the sick principles of institutions in our Czech society.

We want, first of all, to help if we can individuals to communicate what they want to say to the others. We have a center for interlegal consultancy. We work with refugees, with those who lost or didn't get their citizenship, Roma, situations very much influenced by this factor. But we also try to promote dialogue in society when we publish our reports on the state of human rights. We don't want to say that we know what is right and we are not criticizing what's wrong. We want to state our arguments as clearly as we can, but we can also invite people to start thinking about, talking about that. The principle of dialogue, I think, is quite crucial in this context. People, or individuals, or members of collectives and groups talk to each other instead of just fighting with, among themselves, or at least with words. That's, I think, our basic philosophy. And this philosophy, at least for me, is a basis of a political program, or of my personal or my private political position.

This polarization can go in all possible directions, because after the Roma problem, we can start talking about our joining Europe. We can talk about international civil society, about NATO and security.

I still have one project, so to say, on the table. And this project has a working title "From Parallel-polis"—which is my political experience with Charter 77, something very small, very intimate, based on personal relations of a rather small group of people whose common denominator is that they find themselves, or found themselves in a similar or same situation—so from this "to Cosmopolis." I'm just disturbed by the question, to what extent our political experience in this situation is relevant now; what kind of inspiration can come from here in the moment when not only Czechs think about their transitions, or maybe other posttotalitarians, or people living in Eastern Europe. But world politicians now are trying to think about new world orders, the politics of the twenty-first century, or whatever. And to what extent our experience, or this type of thing is relevant, I think, is an inspiration to start thinking big. I don't mean too big, which means in a framework of mankind, but in which ways we can improve even global communication, just taking this point of departure. And, obviously, this question can be translated into different concrete situations. And I think that's what I'm doing and I hope that's what will do in the future as well.

9

Jiřina Šiklová

I told them it will be very bad for you, if you have a mother in prison.
—Jiřina Šiklová, 1998

Jiřina Šiklová, *sociologist, was one of the founders of the Prague Center for Gender Studies in 1992 and is the director of the Department of Social Work at Charles University. In 1998 she served as a member of the Fulbright Commission of the Czech Republic. Ms. Šiklová publishes widely on cultural, political, and social topics, especially women's issues and xenophobia, in a variety of academic journals, as well as the Prague daily* Mladá Fronta Dnes *and the weekly* Respekt. *The interview, conducted in English, took place in Ms. Šiklová's home in Prague.*

I am Jiřina Šiklová. I was born here in Prague on the 17th of June 1935, before the Second World War. From that time I have lived here in Prague and in this same flat. As they say, very conservative people never move, and I never moved. I studied here in Prague. I lived here in this flat with my parents. My father was a medical doctor, an ophthalmologist, and my mother was a teacher in an elementary school. I have one brother. He is a medical doctor, an internist, and he is living here in Prague too. I finished my secondary school in 1953, then I studied at the Department of History and Philosophy. I completed my examinations very well, and I wrote my thesis about the breakdown of the Prague Stock [Exchange] in 1873 in the last century. It was in the time of the Austrian Empire. Then I wrote my dissertation on the history of the YMCA, the Young Men's Christian Association, between the First and the Second World Wars. Then I wrote about the New Left Movement, about the comparison of the students in the New Left in the West and in the East. My dissertation was prepared, ready, but then the changes after the invasion of the Soviet Union started, after '68, and it was not possible to use.

I am married, or I was married. I am divorced. I have two children, a son and a daughter. My daughter was born in 1960, my son in 1963. My husband was a historian and editor of a journal on recent history, *Dějiny součastnosti* [*Contemporary History*]. Then he started with psychotherapy, and we were divorced in 1981.

My daughter is a medical doctor, a pediatrician, and she lives outside Prague. My son is a psychologist and is the head of education programs for children with addictions. He is also a psychoanalyst, and he lives here in Prague. He has his practice now in this flat, my flat, and now we are sitting at his so-called psychoanalytical couch. He has four children. My daughter has two children, and together I am a grandmother of six.

From the beginning of the sixties, it was possible to travel abroad. I was abroad many times with students in Germany, and that is how I had the personal experiences with these socialist-oriented, Communist-oriented students in the West—with Rudi Dutschke,[1] with the *Rote Armee Fraktion* [Red Army Faction].[2] And I have written about the confrontation and misunderstanding between the so-called socialist or left-oriented young people in the West and in the East, or in our country, if we are the East. I don't know. And that's how I wrote and published a book about the students and ideology of the West. It was published, but then destroyed, because it was not acceptable. At the time, 1968, I was an assistant at the Philosophy Department. And in the sixties, I participated in plenty of activities which were possible at the time. They were activities which were connected with the dialogue between Marxists and Christians— discussions at the university about Kafka and about existentialism. It was, from my point of view, a relatively good time. The people arrested by the Stalinists were freed from prison. It was possible to write plenty of things and to translate plenty of things. It was the fight against Communist power, but this fight was relatively progressive and it was possible to interpret it as "the door is open."

But this opening was stopped. It was the reason that I understood that here is one way to change or how to have influence on society. I told myself that the only power I can have is to be a member of the Communist Party and to be active. My idea—and this I have been living all my life—is that it is important to participate in life and not only to be passive. If you are passive, you have clean hands, but really, you are dirty because you are passive, and you have done nothing. I don't like these people who are now saying, "we are innocent, we have done nothing." Yes, you are guilty, or they are guilty, because they have done nothing.

And I can give you an example. I have been canoeing in a kayak, and when you are going through these rapids in the river, and if you go direct you must have a higher speed than the normal water. Only in this case, you have your kayak, your ship, in your hands. I think it is something similar with life too. It is the reason why I think that it is my duty to participate in things which are around me and to do what I think is important.

In '67, in Czechoslovakia there was great criticism against the Communist Party. We were against censorship, etc. In summer 1967 there was a famous conference of Czech writers. Czech writers very often have played the role of politicians, and they have done more in politics more than the real politicians which were only marionettes in the hand of the Central Committee of the Communist Party. And they were persecuted. At that time I told myself it was important to participate in it. There were plenty of people at this time who left the Communist Party, in the autumn '67. But I told myself that now, at this time, it is my duty to participate in it. I became active in the Communist Party in March 1968. I was elected as the head of the Communist Party organization at the Philosophy Department.

I think that what was done in this year '68 was important, that it had a positive influence—not on our country, it was negative. But it had a positive influence on the image of so-called socialism in the Western European countries, on plenty of western European Communists, salon Communists, or cafe Communists. And we have seen that their dream was only to dream. And that it was a very important experiment. But this is history. I participated in all activities which were connected with the year '68, in the students' strike. I was in the press group which was against the Central Committee. I was on the committee of the high school students, and I participated in the activities of the students. At this time the difference between the students and me was not so big. My students, for example, were not only Jan Kavan and Petr Uhl, but Petruška Šustrová, Tomáš Halík, Merek Tyl,[3] and Ľuboš Holeček. And now I am in contact with them, but they are in different positions now.

And when this happened with Jan Palach, he was in the seminar with me, but I could not remember him. And I was reminded about him after he burned. And then I told myself it is too much for me. I said that I will not be a member of the Communist Party. If I was the head of a Communist Party organization, it was possible to change it. And, of course, I was informed what will be the consequences. But I agree with it. And I think that if I have played this role in 1968, that it was normal that I must go from the Philosophy Department. I think that it was the consequence of my activity. My mother very often repeated *pro hubu na hubu* [what goes around, comes around]. And that it's normal. Then I was working at different jobs as a cleaning woman. At the Faculty, at the State Library in the Klementinum, at the Carolinum, etc. It was half recreation, of course.

Then you left in 1969, during the Normalization period?

Yes, I left the position at the Faculty in 1969. It started not directly after the invasion. This really started at the beginning of the seventies. The regime needed time for it. You must imagine that until the end of 1969 the border was open. At first, in November '69, it was announced by the president, Gustáv Husák, that the frontier is not a place where you can go for walks. And the border was once again closed. At this time, plenty of my friends emigrated, more than one quarter of a million. And of course, I have stayed in contact with them, unofficially.

And during the so-called Normalization period, I worked from '71, or '70, in the hospital at the Department of Gerontology. I was there as a so-called social worker, but really I worked there as a sociologist. I prepared some things which were important for the medical doctors, that is, the demographic information to include in their dissertations and these things. I had a relatively good position there. It was very low paid, but of course it was said that I couldn't have, for example, a driver's license. I couldn't have a telephone and could have a salary only on a low level. But it was only the consequences. But the atmosphere in the hospital was rather nice. I had good contacts.

In 1971, in autumn, we started to have contact with people from our emigration, who were abroad. And Petr Pithart[4]—now he is the head of the Senate, the second chamber—returned from England. The contact with Palach Press in England was started through him and through Ľuboš Holeček and Jiří Müller.[5] During the seventies, when Peter Pithart and some of the students were arrested, I was not. I was somebody who was as a "postman," or a "postwoman," between us and exile. And I did this work a very long time. I can say I did that from '72. That was the beginning. But after Charter 77, I was an important person for it until 1989. It was interrupted when I was arrested in '81 for one year.

And all this time I was in contact with our emigration, unofficially. They didn't know my name, of course. It was done through London with the help of Jan Palach Press, then with Pavel Tigrid. He was in Paris. And with the help of Jiří Pelikan.[6] He was in Italy. And in the last years, from '76, it was through the help of Vilem Prečan.[7] He was our historian. He lived in Hanover and he started with the archive of the unedited, or unofficial, or forbidden or illegal literature and publishing in Scheinfeld at the Castle of Schwarzenberg.[8] I was his operative here.

How did you become involved with Charter 77?

I was one of the first persons to receive it. Several people wrote it. I am not the author of it. I know that among these authors were Pavel Kohout and Zdeněk Mlynář.[9] Mlynář was living here, twenty meters from my flat, but he died. Václav Havel was also involved in writing the charter, but I was not in contact with him. And some of these people were informed that I had this contact to the West. At this time it was through one perfect man from Sweden. His name is Peter Teiner. Now he is at the embassy in Washington from Sweden. At that time he was living here in Revolution Street 17. His last name was Pettersson. And through him I sent abroad papers and information about Charter 77. It was prepared abroad for the moment when it could be published here, or would be officially sent to our government.

There was an embargo of this text [Charter 77 Declaration] until the first conflict. This conflict started on the 5th of January 1977. This was my beginning with it. I didn't formulate it. I didn't sign it at the beginning, because it would have been stupid to sign it officially. I played this role—which, sometimes I did not play very well—that I am participating in normal life, that I am not perfect, but I couldn't show what I have done really. But I think that it is normal that you couldn't be visible. But I did sign it, when we saw that this persecution started. Bruno Kreisky[10] from Austria said, "if you are a chartist, you may immigrate." But it was destroyed and I signed it once again in 1981, later, but it was not important.

What were the circumstances surrounding your arrest?

We were in contact with people in the West a very long time. And six times a year, sometimes more often, a truck with the literature arrived. And we sent abroad the manuscripts and articles. It was not the time of e-mail. It was not the time of the diskette, or floppy disk. We didn't have that. We didn't have a telephone. Of course, for example, Václav Havel had a telephone. And my friend Milan Šimečka had a telephone. But, of course, it was only for the secret police or for normal conversation, "Have a nice birthday," not really for communication. It was not possible to use it. And at this time we received, somebody arrived, maybe for two or three weeks, and we sent manuscripts and proclamations, etc. And sometimes this big car arrived, but I was not in contact with this big car, truck. I was only the first contact person with somebody from this car, and I took what was most important for these people. And I told this person, where he had to take the things from this car, and where the things which may be sent abroad are prepared.

This car was perfectly prepared for it. Ivan Hartl and Jan Kavan, they started in London with this so-called Palach Press. They organized it, and they found the money for this car. This car was changed very often, not physically changed, but the make, number, and color, etc. And different people were drivers. And this car was used before for transporting weapons from England to Ireland. It was very well made. I saw it sometimes. It was heavy.

And, you know, I did this a relatively very long time. It is not good to do it long. It is against all the rules of conspiracy, if one person is doing this for so long. It was one reason why I said that somebody should replace me. But it is impossible to say to somebody, "Please take it." And then Vilem [Prečan] promised me that he will do it. But he had a home search, and then he emigrated. The second one who told me he was prepared to take it was Jan Deshart. He was arrested before he could do it, and then he had troubles with his health, neurosis, psychosomatic difficulties, and he emigrated. Prečan emigrated in 1976, July 11, and Deshart emigrated in 1980.

And then Petr Uhl and Jan Ruml[11] told me they had the perfect man who will replace me. His name was Pavel Muraško. He was arrested for so-called Ukrainian nationalism, and he was with Peter Uhl in prison. You know communication with somebody who is in prison is complicated. And he promised me that he will take these things. And I believed it, but I think that he was under the pressure of the secret police. I told him, I will not explain it to you, but we can start together. You will have the "luggage," or the books which should be sent abroad in your flat. And after half a year, I will explain it all to you. I will give you the code, and how it is coded. It was not a play. It looked like a Boy Scouts' game, but it was not a game. Then I explained to him that I will give it to him. It started in January. And in January, during this first meeting, I noticed that I was being observed. But I didn't think that he had done anything. The second time was April 1981. Plenty of people knew about this big car coming. He was not informed. And maybe—it's my interpretation—he made a pact with the secret police in prison under pressure, and he told the secret police at the beginning that it will arrive, therefore, that he couldn't give the oath. But maybe it's my misinterpretation. I believe that people are better.

But, you know, if he really had the interest to give them everything, he could be paid for half a year. What is half a year for the secret police? But he was not informed about when the car was coming. And so I was informed when they arrived. But this man who was the second person for exchanges, my replacement, was not informed when it arrived. But, I think, he informed the secret police about the car. But they didn't know from where it would come. And he didn't know how this car would look, or who the driver would be. They didn't know anything.

And then they stopped this Peugeot. At this time it was white. And they didn't have a translator for the driver. And they thought it should be heavier. They stopped plenty of cars, of course, at different parts of the border. It was going from London to Paris and then through Vienna. And then it happened that the two drivers were arrested. They were from France. Perfect people. They were here for two or three months in our prison. One of them was a jurist, the head of the League for Human Rights. And the second one was a girl who was here many times before. And they destroyed any important information they were carrying on themselves. Then we waited for what would happen next.

And the secret police didn't know who was who and how to organize it, and they started to arrest the people which were on the list, whose books were being exchanged. But my name was not there, and I was arrested at the last moment. It was the 8th of May. During this time somebody arrived by plane, visited me, not just me, but it was organized with the help of the wife of Mr. Šedivý. Jaroslav Šedivý[12] is now the minister of foreign affairs, and his wife was the contact person and she gave me this information. I was very well informed what is dangerous and what was in the car. And I was given the warning for different people for whom it might be bad, but plenty of them were arrested.

In the beginning, fifty people from Bohemia and Slovakia were arrested, but only eight stayed in prison, not more. And the prosecution case had the name of "Šiklová and Company." And this included, at that time, Milan Šimečka from Bratislava, Jan Ruml, Jiří Ruml,[13] and—then later he emigrated to London and was at the BBC and Amnesty International—Eva Kantůrková, Hořec, who else might there be? I've forgotten. But at the time, at this trial were Olga Havlová, Ivan Havel, Jiří Hájek, Jiří Müller.[14] And I had the possibility sometimes to send word from prison, half secretly, and it was a pleasure for me to send, for example, the picture which I made to Pavel Tigrid in Paris, and it arrived. I was told that I will be sentenced for ten years. It was paragraph 98, the paragraph on "*rozvracení a podvracení republiky*, A, B, C." It means "destruction of the socialist system, organized and with the help of the imperialist powers," and for that, one could be hanged. But it was not the right time for hanging. Everything was prepared for the trial, but it never took place.

Then the changes in Poland started in the autumn. There was strong influence from the West—Mitterrand, Margaret Thatcherová [*sic*]—and a great help came from Bruno Kreisky, head of the Social Democratic Party, at this time he was the chancellor of Austria, and some others. Mr. Carter was also involved at this time, and they exerted pressure.[15]

Then we were released from prison, from the trial. But we remained under the watch of the secret police. And I received notice that it is finally finished, that the case was terminated, only after the takeover in 1989, and that I couldn't be against it, that I must agree with it. And it was signed by Václav Havel. It was a pleasure.

When I returned home, I started to work once again in the hospital but in a different department, and I did that not with the contact of Jan Kavan, but with the help of very important people from Germany. The chargé d'affaires from Germany was here, Wolfgang Amadeus Scheuer. Now he is retired and he is in Melzungen. I was in contact with Vilem Prečan with the help of this embassy, the German embassy, and we sent, for example, plenty of materials to Austria. In Austria, in the *Institut für Menschenrechte* [Institute for Human Rights] is the archive of Patočka's work, and Klaus Nellen[16] was the head until this time.

Altogether I was in prison for one year. The conditions in the prison were not bad for me, not only me, but for all of us. I think that it was the influence of the year '68. The year '68 had a positive influence on the Communist power, or the Communist leaders, that they were cautious against treating us very badly. Because it was possible in '68 to open the archives, they were afraid that it would happen once again. It was the reason, I can tell you, that I was never beaten. Of course, I had some conflicts with the people who were criminals who were together with me, but nothing which would be against humanity. Unless you think that it is against humanity that you couldn't have anything in your hand, that you are living only in three square meters with three other people. That may be, but really physically nothing.

It was possible to write, but it was also under censorship. And during this time I have written, of course. Many times what I wrote was destroyed—from time to time when they looked—but it was possible. The conditions now are much better. Eva Kantůrková[17] has written a book about it and there was a film about it, *Moje přytelkyně s domu smutku* [*My Friends from the Bleak House*]. And now it was impossible to make this into a film. They have to destroy it [the prison in its current condition] and they must show how it was at that time.

This time for me was very bad. I really believed that I would stay there ten years, and that I would be a burden for my children. You had the possibility to be in contact with only one person. That is why, for example, all the letters which were written in prison from Václav Havel have only one address. Only to Olga.[18] And it was similar with my children. And I told them it will be very bad for you, if you have a mother in prison. And if I would be forgotten, they would have to stay alive. It was very bad.

But I didn't have the feeling they were living in bad conditions. We had at this time a good organization for helping people who were arrested, their families, and very often I have organized that help, and I believed that the same would be done for my children. And it happened. And they had good conditions. Somebody arrived, gave them money, gave them help. And sometimes my children joke that they had their best time when I was in prison. They lived on a higher level than before the arrest. And people were very nice to them and helped.

For example, my daughter got married. She had the wedding in the very expensive restaurant *U Tři Pstrosů* [At the Three Ostriches] and she wrote to me, "I will have the wedding, and the uncle"—the code name for the person who paid for it—"paid for it as a present for the wedding." For me it was clear that it was paid for by the people who were in exile.

They also prepared for me—when they saw that I might stay ten years in prison—an exchange which was to be on this famous bridge in Berlin. I have never seen it. Sharansky and Solzhenitsyn were exchanged there.[19] You go and this exchange takes place. And then when I was interrogated—my attorney at the beginning was my accomplice, but they [secret police] didn't know it, Judr. Karel Jastovicka. He lived very near Vilem Prečan, and he was informed. And as he was my so-called attorney, he could quickly give me the information. And, for example, he informed me that they, that people in exile, would like to exchange me on this bridge.

And I asked then, "And for whom should I be exchanged?" And this attorney said, this is a horrible question. Then I said, "Excuse me, I must know, what my value is." Oh, you know it is impossible to tell you. And then I said that I would like to be married abroad. And the people from exile organized it, and somebody sent word to me that a man would like to marry me, a Hermann Von Bottmar from Hanover, and that he should marry me *in absentia*. And it was good. It didn't happen, but, in this case, it would be better for me so that then I could receive German citizenship, and then I could visit my children or my children could visit me. But if I emigrated, or I would just be exchanged like Sharansky, then never.

And at that time, we didn't see, we didn't think that any changes would be possible here. I can tell you, that I never thought that this change here would be possible. All my life I was informed that political changes are possible only after a war. And war was nonsense, when the world war was over. And then, this Reagan Star Wars. It was nonsense. And then we told ourselves, change is impossible. Change may happen only slowly. And in the beginning of the eighties, it was the Brezhnev[20] era, no visible changes.

Were you involved in Civic Forum?

In the last year of this so-called Normalization, I was working in the hospital, but I was at times taken under control. And I was in this group of 300 or 500 people which were not usually, but very often under so-called "preventive arrest." It means you were informed that before a state anniversary, before the first of May, before the visit of Brezhnev, before August 21, before October, that these people were arrested for forty-eight hours. If this visit was longer, for example, Brezhnev or somebody was here for a longer time, we were arrested, but we were dismissed after forty-eight hours. We could move two meters in front of the prison in Ruzyně and then once again be arrested. Then we stayed in the prison for ninety-six hours. That was the practice. We were prepared for it, for at this time, we all had at home a bag which was prepared with what was important—coins for stamps for letters, etc. And that was the normal practice.

But in autumn '88, I was visited. I thought that it was the normal preventive arrest, and they were two very important people from the secret police. They pressured me to cooperate with them. And I asked them why just now they came to take me? They told me, "You have value for us only if your friends believe that you have been arrested as the others, and not if you will be." It was a game for them. And they searched my home. Many times. And I was in prison for six days, but I was under control of the secret police, not in the normal Ruzyně prison. It was a problematic privilege. Then I told them, "No, of course, I will not help you." And then they started to be very bad. I was dismissed from my job. They visited me, they visited the hospital. They dismissed my son. He worked in a very bad place, in a home for children outside Prague. And he had to leave. My daughter couldn't go anywhere. She was in Kolín, in Kostelec. And I was living with somebody, Jiří Vacelý. He was a biologist, and he was also under watch. And he was told that he couldn't go to one pharmacological congress in the Netherlands.

But at this time, the situation was different than was normal. This situation was very open. People were helpful. For example, I remember that all the people around observed me. The secret police were here in front of my flat. They were waiting in front of the house. But the people, for example, the very famous actor, now he is dead, Josef Pek lived here. He helped me. Plenty of people helped me at this moment. There was a great solidarity with me. But I was dismissed from my flat.

Then I worked at jobs. Once again as a cleaning woman, but the secret police were so stupid that they visited these places. For example, I was supposed to be the cleaning woman in the National Museum. It was forbidden. Then I started to be a cleaning woman in the Institute for the History of the Theater in Celetná 17. They visited and it was impossible. Then I started with the help of somebody, a dentist, to work on the metro staff, cleaning in the metro. It was forbidden. Then I started in *Vodní stavby* [Water Construction]. And I was in the entrance hall. It was a big factory, a big plant, in Holešovice, Dělnická 12. Then I started working as a cleaning woman in the entrance hall. And they found out and they visited this Mr. Jamsa, the director. You must imagine that it is a big plant. For example, they built all the steamships on the river. And this poor man had a discussion with the police for more than two hours. And I can tell you that this Mr. Jamsa—of course he was a Communist, he was a member of the Communist Party—told them, "No, oh we are very satisfied with her. From the time she started cleaning here, in this entrance hall, the *pissoirs* [toilets (Fr.)] are not smelling. And we have a contract with her until December, and then maybe I will not renew it."

Of course, I was informed about it. But they assigned me not to the entrance hall, but to the second department in Venecka. And it was the department where all the telephone lines were open, an entire telephone central. At this time that was extremely important. At this time I received a tape recorder from somebody from Charter 77. It was impossible to buy here normally. And then daily, I had the possibility to send information to Radio Free Europe, Voice of America, and to the BBC with this tape recorder. I cleaned, then I would go into this other room and make the call. And I used this ordinary wax to attach the tape recorder. It was all done with money from the state. I think that they must have known, that they agreed with it. Or they let it happen. It must be visible in the accounts that they paid for it. But nobody did anything.

Daniel Kummerman was in the same building. He cleaned the windows around it, and I cleaned inside. And it was good for us. He was the courier to Jan Kavan at this time. There was good cooperation between us.

And when this so-called Velvet Revolution started, I was in the Magic Lantern. Then I was at Velčicky, in this so-called headquarters. It was at the beginning. We didn't know what will be or what will not be, or how it will happen. I remember that at one meeting we were all below—Václav Havel, Jan Ruml, Jiří Ruml, Karel Schwarzenberg, Timothy Garton Ash, etc. No, Jiří Ruml was not there. He had been arrested once again. He was in prison at that time. Then Jan Ruml said, "It is horrible, one hand grenade is enough. How stupid we are to be all together in this small place." But nothing happened.

Then Civic Forum started, but I am not one to make official policy. I was present, but I did nothing. I was invited in January to get into politics, I don't know, to be the minister of health or social affairs. But I thought "no." At the last moment I said "no." I returned to the university. I can tell you that I am satisfied with it. Of course it was not easy for me to be confronted with my former comrades, or colleagues.

Then they started, "It is lovely you are here. Our hero." Then they wanted me to be the head of the department. Then I told them, "No thank you."

During this time I was in Spalíček, in Civic Forum, and I was confronted with the people who were released from prison after this big amnesty. For the whole republic, we had 142 counselors who were working with the people who were released from prison. Unimaginable. Eight or nine thousand people from prisons, and they were all in Prague.

And then I told myself that it is important to start with applied sociology or social work. And with the help of the people from Netherlands and from Uppsala, we started it. Together with Igor Tomes—he was vice minister of social affairs. We started this department. I think this department is functioning quite well. I am proud that it ranks in third place with young people among the most desired subjects for study. In first place is English, in second psychology, and we are in third place, applied sociology, or social work. And I am satisfied with it.

I feel a certain prestige that this department is functioning very well. We have set up the curriculum, the so-called minimum standard of education, and everything is ready. And now I would like to have the possibility offering a Ph.D. to our students. And then I could go into retirement. I would like to give my lectures, but I couldn't be the head of this department. It is connected with plenty of stupid bureaucratic things. After this takeover, after this so-called Velvet Revolution, I am participating in an NGO—nongovernmental organization. I am on the Fulbright Commission, on the Foundation for the Development of Civic Society, Foundation Charter 77, Contra Barieri for the handicapped. Now I should be in VIZE. It is this new one, foundation, which is under Dagmar Veškrňová Havlová.[21] It is a foundation which was started by Wendy Wirth.

I would like now to find the money and help from people from in exile to help Vilem Prečan transport this archive from Bavaria, from Scheinfeld, from Germany to a castle near Prague. But it is complicated, the money, etc. Of course, Germany had an interest in buying the whole archive for the new Department of *Bohemistik* [Czech Studies (Ger.)] in Dresden. This is not only the Charter 77 archive. It is all independent literature, before Charter 77, all manuscripts, different manuscripts which were hidden, complete drafts, the first version, second version, etc. For example, what was in *Edice Petlice*—it means *The Padlock*—all the copies of what was published. And also plenty of information that passed between us, commentary, who is who, etc. And it is extremely important. Oh, what a pity that Václav Havel didn't give support for it. He didn't have the time for it. Oh, I agree with him. For him it is the past. It is similar, as, for example, I don't know what I have published. Up to this time, I know perfectly the addresses of my colleagues and my friends, but where something was published and what I have written, I don't know.

Only now when you ask me, I remember it, and I have in my mind that yesterday I had the interview for Vienna about the year '68. And it is interesting about the anniversary of '68, that only people from other countries have an interest in it and not people from here. It is typical for the present situation.

How would you evaluate the ten years since the Velvet Revolution?

I have written about the New Left. And years ago, I didn't think that capitalism was the best solution for a whole society. I studied the Frankfurt School, Erich Fromm, Marcuse, Habermas, Adorno, and I know that it is complicated. And that it is not paradise in the world. And this is the reason, why I am satisfied with this development. I had the fear that here we would be extremely influenced by the West. That we would be in the position of South Korea. That we would be the *Gastarbeiter* [guest workers (Ger.)] in our own country. And that has not happened. I admire that people were able to change so quickly. How quickly they understood, what are stocks, what is the currency exchange, what is banking. I didn't even understand. These things are important. What is it, banking?

Can you imagine that, for example, in 1988, Vilem Prečan sent Václav Havel a check, I know precisely, for 700 pounds. And he wrote to me under my code name, "It is the check for Václav Havel. He must take this check to the bank, and in front of the customer service window at the bank, he will sign it." And then, in the open air, I gave it to Václav, and I repeated it all to him. And he said, "Really, is it possible that I will not be arrested if I sign for the foreign currency in the bank?" And I told him that Vilem Prečan had written me.

You must imagine how complicated it was, these daily changes. It is the reason, or I have written one paper about it, it was published not here but abroad in *Social Research*. It is a quarterly of New York's New School for Social Research, and the paper is titled "Backlash."[22] And it is about how that we sometimes feel like foreigners in our own country. But I think that is normal. It must be. I admire how quickly things have changed. If you imagine that we must change. All our contact was oriented only towards the East, toward Moscow. And now we must change to the West.

We had a very bad situation here in the years 1992 until 1993. At this time, the salaries, real wages, were lower on average by 26 percent. It was on the level of the era before. And then it started to be on the level of the year 1989 at the beginning, at the end of 1994, but very slowly, slowly. But it is a long time for people. It is similar to marriage. At the beginning, it is the big love. After seven or eight years you see that it is only repetition. If it is interesting to you, I have written a paper, "What Did We Lose after 1989?"[23] And it is about that. That we very often lose the things which were important for us at one time, but are now normal for us. They lose their value for us. And we don't know what the value is for us at this moment.

This revolutionary change doesn't just effect Communist power but all our people. I have written about it before the takeover in one paper, "The Gray Zone and the Future of Dissent."[24] And in this I have written that this "gray zone"— they are these people which are not dissident, not in the *nomenklatura*,[25] not in the silent majority—but they are people on the border of it. They didn't lose their positions. They didn't lose their qualifications. They were small, dirty, collaborated with the regime. They were not heroes, but people as, for example, Václav Klaus, Miloš Zeman, etc., are now at the head. Then these people—but nobody knows their names, nobody knows them—will be the new leaders. Therefore the dissidents will not have the qualifications to be the power holder, and to engage in politics, because they had an ambivalent attitude towards power.

And that they have an ambivalent attitude towards power is very bad. If you can have the power then you must take it, and you must dip your hand into it. I think that it is the normal development. I know the situation in Poland and in

Hungary. I can tell you that I was never for Václav Klaus. My political orientation is more on this former dissident. In the election before the last, I supported Jiří Dienstbier's party, or the Civic Movement. In the last election, I supported the Union of Freedom—Jan Ruml, Vladimír Mlynář, etc. This is my orientation, my political orientation.

I have some slogans which helped me from childhood. One of them is from Confucius: "You should live like you wish yourself in the last moment of your life." Before death. And the second one is from Marcus Aurelius. "In all places in which it is possible to live, you can live relatively well." And this has been my experience. I think that during the next year, we will be a normal, relatively poor, central European country. We will be boring. That is all. I don't see any catastrophe.

I have only one fear, if the situation in Russia, in the former Soviet Union, will be very bad. I was many times in Ukraine. I moved among the students. I have organized—not I alone—repatriation. I know what will happen. Then these people will go to the West through us. And it will be dangerous for us, that the right-wing oriented parties have started here. And it is such stupidity which is in people very often in the West, that the people repeat, "You are racist," etc. We are not. It is not racism. It's xenophobia. We were closed for a very long time. The border was not only for us that we could not go to the West, but nobody could come to us. And we are not prepared for foreigners. And we are at this moment in this position, excuse me, like the prostitute, who would like to be a very good mother and wife, housewife, leader of the household. She must, in this case, do more than other normal women, a normal wife. And we must now show to the West, how perfect we are. That we are not racist, that we don't have these problems, etc. But it is complicated.

10

Petruška Šustrová

I regarded it quite a useful thing, to abolish what Orwell called "the Ministry of Love."
                                                    —Petruška Šustrová, 1998

Petruška Šustrová, *journalist, was deputy minister of the interior of Czechoslovakia 1990-1991. She has published widely on a variety of political issues relating to the transition of post-Communist states and contemporary Czech politics. Her articles have appeared in the online weekly service of the Network of Independent Journalists (www.idee.org) based in Split, Croatia. She is currently a columnist for the Prague daily* Lidové noviny. *Ms. Šustrová is the author of* Politické tanečky [Political Dances] *a collection of political commentaries broadcast on Czech Radio Regina, 1999-2001 (Praha: Academia, 2002). The interview, conducted in Czech, took place in Ms. Šustrová's home in Prague.*

I am from a broken family. I have a mom and a younger sister, a year and a half younger, and I also had a brother who was ten years younger than I. And mom was in the Communist Party which she joined in 1945. My grandpa collected money for families of political prisoners during the war. The Nazis arrested and executed him.

I went to school just like any other child. I grew up in Prague, and when the year 1968 came, I was twenty-one years old. I spent my childhood like the majority of children in the fifties, that means that I was a Pioneer. We went on trips. From time to time they bored us with some ideology, which was to us about as much—or to me it meant about as much as spelling or multiplication. I simply did not think it was important at all. And in 1968 I was learning things that till then I had had no idea about, because there were no books being published here from which a person could find out what was really happening. There was no information in the newspapers, and we did not have anyone in our

family or in our surroundings who would have been somehow politically persecuted. My mom was an editor. She worked in the publishing company *Detská
kniha* [*Children's Book*] and then in the magazine *Sešity* [*Notebooks*], and so for
me, what I was finding out in 1968 was a complete shock.

When in 1968 the tanks of the five countries came, we of course did not like
it, but even during the Prague Spring movement I was aware that what was happening here was not all right at all, and of course we all hoped for some reforms.
And I imagined that the reforms should be somehow within the system. When I
heard the opinion that the Communist Party should be one of more parties, that
was for me quite new, surprising. I did not understand it, and because I was at
the time at the Faculty of Arts I, of course, participated in student strikes, the
student movement. And I did not like at all how quickly, after August '68, the
interest and political activity subsided, because, when during the spring and
summer there were various meetings, that was very interesting. It seemed to me
that the city came to life, that the whole country came to life, and that it was as I
thought it should be, that people on the radio, in the streets, on television talked
about things they found interesting. And of course I did not like it when people
were becoming reconciled to how the freedom was gradually being curtailed,
how censorship was being introduced. And so we established—when it was
clear that in the student environment we would not stir further resistance or
some activity, because everyone was afraid—the so called Revolutionary Youth
Movement [*Hnutí revoluční mládeže*]. And we wrote pamphlets, translated various political texts that were related to the essence of the system, and we tried to
revitalize the former activity. We were in contact with labor unions that did not
want to accept the situation, and at the end of '69, the state police found out
about our organization and we were imprisoned.

I returned from prison at the end of '71, and at that time the majority of my
prison mates, my friends, got out as well, and we were still trying to do something useful. I don't know if it can be called opposition activity, probably yes;
we collected among ourselves money for families of political prisoners we met.
When there were some petitions, we tried to sign them. And then, in 1976, when
the police arrested musicians from the group the Plastic People of the Universe,
we also put together some petitions, gathered signatures for them, and sent them:
one to the chairwoman of the court which was to try the young men, and the
other to, I don't remember that one, Petr Uhl would know that.

And shortly after that Charter 77 was organized. I signed it in December
'76, and my activities in the charter varied. Mainly, we copied various texts and
documents, letters, open letters, but also columns, on a typewriter, and we gave
these out to more and more of our friends. And in 1978 the Committee for the
Defense of the Unjustly Prosecuted was established which documented the cases
of political prisoners. That means that the reports were based strictly on the official documents: on the charges, prosecutions, and sentences, and we described
what the person was accused of, and we also tried to note what the true reason of
the repression was.

In 1979 ten of the members of the Committee for the Defense of Unjustly Prosecuted were imprisoned, and so we, twelve of us, in a way took their places. And international reaction was quite strong toward this trial of the whole group. And so even though we still went to interrogations, were subjected to home searches, and various forms of abuse, we were not taken to prison, the regime did not send us to prison. In 1985 I was a charter speaker, and in the years from '79 to '89 I worked in the Committee for the Defense of Unjustly Prosecuted. Apart from that I was in the editorial staff of a *samizdat* magazine *Středni Evropa* [*Central Europe*], and I helped in the magazine *Informace o Chartě* [*Information about the charter*],[1] in *Kritický sbornik* [*Critical Journal*], and in various other *samizdat* [publications]. We traveled to unofficial concerts, went to unofficial exhibitions. There was also unofficial theater. There were many cultural activities.

And as far as political activities were concerned, even before I was a [charter] speaker, I participated in the preparation of various documents and helped the speakers with different technical tasks, and I also went to various discussions. These were discussions, in part, within the charter among ourselves, but also professors came from Oxford, or French philosophers, for instance, and various Protestant lecturers from Holland. And there we also talked about many different subjects, not only about politics, but about philosophy, political science, history, or perhaps about the history of theater; simply, the apartment seminars, as they were called, or "Patočka's University."

Those were not something that would offer general education but were more like certain pieces of education, because the variety of the people was very broad. People of all kinds of specializations came, so that one week there was, for example, a lecture on—how should I put it—on the philosophical significance of the English terms "shall" and "will," about the difference between them, which for someone who did not know English sounded as if they were from Mars. For those who could speak [English], it was probably very interesting, but not for me. Then again Roger Scruton[2] gave a lecture about the difference between fantasy and imagination. I have to admit that I don't see any difference between fantasy and imagination—in Czech the word *fantazie* incorporates the meaning of both. Those were simply certain points to hold on to, and a person who became interested could get information about authors who wrote on that topic. Those were like a slightly open window toward education, but in itself it was not, of course, an education, because it was very accidental.

How did being a speaker for the charter affect your family life?

On the whole not much. The repression was a little more frequent or harder. I went to interrogations more often, but not too much, because the worst persecution was here before, in 1980 and '81 when Solidarity was becoming stronger in Poland. So the local regime was probably very afraid of that and, therefore, persecuted the members of the charter really hard, including physical attacks, though I was never beaten by anyone. But I also had to listen to insults, threats. It was simply not very pleasant.

And when I was charter speaker, it was worse only because when there was a visit by a Western politician—which caused either hope or suspicion, depending from which side you looked at it, because he would want to meet with members of the charter—the speakers were under a strict watch. This means that they could not leave the apartment, or they could, but two secret police agents would follow a step behind them in the street, which looked simply terrible. It was shameful.

But at that time people already listened a lot to foreign radio stations, and so I did not much mind all this, because my neighbors from the house or the street knew, of course, what it was all about and they behaved toward me in different ways. Some of them had a quiet sympathy but, of course, did not do anything for us. And others would, for example, stop saying "hello" to us and avoided us, because they did not want to have trouble. For the children, well, that depends on how you put it for them, because, for instance, a home search is a very unpleasant thing. But for children it is also in a way an adventure, even if an unpleasant on. I think that it was more that the repression drew the families closer together, because it was so obviously unjust, that in a way, the outside world was separated from the family and from the whole dissident environment. After all, we knew that we were not doing anything—anything either illegal or bad, and the attacks from the outside were so nonsensical, unjust, that they in fact made it easier for one to maintain that position.

What were your activities during the Velvet Revolution?

In the spring of 1989 we agreed with some friends to publish a magazine of the kind that we missed in the *samizdat* spectrum. We called the magazine—for some reasons that I don't, that I simply couldn't understand even then, it was probably fate—*Sport*. But it, of course, did not have anything to do with sports. It was simply a political-social magazine in which there were reports, analyses, interviews. From the spring of '89, three issues were published, and the fourth issue was written and transcribed on stencils, but we did not have time to spread it around, because November 17th came and we established an independent press agency which published daily bulletins. In the bulletins we included brief, a sentence long or longer, pieces of information about all the activities that we heard about. We made copies and carried them all around and distributed them as our action radius would reach and as far as our news vendors were able and willing to walk and go. But we got help from, for instance, the taxi drivers. It was spread around by Civic Forum. It was in fact the only periodical that Civic Forum had. But it was not an instrument of Civic Forum.

Actually we soon had conflicts with them because they thought that since they distributed it, they could also dictate what and how we should write, they could not allow us to criticize Civic Forum itself. So we had a discussion where we got into an argument and we clarified some of their assumptions for them.

We explained to them that the money that people brought us they brought for the bulletin, for our work, that it was not Civic Forum's money. It was simply a custom of the Communist regime not to be allowed to criticize those that one sympathized with, but that we wanted to maintain a critical distance as journalists.

Well, this independent bulletin later became a weekly magazine *Respekt* [*Respect*] that exists even today. And I in fact spent the whole Velvet Revolution, or actually more a takeover, at Saša Vondra's[3] apartment, then in the gallery U Řečických, simply depending on how the editor's office of the independent bulletin was moving. I myself never went to any demonstration. Actually I did, but earlier, while they were still real demonstrations. But those manifestations of sympathizers, those I always just watched on TV.

What have you been involved in since the revolution?

From March 1990 I worked in so-called civic committees. These were groups of people that were to investigate past activities of the agents of the state police and suggest to the Ministry of the Interior whether those people could stay at the ministry or whether, according to our opinion, they had done such things during their service that they now had to leave. I was there for two months and then, when Jan Ruml went to work as deputy minister of the interior, he took me with him as his advisor.

And after about two weeks at the Interior I found out that we in the [civic] committees had very incomplete information, that we actually made such accidental decisions, that we didn't actually know what was happening. And so we agreed to be on the safe side and lay off the state police agents who worked against the so-called inside enemy, which means the forces of repression against the citizens; to lay off all of them, regardless of the decisions of the committees. The committees simply could not, did not have enough information for making decisions. But that did not work out very well, because Parliament did not pass the particular law. And the secret agents that we were firing from the Federal Ministry of the Interior were being hired at the Czech Ministry of the Interior, because we, of course, did not understand legal amendment, and even if we had understood it, we would not have had control over what the Parliament did or did not decide.

And on the other hand, Parliament, of course, did not know about this legal problem, and so the whole thing succeeded only partly. Nevertheless, the state police as an organization was simply dissolved. That was why I went to work at the ministry. I regarded that as quite a useful thing, to abolish what Orwell called "the Ministry of Love." In that we succeeded, I think.

And then I was the deputy of the minister. And I was—that was until August 1991, when there was a lot of restructuring at the ministry, and we thought that the first phase of our work was finished. And I wanted to leave then, because I am not an office clerk. I never wanted to be a state clerk. It is not for me. I am terribly messy. I have a system that no one can adjust to. I am simply not suited for group cooperation of the kind that there is in the offices, and I did not enjoy it. I saw that without constant intrigues it was hard for one to get things done. So I went back to *Respekt* and then from *Respekt* I went to *Střední Evropa* [*Central Europe*] where I had been before, because for two years I was not at home at all. I left in the morning, came back at ten in the evening and the children were growing up, and they grew like wood in the forest, very fast. My husband and I got a divorce, in part, because it was hard for him to accept that I was not home at all and apart from that, it was unpleasant for him. He thought that my career was an indication of my desire for power. Sometimes it happens that it is hard for the husband to accept the [wife's] career. We later got back together, and we continue to live together, but at that time, the family was falling apart. And at *Respekt*, even when it was a weekly, I had to be there, while for *Střední Evropa,* I could work at home. So I wanted the children to recover a little from it, because it was not their fault that some Velvet November came.

I was there until the fall of '93. And then my friends persuaded me to go and work in *Deník* [*(Czech) Daily*]. I thought all my life that newspaper reporters were a kind of servants, something quite inferior. But it really was very hard to respect the commentators when you read the Communist papers. Well, I could not even read newspapers in the eighties, the seventies. I thought I was reading about some towns that did not exist at all. I read, for instance, about Jičín, from where I had a lot of childhood memories, because I lived there at my uncle's for about half a year. I went to school there. I loved what I was reading about Jičín. I thought to myself that that was Jičín on some other planet, it simply was not like that at all. And when I came to *Deník* in '93, I thought to myself that in fact I was—because from '82 until November '89 I did not find any job—I thought that I had sat at home long enough and that I had enough energy, and that I enjoyed it.

So I was in *Český deník*, and then in the weekly until the time that it stopped in September '96. And from September '96, I simply did not find a newspaper job, because in Czech newspapers it was not allowed to criticize Klaus, only in *Právo*, but I simply could not work for *Rudé právo*. That paper had written very badly about me. But, of course, I respect, for instance, Petr Uhl or other people that they do not—if it does not bother them, I do not hold it against them and do not disapprove of them on any moral basis, but I myself could not do that, no.

I was translating at home for about a year, and then, luckily, *Lidové noviny* [*People's Newspaper*], decided to try one more editor in chief. Pavel Šafr and I had known each other before, because we worked together on the *Petice smíření* [*Petition of Reconciliation*] and so he asked me if I would come to *Lidové noviny* to be a commentator. And I have been there since September of last year, and as long as Šafr is there I will probably stay there and then they will fire me again.

How do you evaluate the last ten years in the Czech Republic?

Well, you know, I have had in the last ten years, or nine years, the opportunity to travel through almost all of Eastern Europe. I have been to almost all the countries, so I can make some comparisons. And I think that—of course the freedom, the disappearance of censorship, opportunities to travel, the flow of information—that, I simply cannot imagine a person who would not evaluate this in any other way than as extremely positive. That is a great thing. But at the same time, I think that in [people's] thinking, in all the countries, perhaps apart from Estonia, there has survived the Communist mentality, that the Czech and the Slovak, especially, are inclined toward strong leaders, that they are looking for a way in which somebody would do it for them, in which someone would lead them to a free society.

I think that, for instance, my husband or some of my friends expected that when after November, freedom broke out, the people would change. But, of course, the people have not changed. That is a thing for one or two generations, and when you are in contact—because I work with many people in Poland, in Bulgaria, throughout Eastern Europe—with people who are like me, who are also former dissidents, who read a lot, who are either journalists, politicians, or people who work for nonprofit organizations, so we all complain that it is not as it should be.

For me Czech journalism is desperate, because journalists go and ask the politicians what they mean and they try to make friends with them so that they would get information from them, and they do not, are not able at all to have a critical distance. And they plagiarize from one another. They do not speak [foreign] languages, do not read the international press, apart from exceptional cases. Of course, they are not studying and just stubbornly support the political party that they happen to be fans of at the time. They do not act as journalists at all. And in the intellectual professions it is everywhere terribly similar to that. The people do not know how to live in freedom. They know how to live freely in that they buy some canned food and go for a vacation in Croatia and they do not mind at all that there is a war two hundred kilometers away. They hate refugees, they do not like foreigners, scorn the Gypsies. These are all things that are—it is not visible at first glance—but if you live in it, it is hard to overlook.

Well, it is sad, because while there was Communism here, you somehow excused the citizens, because they were scared and because there actually was a real danger. But now there is no danger for anybody, and it is somehow, it will still take, the transformation is going terribly slow. And Czechs, moreover, I don't know if all nations have it. I don't know. Maybe you are more critical of your own nation, because you can see it more closely and you know it better, but Czechs have a certain tendency to think that when they succeed in something they are the best in the world, without having any comparison to how things are next to them.

Really, journalists here simply have no idea how things are in Poland, how things are in Hungary. They simply don't know anything about it—maybe those in the international columns, and those who follow the events. But when I wrote that the right-wing government in fact did not have broader barriers or broader possibilities than the left-wing government in Poland or in Hungary, the editors in chief did not want to publish that. They insisted that it was not true, that I should watch TV, that they are saying something completely different there. Well, they are. But these are, of course, all things that are all quite minor in comparison with the change of the regime. I don't know. I have learned in my life to look at things critically, and I think that you should always try to see things critically.

I, of course, did not finish college, because I went into prison and then there was no thought of studying anymore. But I think that here in the seventies I actually gained an education that could not have been gained in college, because I considered the people who were my friends to be the highest quality people of the generation, who, under normal circumstances, would of course have taught at colleges. They would have taught history, literature, political science, and we, because as far as work, it was so that all the jobs were, well, simply physical jobs, and especially older people looked for perhaps a night-guard job or some job that would not be too demanding. And all the jobs paid terribly little. We had discussions long into the night, sometimes until morning, about various issues and, of course, because we did not have anything to lose anymore, we could talk quite openly, and that was something that simply did not exist in schools.

And so, simply, my friends recommended literature to me. We studied languages. I can only read English and translate from English. I cannot speak and understand spoken English, because I never had the opportunity, or the opportunity was always so short that it did not have much effect. But I think that, actually, life among dissidents in fact gave you opportunities comparable to the opportunities of the free world. We may have lived in a ghetto and paid for it by various [types of] persecution, but that provided us with the critical approach and freedom of thought. Because we did not have to think about whether the response to a question would be appropriate or not appropriate, and we could be more open.

11

Petr Uhl

I see in the European Union a common means against the globalization coming from the United States.

—Petr Uhl, 1998

Petr Uhl, *engineer and journalist, was an activist in 1968 and during Normalization until his arrest and imprisonment in 1969. A signatory of Charter 77 and a founding member of VONS, Mr. Uhl has long been a prominent advocate for human rights both in his home country and abroad, for which he was imprisoned 1969-1975 and 1979-1984. From 1989 to 1990, Mr. Uhl was a member of the advisory council for the Coordinating Center of Civic Forum. Since 1996 he has been the editor of the Prague daily* Právo, *and since 1998 the commissioner for Human Rights of the Czech Republic. The interview, conducted in Czech, took place in Mr. Uhl's home in Prague.*

Basic information is that I was born here in the neighboring street on October 8th, 1941. My parents lived in this house two stories above us, and I have also lived in this house all my life, with the exception of the nine years I spent in prison. And I went to school and studied first at a general high school and then at a technical college. I graduated from high school in '58 and from college in '63. And then I worked at various jobs, for a longer period as a teacher at a high school, at an engineering high school where I taught mechanical engineering.

And so when I was twenty-seven, or twenty-six, the Prague Spring came, the Czechoslovak Spring, a kind of democratizing spring. I was not a member of any political party, nor was I a candidate. I was nonpartisan. I was single at the time and didn't have any children. I had traveled, since '65 to France and to Western Europe, and during the Prague Spring I began, I became involved in the ideological association the Left [*Levice*], which was a kind of a civic group, and after the Soviet armed invasion in the student movement, even though I was no

123

longer a student. There we established a group that was called the Revolutionary Youth Movement and that was extremely leftist. I myself was close to revolutionary Marxism, Trotskyism, and, gradually, we descended into the political underground.

And for our activities, which were based on nonviolent resistance against Normalization, in pamphlets, in texts, analyses, meetings, in establishing a certain organizational structure, we were arrested in '69, a year after we were founded, which means toward the end of '69. I was sentenced to four years. The trial—that took a long time. We were not sentenced until the summer of '71. And after four years I got out.

I married a girl[1] who was also in prison for two years, and we had two children. Together we founded Charter 77 and the Committee for the Defense of the Unjustly Prosecuted. And for my activities in this committee I was in fact arrested. I think fourteen of us were arrested at that time. And after forty-eight hours, four were released and ten were kept in detention. And out of those, six were tried.

That was in May '79. And in October we were sentenced, and in December there was an appeal, the appeal process. And there I got five years, the most of us all. Václav Havel got four and a half, Václav Benda four, Jiří Dienstbier three years, Otka Bednářová also three years, and Dana Němcová two years of probation. After I got out in '84, I found out—I had already known in prison—that my wife had continued to publish *Information about the Charter* [*Infoch*], of which I was the editor in chief, which I founded.

So I again took charge of the publishing, again began working in VONS, and also in the charter. My wife was in '86 a charter speaker. And we continued to develop Polish-Czechoslovak solidarity, and "Memorial"[2] came to us from the Soviet Union, a branch of which we founded here.

We cultivated contacts with friends from the GDR, the German Democratic Republic. A year before November '89, in the fall of '88, we established the Eastern European Information Agency, which, as a matter of fact, published what CTK [*Československá tisková kancelář*], or "Czechoslovak Press Agency," could not or would not publish, that is, about repression, about the activities of the independent movement. We worked in Moscow, Warsaw, Prague, Budapest. We had correspondents in Sofia and Vilnius.

We were connected with other Soviet press agencies that were already then independent. We exchanged information. And then came November. I was arrested again, for a week, because I published, in the name of the Eastern European Information Agency, false news of the death of the student Martin Šmíd, who was, reportedly, beaten to death on *Národní třída* [*National Avenue*]. It was not true. I did not know that it was not the truth. I thought that the information was trustworthy, and I published the news. Then I was released.

I became involved in Civic Forum. I became a member of the council in December, and in February I became the executive director of the Czechoslovak Press Agency where I was for two and a half years. In June I became a representative of Civic Forum in the Federal Assembly, where I worked for two years.

Then, when I was recalled from the executive position, I stayed on in CTK for two more years and worked as an ordinary editor and then as a publishing editor in a higher position. And then for not quite two years I was the editor in chief of *Listy*, and now I have worked, also for not quite two years, as an editor of *Právo*. Apart from this, I have held for seven, eight years, a small mandate in the Commission for Human Rights in Geneva, in the Committee for Unfounded Detention. That's just about all of my life. And also, I forgot to say that when I got back from prison we had a third child who is now thirteen.

Can you talk more about the Committee for the Defense of the Unjustly Prosecuted?

It may be interesting. Now here is just a supplement from my publishing company. There are actually all the annotations of the information on Charter 77, including all the reports of VONS, because all the reports of VONS, and there were a lot of them, it goes into four digits. I don't know if 1,300 or how many, 2,000, were published. I don't know how much there is in this particular one, but each issue begins with the report. So this is report number 191, "Solidarity with S.," for I don't know who. These are successive reports of VONS as they were being published by *Infoch*. This book you can purchase. You can even get it from me. It is only in Czech, of course.

VONS did not in fact become, it was not a part of Charter 77. We thought—the charter speakers at the turn of the years '77-'78 were Marta Kubišová,[3] Ladislav Hejdánek, and Jiří Hájek, who then passed his position on to Jaroslav Šabata[4] sometime at the beginning of the year, I think in February or March '78. So they thought there was a certain obligation to defend political prisoners, prisoners of conscience. And they did it in a not very effective way, well, it was rather chaotic. And, on the other side, Jan Tesař, already in the summer of '77, had the opinion that we should organize a group of people that would be involved in the defense of political prisoners.

And we had meetings already in the fall of '77 and at the beginning of the year '78 with the intention to establish such a group. In the middle of this came the repression at *Náměstí Míru* [Peace Square]. In the House of Railroad Workers, where there was a ball, a ball of the railroad workers, and Václav Havel, Pavel Landovský,[5] and Jaroslav Kukal were arrested there and held in detention for six weeks. A committee was formed for them, just for those three. In fact we were allowed even to be represented at the trial through counsels. We saw that it was a good thing and when they were released from detention, Václav Havel highly recommended that we establish ourselves.

We wanted some support from the charter, something like the charter announcing that we were one of its organs. And Ladislav Hejdánek, who was a strict charter fundamentalist, even somewhat stricter than I was—I was also a fundamentalist, but in this case I was for a break in this fundamentalism—so he threw us out, that is me and someone else, and he said that it could not be a charter organ and that we could establish it on our own outside of the charter. So we established it in the spirit of Charter 77, in the spirit, not as its organ.

The charter had its three speakers and its documents. Nevertheless, almost everyone, in fact everyone at the beginning—it was not until later that there was one person who joined and who was not a signatory of charter—we were all signatories of Charter 77, and also, it did not make much difference. The state police did not differentiate between the two like we did.

The purpose—you surely have the founding declaration, it is in the archives, Jiří Gruntorád[6] has it—is to support people who have become victims of unfounded police and juristic prosecution. That means not only, not just people, political prisoners or prisoners of conscience, but also those who were denied, we would say in today's terminology, the right for a just trial, the right to due process. And so—which was very common—here it was, moreover, contaminated by a certain imposed criminalization of conduct. That means that political action was criminalized and, on the other hand, those who were politically active were trapped into, or were accused, artificially initiated criminal charges, where there was no illegal conduct.

So VONS in fact was active for a year and then was destroyed, or there was an attempt to destroy it by arresting the majority of the people. Nevertheless it was not destroyed. Twelve more people became members after our imprisonment, and those people continued under difficult conditions, especially in '80 and then also in '81. The activity was minimal because the repression was strong. The Czechoslovak State Police was afraid of the Polish development, but as soon as Jaruzelski[7] suppressed Solidarity in Poland, they calmed down a bit and relaxed. Not because of some natural humanism, but because there was pressure from abroad, and trade contacts and other cooperation, scientific and in all other areas, depended on their concessions in this field.

Therefore, there were not so many imprisonments since '82. Not until toward the end, in the years '86-'87, there was again a certain relapse because they could feel that the system was crumbling. So they again imprisoned more, but, mainly what they started doing two, three years before the November revolution, they started a certain mass repression, petty, to put people in jail for a few days, give them probations for the signature movement "A Few Sentences" and for taking part in demonstrations.

Usually these were judged to be misdeeds or even minor offenses, and so their attention was suddenly kind of spread out over a wide circle of people, and we felt relatively free. So these were the activities of VONS in a certain broader context.

Were there people involved with VONS in Moravia and Slovakia, as well as Bohemia?

In VONS there were practically only, or the majority of people were only from Prague. The people who were not from Prague, that was Ladislav Lis,[8] Magor, or Martin Jirous, and two or three others—then Roubal, now I don't know, can't remember his first name, he later committed suicide—they were much less involved in our work. There were people from Brno. Those were Petr Pospíchal and Petr Cibulka, who participated in our work because they were entrusted with certain assignments there, and, really, there were not many others. And also Petr Pospíchal was in contact with Ján Čarnogurský,[9] who was in Bratislava and who was, as a matter of fact, the only person from Slovakia or practically the only one who consciously and systematically cooperated with VONS on a certain long-term basis and brought to our attention especially the cases of repression for religious activities. And so it was not from the whole republic.

It is important to say that the repression in Slovakia was substantially weaker and that it was really to a large degree concentrated on the religious activities, but also that there were many counties that we did not cover. Nevertheless, we had certain sources of information from individual counties in regard to the activities of young people, their cultural happenings, concerts, that were affected by repression, so, we had sources in the, in the natural network of acquaintances and friends in what was then called the underground, the cultural underground, where the people knew one another, were connected to the *androše* as we called them, from Prague, and they passed on the information. Sometimes it was confused and inaccurate, so additional research was needed later. But we succeeded, at least in the environment of these people who knew one another like that, in actually mapping most of the reprisals, especially in the second half of the eighties, probably not yet in the first half of the eighties.

We did not successfully cover the so-called solitaires who protested on their own, alone. For instance, they would write anonymous letters. Or they would tell a certain official or boss off and call him a Communist pig and for that—which is still illegal today—they got maybe, I don't know, a year or two. And so we did not catch that, because the regime resolutely did not publicize this kind of repression. They practiced it but did not generally publicize it.

How do you evaluate the last ten years?

The evaluation is double: on the one hand, from the point of view of VONS, and on the other, from the point of view of unfounded juristic and police prosecution. VONS, I believe, has actually not been disbanded yet, or it is not quite clear. It has somehow frozen its activity or has been preserved, but has not been disbanded. It was not until two years ago, I think, that it was expelled or crossed out from an international organization that is called, I will say it in French, *Fédération Internationale des Droits de l'Homme* [The International Federation for Human Rights], into whose member league it was accepted in December 1979, shortly before the appeal process. It was argued that the FIDH, that is the French abbreviation of the federation, is an organization which has the status of an organization associated with the United Nations. Which was true, or it is even still true today. And so this was somehow, this was supposed to help us, and it probably did. Nevertheless the federation FIDH, since the beginning of the year '90, pressured VONS to transform itself into a regular league.

That means, to cover not only unfounded imprisonments but also to cover things related to that. VONS did not do just imprisonments, but also prosecution, home searches, simply all the police procedures associated with the imprisonments. But the federation wanted VONS to also monitor the general freedom of expression, freedom of assembly, religious freedom, freedom of artistic expression and scientific exploration, simply all the freedoms that exist, to deal with these in full breadth, to include national minorities, racial discrimination, violation of children's rights, discrimination against women, and so on. VONS was not able to do that.

Most of the people left, actually because they became ministers, presidents, members of Parliament, and I don't know what all else, and some ministers even stayed there. What was curious was that for a long time the minister of the interior was still there, and, which I personally tried to talk him out of. A few people stayed in VONS, one or two even—no, I wouldn't say that—simply, only a few people stayed who wanted to use VONS as a political instrument for punishing the sins or crimes of the old regime. And they tried, through VONS, to screen judges, prosecutors, to initiate certain campaigns against certain people.

And I left VONS around the year '92 because it was not willing to support the then imprisoned editor in chief of *Rudé právo*, not because VONS thought that his imprisonment was justified or because there were any doubts about the lack of justification, but simply because he was a Communist. And they simply said we had the right of veto in VONS, which meant that it was enough for one person to hold this view, and there were even two people who supported this. So it was not allowed to be brought up for discussion and there was only one reason: we don't know if the man's imprisonment is justified or not, but we are not interested because he was a Communist.

Well, to me this seemed a violation of ethics. I also was not too comfortable when we supported Mr. Polanský who was a follower of Jozef Tiso[10] and fascism. And we even defended him for that, to a large degree, and because we thought that there was a violation of the freedom of expression, and we tried to separate the fascism of our client from the avoidance of the law or from the illegal behavior of the state organs. Well, I was not active in VONS after that. Not a long time ago, maybe a half a year ago—sometime in May, it was about two months ago—we had a commemorative meeting, where I learned that VONS had not even been officially disbanded, but that there was no activity, no meetings.

And now the other side of the development since the revolution. . . . The other thing that I wanted essentially to say in my answer is, then, whether since the year '93 in the Czech Republic and between the years '90 and '92, inclusive, in Czechoslovakia, there has been the violation of human rights in the area that VONS had delimited for itself, so that its activity would still be needed. I think that gradually yes, such violation of human rights exists, it is at the same level as in other European countries or in the United States of America.

I am saying this because of my experience as a member of a working group for unfounded detentions at the Human Rights Commission at the United Nations. I do not think, and I am fully convinced, that violation of human rights is programmatic, that it is systematic, that it is intentional on the part of the state power structure as it was during the old regime when it was really a means—one of the means of power politics was illegal repression.

It is not like that anymore, a democratic order of human rights is guaranteed, in the Slovak Republic as well as the Czech Republic, in both successors of Czechoslovakia. It is guaranteed by the constitutional order in the Czech Republic and by the Constitution itself in the Slovak Republic. That is so, because included in this constitutional order, or the Constitution, is a Deed of Fundamental Rights and Freedoms that we put together and passed and which was adopted by both the successor states. And there is an entire system of laws, especially judicial protection which is provided, or which can be provided, which is ineffective, slow, anything you want, but it exists. And so I don't think that VONS would be especially needed.

Nevertheless, it could be needed. Sometimes the state organs have a tendency to imprison a person, or prosecute a person who is guilty only of, or who is mainly guilty of—and they find something else on him, something secondary—using his or her right, of applying his or her right which is granted according to international documents, according to the General Declaration of Human Rights, according to the International Treaty on Civil and on Human Rights, and possibly according to the European Agreement on Protection of Human Rights and Fundamental Freedoms.

And these, these names [of documents] are quite exact, in case this would be translated. I didn't make a mistake. No, I know that I didn't. I paid special attention to that. And so this tendency exists here and such cases come up from time to time. For instance, recently they stopped the prosecution in twenty-two cases out of about thirty people who were accused in regard to an ecological-alternative demonstration in Prague in May. The people were accused simply because the police thought that billboards should not be demolished and windows broken in McDonald's. I agree with that, but they did not accuse those who did those things but some other people, and they could not prove it, and, basically, they accused the people because they were also present and otherwise were using their right of freedom of expression and freedom of assembly.

Much more serious is the sphere of due process, just prosecution and trial, where there are numerous indications that due process is not quite guaranteed in all cases. And the only question is whether the violation of international and also national rules that govern this process has reached such intensity and such breadth that it is possible to say that the given situation of the given accused person is unfounded, detention in the sense delineated by our working group.

There would probably be very few of these cases here. I don't know of any. There has not been any in our working group yet, and if there were, I would not be allowed to participate in the decision making. But from my experience, I know that we have such cases every now and then and that the decision making is hard. We always require serious violation. This happens in the Czech Republic, I think, only exceptionally.

I don't know if—I simply answered the question, the subquestion, essentially by saying that the democratic order of human rights is basically maintained in both the two republics, in both the Czech and Slovak Republics. It is possible to go further and say that not only the democratic order is being maintained but that there has been built, in a way, a pluralistic democracy of the parliamentary type—and I'll be speaking now only about the Czech Republic and not mix Slovakia into it, because, nevertheless, the development is slightly different.

Here, essentially, a civil society has not been established; there has been, for now, a strong opposition against any regionalization and decentralization and against territorial self-government. The state has done very little for protecting the law, or for protecting the rights of people, especially in the area of private property, especially in regard to economic criminality, and that, apart from the law.

There is, of course, a lot to be done in restructuring companies, and in productivity, in which the Czech Republic is at one-third or one-half the level of Western European societies, or at least of the northern part of Western Europe. And these are things that we need to catch up on. I personally think that it was unfortunate to break up the common foreign policy of the Vyšehrad Group, that is, Poland, Hungary, the Czech Republic, and Slovakia, that the government and the society of the Czech Republic did not work on getting closer and entering the European Union.

I see in the European Union a common means against the globalization coming from the United States. I see in it a certain basis for social security and social protection, protection of social rights against the wild capitalism that we have here. And so I see in it a certain rescue more to the left than somewhere to the right. And Klaus, of course, and the democratic right sees this too, and that is why they are a little reluctant to enter the European Union. And I think that with social democracy, the Social Democratic Party, if it has more influence in governing the country, it will be easier and better.

On the other hand, I am against the expansion of NATO. I think that it still should be approved by a referendum. If there was a referendum, I would, of course, democratically give in and would not organize any more activities against NATO. But as it is, I do not like it very much. And in the sphere of human rights, I think that progress is very slow, and, even with the new freedom and with a certain liberalization of everything, which is welcome not just by me but by the majority of society, there has been an increase, or a release, of racial prejudice. We have prejudice. We have found out that in Russian, German, French, English, and in Czech it is formed in the same way "pre-judge," *predsudek, pred-sudok*, and even in German *Vorurteile*.

So, there are racial prejudices that had always existed among the people and that have now grown even deeper, have been released. A certain tension is developing, and the government started dealing with these things late and ineffectively. Actually not until last year Pavel Bratinka,[11] and now his successor Vladimír Mlynář,[12] addressed these issues a bit. So this is my opinion regarding the last ten years.

12

Jan Urban

*As a dissident . . . who was constantly on the run, you had no expecta-
tions.*

—Jan Urban, 1998

Jan Urban, *journalist and historian, filed news stories for Radio Free Europe
and the BBC as a dissident during the seventies and eighties. During the Velvet
Revolution he managed logistics for Civic Forum and remained active in that
organization until after the elections of 1990. He was editor in chief of* Transitions *magazine, founded in Prague in 1994, dedicated to fostering independent
journalism in Central and Eastern Europe, the Balkans, and successor states of
the former Soviet Union. The former* Transitions *magazine is now the internet
magazine* Transitions Online. *Mr. Urban continues his work as a journalist for
Radio Free Europe/Radio Liberty, as well as for Czech Radio [Český rozhlas] in
Prague. The interview, conducted in English, took place in the offices of* Transitions *magazine.*

Forty-seven. That's how old I am. Married. Two daughters. Studied philosophy
and history at Charles University in Prague. Because of my family tradition, I
got involved with the dissident movement quite early. But because of the nature
of the things I was doing, for most of the time, I did not belong to the kind of
upper echelon of the dissident movement. But in '87 when the police got too
close, it was kind of a proven technology, that the better known you were, the
safer, at least we believed that.

So I was sent by Charter 77 in December '87 to Moscow to meet with, at
that time, Soviet dissidents and make a kind of public relations stunt, or scandal.
And that worked in my case. Overnight I became one of the known names and, I
think today, mostly because of my knowledge of English, I became a target of
Western journalists. And so that kept me busy until November '89. I was in-

volved in many dissident groups and helped to found the Eastern European Information Agency which was the one and only, in history, dissident movement that was organized internationally. And in November '89, I was a part of Civic Forum. And because I had some instinctive distrust of politics as a craft, I was in charge of logistics. And because everybody else ran into the executive, or most of the people ran into the executive, I was left there to lead Civic Forum in the last four months before the elections in June 1990. But already in January I kind of secured myself and publicly promised to step down the day after we defeat the Communists through free elections. And I did that, and work as a journalist since.

How were you able to travel to Moscow?

I didn't have a passport for seventeen years. And I used the fact that my family moved two or three times in a very short time, so I applied for a passport in one district of Prague. And to my great surprise, I got it. Two people were assigned to try to get to Moscow, and each of us prepared the tourist trip absolutely individually, without any contact. And we first met at the airport quote-unquote by chance. And Professor Věněk Šilhán, who was the second guy, went first to check in. We got our boarding passes, but at the passport control check he was detained. In Prague. And he was a real pro. He created a huge commotion, scandal. There was a bunch of, I remember, fat Russian ladies who were in an absolute panic.

You know, why the hell is this old guy screaming and fighting with those nice guys? And he needed that, because in '87 it was precomputer times, we had on us, though it was on thin paper, quite some documents and letters. And so he created this commotion, and he was able to give it to me in the crowd. I was scared shitless. The plane was delayed for forty-five minutes. He was accused of smuggling diamonds. Yes. But fortunately enough, this helped me to get through, and I made it to Moscow.

As an individual tourist, I had hotel accommodation. I just left my luggage there. It was freezing cold. And I knew I have to make it to Lev Timofeev, who at that time was one of the leading dissident figures. And he was running the group calling itself Press Group Glasnost. And they organized the first independent international human rights seminar, kind of testing Gorbachev's *glasnost*. And it was dark. It must have been somewhere around eight or nine, or maybe even later at night. And it was quite far away from the center. I went by metro and walked through those dark concrete blocks of flats. And I rang the bell. It was a kind of a shabby block of flats. Stinky.

There was a metal door, very uninviting. And I had no other address. And somebody opened it. I introduced myself, and there was a roar. There were a few people there. And they started to embrace me, because, as it turned out, I was the only one from outside the Soviet Union who made it through. And so they were really glad that somebody came, was able to come. And I met with—I mean it was a stellar, extremely fortunate for me, moment, because I was able to meet people like Father Gleb Yakunin,[1] Sergei Kovalev,[2] Zviad Gamsakhurdia[3] and his Georgian colleagues. Later I even met with—which was one of the turning points in my life—Andrei Sakharov and Yelena Bonner.[4] So it was a great success, and it helped a lot, because we somehow, something clicked between Andrei Sakharov and myself, and he even said in public that he will keep an eye on me that the Czechoslovak (at that time) police doesn't bother me too much.

Can you describe when you first felt yourself in conflict with the regime?

August 21st, 1968. Until that moment, I think I was growing in this kind of Czechoslovak Communist tradition. My father was a Communist since he was eighteen, which was in '39, when he joined the anti-Nazi resistance and spent six years in the Communist anti-Nazi resistance. And after that, it was just very simple.

Can you describe what your activities were at the time of the Velvet Revolution?

There was enough or even too many people who could take care of politics, but there was of course the need to organize things like how to feed those who care about politics, how to get them clean shirts, how to organize secret negotiations with the Soviet embassy, to organize press conferences, and kind of run the whole show. So that was my job, and the job of many wonderful people from the Magic Lantern Theater. Without them there would be no Velvet Revolution at all.

Can you talk about the circumstances that took you to Bosnia?

When you are on the run, or in a fight for some time, everything becomes a fight and your mind, everything becomes part of a struggle, or a craft, whatever you want to call it. And towards the end I didn't like it. And because it was, not to make a mistake, and you were not allowed to make a mistake, because every mistake would be the last one. You had to become a kind of monster, because you couldn't trust anybody, no exceptions. You had to lie twenty-four hours a day. Not because you wanted, but because you needed that there is a kind of informational mist around you, no clear facts.

The less people know about you, about things you are doing, the better. You deliberately disinform. You constantly test people. You have to make clear to the other side that you can't be blackmailed. It becomes tougher when you have children and a family and parents who may be ill. And you become a tool and you know it cannot be different if you want to survive, but you don't like it. And in the end, you are not just made paranoid.

So then the change came and as I said, I didn't plan it, I didn't expect to see it. So when it came, the first chance I had to get out from anything that reminded me of the fight, including politics. But I wanted to understand what happens with people like myself, what happens with people who live for many years in the society we had in prolonged conflict. So I started to study postconflict situations all around the world. And this brought me to Central America and somewhat logically, quote-unquote to Bosnia in the end.

And it was a kind of growing up, or a kind of eye-opening experience, because until the very end we had too great expectations and too great naïveté about the United States and about the human rights policy. And to see this unbelievable hypocrisy that the so-called international community performed in Bosnia, was really an eye-opening experience. I went there the first time in 1993, then I've been there more than twenty times in wartime, and I spent all of '96 there.

What is the philosophy behind Transitions?

It's a great toy. In those "good ole bad days" when we needed to debate something with our Polish colleagues, we either met in the mountains or we wrote articles for the Western media, the Western press. And at that time it was fine, because there were no computers, no e-mail, and we didn't have more options. To do the same twenty years later is simply stupid. I want this magazine to be this kind of meeting place, meeting spot for people from the region who share, despite zillions of differences, several decades of common experience with a very funny way of societal organization. And exactly in a time when things become very complex and very difficult, Western media and Western elites are losing interest in this region, or are picking up individual problems, not seeing the larger picture.

So, I want this magazine to serve as a kind of a meeting place and debate forum both for East and West and for those Eastern elites. Also, because exactly in this time, for instance, even the large Western media are withdrawing their correspondents from the region. There is less and less reporting. And media in this region, which as we count, consists of twenty-seven countries with more than 300 million people, do not have the means to send correspondents, their [own] correspondents to the region, so we are trying to have a network and service these media. That's the motivation.

Can you give an example of a particular issue the Western media has focused on?

Kosovo. Russia. The economic crisis.[5] I mean, let me give you an example. I was at the end of June, July, negotiating with one big bank, a Western bank, on an advertising contract. And it was just after we published a special issue on Russia in which the leading article started with a sentence that the devaluation of the ruble, that is so much talked about, has already taken place in people's heads and that is what counts. And I didn't get the contract.

And the marketing people from that bank told me, "You know, you are so pessimistic. We in the financial sector, we want to be seen as supporting something positive, something stabilized. You are not writing about successes, you are writing only about problems. You have to admit that Russia got its ruble inflation down to 6 percent and it is holding." And I was staring at them, and I could not believe my ears. Two months later, Russia collapses. The Western media are in panic, but so many people saw it coming. It's just that it was not really popular and sexy to write about it too early.

The same is happening with Kosovo. I mean, so many of us, but also in this case many writers and journalists in the West, we were writing about it for years. Everybody saw it coming. And it was just too painful to see Dick Holbrooke,[6] who two years ago was patting Milošević[7] on the shoulder and writing about him and telling stories about him as the most important peace-making tool, or individual, American foreign policy has in the Balkans. And the same Dick Holbrooke is now threatening the same bastards as if nothing happened. As if there was no past.

What is your personal perspective on the last ten years?

I don't think that I can answer that, because as a dissident, as somebody who was constantly on the run, you had no expectations. You just wanted to make it to the next sleep. To plan for tomorrow would be stupid, because to have expectations was stupid. It slowed you down. It was a load you didn't want to carry. And also, we knew nothing about society. Dissidents in Czechoslovakia were a very closed group with no experience about what people think about what they want. And I think that there is one significant little illustration.

The absolute majority of dissidents were working in jobs where they did not meet with other people—window cleaners, stokers, and stuff like that. I belonged to a small minority. To have a job as I had, bricklaying, where I worked with quote-unquote ordinary people, and was confronted with what they think, what they want, and so, there was no expectation at all. It was a kind of sigh of relief. We made it, though we thought we will never see it. And the rest was just absolute improvisation.

Of course, I'm critical about certain things. But I'm enjoying every single new morning, because it's so beautiful to recognize that whatever stupidity or mistake I make, it's my mistake. And I don't depend on anybody's evil mind. I don't have to run. Of course, I regret that my homeland which was Czechoslovakia did not survive. I regret that most of my compatriots, instead of kind of strengthening up their backbones when they got the chance, just opened their mouths. I can regret many things, but I don't think I need a perfect world. I think that if it's livable and tolerant enough, it's fine with me.

What are the problems you think are facing the Czech Republic?

The Czechs. I think that my compatriots remind one of young kids who wake up and look around sleepy-eyed, not really realizing where they are. And we really—it's easier for me to say "they"—they are still ideology addicted. This, I think, is my biggest critique after the period of '89. The simplicity of the swing from shutting up or even believing whatever the Communist Party said to another ideology this time, this kind of extreme, Chicago-style liberalism. The facts did not matter. It was this religious, fanatical belief in ideology and the leader. And I think that only through the last elections this year—when for purely manipulative reasons, a few guys who wanted to stay as near to power as possible—we had a very right-wing party in a sense "marrying" social democrats.

And whatever the motivation, the result I think is very healthy. For the first time people can realize that politics is not and should not be about ideology, that it's about power. It's about making deals, making compromises. And with God's help, if the nation and the economy is lucky, things can get slowly better. But it's not about black and white, an "either" "or," "us" and "them," struggle. But this realization is only now, nearly ten years after the change, slowly starting to come out of the ground. And specifically, I think, we are running downhill toward a very difficult period with the Czech economy. And I think it's healthy, because we simply have to realize that things have their price and that we cannot live on promises. So, I'm curiously watching what is happening and how people react and thank God I can still be curious.

Do you have any last words for posterity?

For history? Stay curious.

13

Reality Czech

*We are not heroes . . . we simply did what we had to do to make life
livable.*

—Eda Kriseová, 1998

The interviews presented in the preceding eleven chapters provide the outside
observer a unique glimpse into the personal experience of those individuals
popularly labeled as "dissident" during the Communist era of Czechoslovakia.
The value of this approach to history—history from the witness of the participant—or, "oral history," is in this case twofold. First, the personal narratives
shed light on "dissent" as a phenomenon both in Communist Czechoslovakia
and in the broader context of totalitarian systems.

Second, the narratives allow a means of comparison of the views of an
"elite" group within a society, in this case the so-called dissidents, with the
views of the broader public. In regard to this volume, such comparisons can be
drawn with reference to the periods of both Communist Czechoslovakia and
post-Communist Czech Republic.

The following chapter consists of two parts. In part one, the briefer of the
two, I will discuss a few specific characteristics of "dissent" as it relates to the
Communist era of Czechoslovakia as revealed in the narratives of the preceding
chapters. In part two, I will draw comparisons between the conclusions and
opinions expressed by the eleven narrators with those of the broader public in
reference to the post-Communist era and the future of the Czech Republic, specifically in regard to economic progress, political sophistication of the electorate, international integration, and xenophobia.

The Dissident Voice

As mentioned in chapter one, the term "dissident" is problematic for those who bore the label in the context of the Soviet Bloc prior to the revolutions in Central and Eastern Europe in 1989 and the collapse of the Soviet Union. In the West, the term carries primarily positive connotations. Within the context of the Cold War, according to the Western understanding of the term, a "dissident" was one who championed ostensibly democratic values such as the freedom of assembly, the freedom to express an opposition political view, as well as intellectual, artistic, religious, and entrepreneurial freedom in opposition to a totalitarian government or system. Indeed, prior to 1989, Western governments and Western public opinion relied on information gathered through contacts with "dissidents" in the East Bloc, for the most part through journalists and *samizdat*, to gain a truer, more reliable picture of political and social conditions in those countries.

During the 1970s and 1980s, Western media coverage of the persecution of high-profile dissidents such as Alexander Solzhenitsyn and Andrei Sakharov in the Soviet Union, Lech Wałęsa in Poland, and Václav Havel in Czechoslovakia, to name a few, contributed to the positive, one might say even "heroic" image of the "dissident" in the West. Newspaper and television reports of Solzhenitsyn's expulsion from the Soviet Union and Sakharov's exile in Nizhnyi Novgorod [Gorky] and the imprisonment of Wałęsa and Havel garnered public sympathy for the plight of the dissident and bolstered the image of the dissident as hero in the struggle between "Us" and "Them," "Good" (the West) and "Evil" (the East Bloc).

In their home countries, however, the so-called dissidents suffered under the label. The Communist regimes of the East Bloc took every opportunity to discredit and vilify the "dissident" in the esteem of the public at large by painting the "dissident" as a malcontent and troublemaker. The government of Czechoslovakia was no exception, for "since the Party was always right about everything, even retroactively, those individuals who ceased to be humble and obedient Party followers were automatically considered to be its deserters and, therefore, enemies of socialism."[1] As Havel explains:

> A "dissident," we are told in our press, means something like "renegade" or "backslider." But dissidents do not consider themselves renegades for the simple reason that they are not primarily denying or rejecting anything. On the contrary, they have tried to affirm their own human identity, and if they reject anything at all, then it is merely what was false and alienating in their lives, that aspect of "living within a lie."[2]

Almost immediately after the launch of Charter 77, the government initiated a two-pronged strategy to counter any effect the charter might have on public opinion. While the StB harassed and interrogated charter signatories, including the three speakers, the government proceeded to attack Havel personally in articles in *Rudé právo* and broadcasts on Czech Radio, even alleging links between

Havel and the CIA. In addition, the government convened a "congress" of popular celebrities, including actors, singers, journalists, television personalities, and sports stars, who through speeches and statements to the press extolled the virtues of socialism and criticized the actions of the chartists. The so-called anti-charter set about to compete against the charter for influence in the public arena. Keane maintains that the government campaign was a tactical error: "The Party leadership did not grasp at the outset that by 'going public' about the *Charta* it not only provided it with free publicity. It also placed itself on a level playing field—the battle for public opinion through reasoned argument and rhetorical controversy—with which it wasn't familiar, and in which it had trouble winning against its opponents."[3]

It is clear from the personal narratives that none of the narrators simply woke up one morning and made a conscious decision to become a dissident. "We are not heroes," comments Eda Kriseová, "we simply did what we had to do to make life livable."[4] Kriseová's statement encapsulates the nature of "dissent" as it emerged in Czechoslovakia in the late 1960s and as it was practiced right up until the triumph of the Velvet Revolution in 1989. The writers' mini-conferences, the home seminars, the "illegal" concerts, even the *samizdat* editions of literature, philosophy, and science, were all manifestations of the attempts to live a normal life, albeit outside of officially sanctioned venues and media.

Scores of individuals found themselves to be "dissident" rather accidentally. Daniel Kummerman found his very existence, his personal identity as a Jew—a condition beyond remedy—to be an object of the, at times more or less subtle, anti-Semitism of official Czechoslovak culture. Dissidence was for Kummerman, therefore, something of a birthright. Ivan Havel, punished by the regime for his bourgeois family background, tried to make his own way as a philosopher and cyberneticist in a struggle against the obstacles placed before him by the regime.

Věra Jirousová, essentially uninterested in politics per se, through the exercise of her intellectual and professional interests in art history and music, found herself stymied by and isolated from official culture and drawn to those with whom she shared common interests, and, who also happened to be "dissidents." Kriseová, Kocáb, Němcová, and others found themselves in "dissent" through the struggle to maintain and preserve their personal artistic and spiritual integrity, two realms which in the view of Western democrats ought to lie outside the purview of the state.

Kriseová's statement further reflects Václav Havel's description of "dissident" life as "living within the truth." According to Havel, living within the truth meant "serving truth consistently, purposefully, and articulately, and organizing this service."[5] The aim of Charter 77 and VONS in publicizing the government's violations of international agreements on human rights and the Czechoslovak legal code was to serve the truth.

"Living within the truth" describes the endeavor on the part of the "dissident" to live as if all the human rights and freedoms stipulated in both domestic and international law were in fact "real" in the attempt to maintain one's human dignity. Chartists and VONS members issued statements openly to the general public and directly to the government, acting in full faith in the legal code that they had the "right" to carry out such actions. Persecution on the part of the state for these activities only increased the esteem of the dissidents among the public and the international community with the effect of yielding to the dissidents the moral high ground.

Strict adherence to the legal code benefited the "dissident" in a number of ways. One, every "dissident" took pains to learn the letter of the law, acquiring an understanding of the rights due to any citizen according to the law, e.g., the maximum length of detention, the right to counsel, etc. Knowledge of the law served on the one hand as a weapon against possible or potential abuses by the state, in particular the StB. On the other hand, a knowledge of one's legal rights served as a psychological comfort during times of arrest and imprisonment; foreknowledge of what to expect potentially eases emotional suffering and stress.

One of the salient and most profound characteristics of "dissidence" and what Barbara Falk describes as the "oxymoronically titled 'Velvet Revolution' in Czechoslovakia" was the commitment to nonviolence. In Poland, Falk continues, "over time nonviolence became less of an indispensable condition and more of a morally-inspired credo."[6] The same could be said in regard to Czechoslovakia as well. Not a single Charter 77 or VONS document nor any statement by Havel ever advocated the use of violence as a means of protecting or preserving human rights.

The commitment to nonviolence on the part of dissidents meant that any violence in the struggle for human rights would be exercised by the state apparatus. The 17 November "massacre" is a case in point. Had state and party authorities prevented the violent attack on the marching students, the Velvet Revolution might never have happened or, at least, might have been delayed. The attack on the students galvanized all sectors of the opposition and solidified public opinion in support of a political opposition which called for an investigation of the incident and punishment of government and party officials held responsible.

Ivan Havel's statement "we were proud that it was velvet," is indicative of the moral significance of nonviolence to the opposition movement. Likewise, Michael Kocáb's account of his negotiations with Soviet embassy officials during the frenzy of the Velvet Revolution underscores the attitude of "dissidents" toward violence. When the Soviets expressed concern that demonstrators or Civic Forum might advocate the use of force against Soviet troops stationed in the country, Kocáb assured them there were no plans of that nature and that "the times of bloody revolutions had been over for a long time."

It is understandable that the nonviolent stance of the revolutionaries of 1989 puzzled the Soviet officials. Historically, the seizure of state power by opposition groups through revolution or coup d'état has been accompanied by execution and very often also by bloody civil wars; nonviolent revolutions are indeed rare. Kocáb continues about the Soviets, "they still lived in the dogmatic captivity of the experience from the year 1917, their own Bolshevik revolution, and thought that all takeovers of state power were necessarily accompanied by lampposts full of hanged men, that simply, blood had to flow" (see chapter four).

The insights provided through the "oral" narratives presented here are instructive on several levels. The narratives provide an intensely personal perspective on "dissent" within the socialist Bloc, the Velvet Revolution, and the transition from totalitarianism to democracy from the inside out. The experiences of the narrators can be viewed as a lesson in the practice of both individual and collective nonviolent resistance to oppressive, monolithic government; the methods of maintaining individual survival; and the performance of civic duty in spite of risks to one's family, livelihood, and personal health and freedom. The narratives are a testament to the endurance of the human spirit in the face of adversity and can serve as a reference for other individuals and groups who might find themselves in similar circumstances in the future.

Czech Transition

The eleven personalities represented in this volume have commented either directly or indirectly on virtually every aspect of the transition from the beginning as Czechoslovakia, then after 1993 as the Czech Republic, divorced from its federal partner the Slovak Republic. In the remainder of this chapter I will present a summary of some of the salient characteristics of Czech society as it has developed over the course of approximately ten years since the transition began in 1989. I will make comparisons between the conclusions and opinions drawn by the eleven narrators regarding certain aspects of the transition and the results of public opinion surveys and other data. I will discuss how the opinions of "elite" members of Czech society compare with the public at large regarding topics such as economic progress, political sophistication of the electorate, and xenophobia.

Several of the narrators imply dissatisfaction with the inequalities introduced by unbridled capitalism. The narrators express unanimous support for the system of government by parliamentary democracy and have no nostalgia for the old totalitarian regime. At the same time, they fear that the general public does not appreciate democracy as they do. Is this indeed the case? Are the concerns for the future development of society in the Czech Republic expressed by the narrators merely those of a small minority of the population, or do those concerns resonate across all sectors of the population? In the following discussion, I will attempt to provide answers to these and other questions, with the aim of providing a more complete picture of the Czech Republic's progress thus far in the transition to a free, democratic society.

I do not in any way contend that the value of the narratives lies in how the views expressed mirror those of the public. My aim here is not to "validate" the opinions of the narrators by showing how closely they correspond to the results of public opinion surveys. The narrators represent an "elite" group within Czech[oslovak] society—each person has achieved a measure of celebrity through his or her past as "dissidents," their contributions and activities in the effort to construct a civil society, and in their professional fields as writer, journalist, philosopher, etc. Moreover, the narrators are well-educated, well-informed members of Czech society who for at least three decades have been actively engaged in the political and cultural life of the nation. The reader might ask, "Are the views of the narrators in some way skewed by their access to power and their celebrity status?" It is a fair question.

It is evident from the narratives that each of the authors is deeply concerned about the future of the Czech Republic and the aspirations of its people to find their place within Europe and within the global community. My motive in asking the interviewees to comment on the progress of the transition since 1989 was to determine to what extent the aspirations and hopes of the narrators for the country had been realized, and to determine which areas in their view required further attention. My aim in the remainder of this essay is to discuss those areas of greatest concern as expressed in the narratives and to illuminate where those areas of concern intersect and diverge with those expressed by the broader public.

One of the main sources of the material presented here is data collected in surveys conducted by the Centre for the Study of Public Policy at Strathclyde University in Glasgow, Scotland. The center has published the results of its surveys in a number of volumes covering a variety of topics, incorporating data collected from its "Barometer" surveys. The New Europe Barometer is based on data gathered in the ten post-Communist countries of Central and Eastern Europe which are potential members of the European Union (EU): Bulgaria, the Czech Republic, Estonia, Hungary, Latvia, Lithuania, Poland, Romania, Slovakia, and Slovenia.[7]

The discussion here will focus on the Czech Republic, but where instructive, I will introduce results obtained in other countries in order to draw comparisons with the Czech Republic. It is important to bear in mind that the data quoted here represent opinions of persons who voluntarily answered survey questions and are relevant and useful to the researcher only as an "indicator" or "general tendency" of broader public opinion rather than an absolute.

In the years since 1989, the country that was at that time Czechoslovakia has undergone a total transformation. One of the first acts of the new government, largely symbolic, in 1990 was to rename the country the Czech and Slovak Federated Republic (CSFR). The name change was an olive branch to Slovaks, who felt themselves the stepchild of the federation during decades of Communist rule—despite the fact that since the 1960s the top leadership post in the Czechoslovak Communist Party (CCP) was held by Slovaks, both Dubček and Husák. In 1992, Slovak nationalists forced the issue of Slovak independence. Václav Havel resigned as president rather than preside over the breakup of the country. As a result, on 1 January 1993, both the independent Czech Republic and the independent Slovak Republic, or Slovakia, came into being.

Since 1993, both the Czech Republic and the Slovak Republic have held a series of elections. Development of the institutions of civil society has proceeded apace earning for each country the "Free" designation by Freedom House—the Czech Republic since 1993 and Slovakia since 1998.[8]

Transition to Democracy: Where's the Party?

By all accounts, the Czech Republic's transition from Communist-dominated totalitarianism to democracy has been one of the more successful among all the transition states. While there have been setbacks, the country's electoral system and economy have remained stable throughout the transition. Likewise, the country enjoys a high degree of confidence among the Western powers. The Czech Republic joined NATO in 1999, and was one of eight nations invited to join the European Union in 2004.

Czechs themselves are, for the most part, satisfied with the change in regime and the move toward market capitalism. Perhaps the greatest disappointment has been the realization among the population that the transition has not taken place at a quicker pace, both in economic terms and in terms of people's perception and understanding of what a democracy should be. In chapter two, Ivan Havel talks about his own disappointment that others are disappointed with the pace of the transition, and that the public tends toward a nostalgic view of the totalitarian system, "they do not see how different it is, that they can read various opinions . . . that they can go abroad wherever they want." In chapter six, Daniel Kummerman expresses his own disappointment that the Czech public has not fully embraced democratic values, "I did believe for some time that we are maybe in for some economically bad years, but that democracy somehow was deep in the genes of this nation and that the very moment we get rid of the Communist regime we will be more or less democratic."

Old Regime versus New Regime

Insofar as survey data provide an accurate picture of reality, there is not so much disappointment and nostalgia for the old system as Havel suspects, and Czech citizens are much more politically savvy than Kummerman surmises. For example, when surveyed about their views of the "old regime versus new regime," the majority of Czechs (60%) "disapprove" of the former Communist regime, while only 31% "approve." Czechs give the current system of free elections with competition among multiple parties high marks with 76% approving and only 17% disapproving.[9] In contrast to the Czech Republic, only 26% of Hungarians, 29% of Slovaks, and 21% of Slovenes "disapprove" of their own former Communist regimes, while "disapproval" of the current system of government is highest in Slovakia (51%) and in Lithuania (42%).[10]

Czechs show a tremendous amount of faith in the stability of the current democratic system as well. A majority of Czechs (72%) describe themselves as "confident democrats," meaning they both consider the suspension of Parliament unlikely and would disapprove if suspension were to occur. Only 21% of Czechs consider themselves "dejected authoritarians," that is, they approve of the suspension of Parliament and consider suspension likely. The highest percentages of "dejected authoritarians" are found in Lithuania (35%), Slovakia (25%), and Latvia (26%).[11]

Likewise, endorsement for "undemocratic alternatives" to the current democratic system is extremely low among Czechs. Only 18% of Czechs support the return to Communist rule, 1% would approve of putting the government in the hands of the army, and 13% would prefer a dictator. Election results corroborate the data collected in opinion surveys. From 1990 to 2002, electoral support for the Communist Party of Bohemia and Moravia has fluctuated from 10% at its lowest margin in the 1996 elections to 18% in a surprise showing in the June 2002 elections, still quite far from achieving a majority.[12]

In sharp contrast to Czechs, 47% of Russians surveyed favor a return to Communism, 15% favor rule by the army, and 31% prefer a dictatorship. Indeed, the highest support for dictatorship is found among the former Soviet republics of Estonia, Latvia, and Lithuania, in addition to Poland and Romania, each with more than 30%, or one-third of the population.[13]

Electorate's Understanding of "Democracy"

By the end of 2002, Czech voters had cast ballots in free parliamentary elections five times, gaining experience in and understanding of the practice of democratic government. It is now possible to examine a large body of data concerning Czech attitudes toward and understanding of a free democratic system of government.

Social scientists have conducted a number of studies on the Czech Republic's transition to democratic government. These studies have probed, among other things, the development of party loyalty among Czech voters through the course of the transition and the correlation of party affiliation with wealth and social attitudes. Researchers have established, for example, the correlation between the party affiliation of Czech voters on the left-right axis and support for a socialist or market economy. From 1991 to 1995, voter support for the market economy changed from "unconditional" to more reserved support, while voters identifying with the left "ceased to accept the liberal market economy as a condition of a successful road to prosperity and they returned to the socialist model."[14]

Survey data reveal that the majority of Czech voters have a well-formed understanding of the left and right wings in politics and are able to define what democracy means to them. In response to the question "what does democracy mean for you," 87% of Czechs asked could provide a definition, and "political freedom" emerged as the most important attribute of democracy in the value hierarchy of Czechs. Indeed among transition states, the highest proportion of respondents able to define left and right wing and democracy is found among Czechs and Poles. Among Czech respondents, 74% could define what "left wing" and 72% what "right wing" meant to them. Among Poles, 60% were able to define left wing, 58% right wing, and 81% democracy. By contrast, in Spain—a "Western" democracy—the percentages are much lower at 48%, 48%, and 70%, respectively.[15]

The perceptions Czechs have of democracy as quoted from survey data appear to refute Kummerman's opinion, "most people not only don't know what democracy is about but they don't even care what it is about." How can the discrepancy between scientific data on the one hand be reconciled with well-informed opinions of an educated observer and member of the same society as the survey population on the other? The solution is simple. Kummerman's observation is valid, but only in regard to a minority, roughly 20%, of the population. In political practice, the views on one side of the spectrum are in constant conflict with views from the opposing side of the spectrum, no matter how small the population expressing the opposing view. Kummerman's skepticism will perhaps lift as the percentage of Czechs who cannot define democracy decreases. Research supports Kummerman to a certain degree, for as Simon concludes:

> In the early 90s the establishment of the institutions of democracy and market economy in the previous "state-socialist" countries brought substantial changes, but the influence of the ideologies and ideas of the old authoritarian systems remained even after the systems and their institutions ceased to exist. The democracy-image of the citizens of the region is built from the experiences gained during the collapsed communist system and it is going to be built from those experiences for a long time.[16]

Political stability supported by improving economies and living standards through time can only improve the "democracy-image" of citizens of transition states, including the Czech Republic.

Economy: From Zero to Gucci

Support for any country's political system is, to a large extent, dependent on that system's ability to respond to the needs of citizens. Dissatisfaction with the former Communist regimes of Central and Eastern Europe grew in response to declining living standards and the citizens' perception that their economies and living standards were falling far behind that of their Western neighbors. Long lines for food, empty store shelves, and the thriving black market—with its available but expensive items—drove those perceptions. Opposition groups in the region saw political reform as the only means of bringing about needed economic reform that could improve the lives of citizens.

In Poland, the opposition movement *Solidarność* [Solidarity] was born in 1980 as a free and independent trade union of shipbuilders for the purpose of improving labor conditions and the living standards of workers. Solidarity ultimately prevailed and brought about the demise of Poland's Communist regime in 1989. In the Soviet Union, Gorbachev's attempt to improve the economy without relaxing the Communist Party's hold on power failed and the Soviet Union collapsed.

In discussing the Czech Republic's economic success since 1989, Ivan Havel notes: "I read in the papers that the effective income is going down. But I see more and more restaurants, more and more shops. And I see Czech people in the shops and restaurants, not only tourists. And I see new buildings being painted and reconstructed."

At the time Havel made this statement, in summer 1998, the Czech economy was attempting to climb out of a recession that began in 1997. Unemployment had risen steadily from a low of just under 3 percent in 1995 to more than 9 percent by 1999.[17] But how does Havel's perception match with the Czech Republic's overall economic performance since 1990, and what has been the effect, if any, on the country's transition to democracy in general? And has the Czech Republic's experience been typical of the transition states as a whole? While the answers to these questions are complex, some general comparisons can be made and certain conclusions can be drawn about the long-term prosperity of the Czech Republic and its further transition to civil society.

In the early 1990s, the failure of democratic transition governments to make dramatic improvements in living standards meant the loss of elections and opened the door for the reemergence of Communist parties. Solidarity leader Lech Wałęsa sailed to the pinnacle of power in 1989 only to suffer defeat in his bid for the presidency in 1995, due in part to Poland's rising unemployment in the early 1990s—from 6.5% in 1990 to 16% in 1994.[18] Aleksander Kwaśniewski, former leader of the Polish Communist Party, organized a new coalition of leftist parties, the Democratic Left Alliance (DLA), and defeated Wałęsa receiving 52% of the vote to Wałęsa's 48%. Kwaśniewski repeated his victory in the 2000 presidential election receiving 54% of votes to Wałęsa's 1%.[19] In the most recent parliamentary elections held in September 2001, Kwaśniewski's DLA, in coalition with the Union of Labor, garnered 41% of the vote and 216 seats in Parliament to Solidarity's 5.6%—reorganized in a coalition under the name Electoral Action Solidarity (AWS).[20]

Czech Republic's Economic Success

In contrast to Poland, the Czech Republic's economy remained strong during the early 1990s. The Czech economy maintained the lowest level of unemployment not only among the transition states, but outperformed economies of major European powers and the United States, making it second only to Japan.[21] Analysts cite a balanced budget and the devaluation of the Czech crown as factors in keeping both unemployment and inflation low.[22] Average unemployment for the years 1990-1994 was 2.8% in the Czech Republic, in contrast to 10.6% in Slovakia, 9% in Hungary, and 12% in Poland.[23] After a steep decline in the early 1990s reaching a negative 14.5% in 1991, the Czech Republic's GDP posted steady gains through 1995 to just over 6%. From 1997 to 1999, GDP dipped slightly then rebounded to 3.5% growth in 2001. Economic forecasters predict GDP growth at 3.6% in 2004.[24] While GDP lost ground 1997-1999, average annual inflation rose to 8 percent in 1997, 9.7% in 1998, then decreased dramatically in 1999 to 1.8%.[25] Unemployment and GDP data for a number of transition states are summarized in tables 13.1 and 13.2 in the appendix.

The strong economy during the first five years after 1989 no doubt contributed to the staying power of the Civic Democratic Party (ODS) in the government with Václav Klaus as the prime minister, limiting the chances for a resurgence of Communists in the government as happened in Poland. Klaus's ODS captured nearly 30% of the vote in the 1992 and 1996 elections. The ODS lost power only after the brief economic downturn in 1997. In the 1998 elections the Czech Social Democratic Party (ČSSD), led by Miloš Zeman—subsequently prime minister—defeated ODS with 32% of the vote to 27% for ODS.[26]

Survey data reveal the strong satisfaction Czechs feel toward the economy in spite of setbacks of the late 1990s. Although one of five transitions states— including Poland, Slovenia, Slovakia, and Hungary—where the GDP is higher than it was in 1990, the Czech Republic is distinctive as the only country where "less than half [the population] view the old economy through the haze of nostalgia."[27]

Czechs enjoy a high standard of living among citizens of transition states as well. Growth in disposable income allows for the acquisition of luxury items such as color televisions, VCRs, cars, and Internet access. In the Czech Republic, 98% of households have a color television, 50% a VCR, 62% a car, and 33% have access to the Internet. The Czech Republic is topped in these categories only by Slovenia in car ownership (86%) and Estonia in Internet access (38%). By contrast, the percentages for Russia are 82% (color television), 39% (VCR), 28% (car), and 8% (Internet access).[28] The European Union's regular reports on progress toward accession also include data on cellular telephone subscriptions as an economic indicator. According to this report, in 2001 approximately 68% of Czechs held cellular telephone subscriptions compared with 76% of Slovenes, 49% of Hungarians, 29% of Lithuanians, and 25% of Poles.[29] Data on the five consumer products discussed above are summarized in table 13.3 in the appendix.

International Integration: Good-Bye Warsaw, Hello Brussels

The two most strategic arenas for international integration of transition states are NATO and the European Union. The enlargement of both organizations through the admission of former Soviet satellite nations and former Soviet republics will have far-reaching consequences for issues in European and global security. The Czech Republic's membership in NATO and EU are linked together in that the country's entry into NATO "accelerates the pace of the catching up, for it solidifies the irreversibility of the transition process and strengthens the country's candidacy for early European Union . . . membership."[30]

The most important measure of the success of the Czech Republic in its transition from a centrally planned to a market economy will be its accession to the European Union. The Czech Republic submitted its application for membership to the European Union on 23 January 1996. The European Council launched accession negotiations with six Central European nations, including the Czech Republic in March 1998.[31]

Eda Kriseová (chapter five) sees her country's admission to the EU as a positive signal for continued peace and prosperity: "My only hope is that they will be invited into the European Community, and they will adapt. I don't think the Czechs are able to exist separately. They always functioned well in the big empires or unions. . . . They were revolutionaries, but they were not able to rule themselves. They were always working very well together with the others. The best quality of their character is the ability to adapt—in better conditions and also in worse." Petr Uhl (chapter eleven) sees EU membership as a protector of national sovereignty and common European interests, "I see in the European Union a common means against the globalization coming from the United States." How does the majority of Czechs view the membership of the Czech Republic in the European Union? And do Czechs support their country's entry into that organization?

Lukewarm Support for NATO and EU in Czech Republic

The Czech Republic, along with Hungary and Poland, officially joined NATO in March 1999. Support for NATO membership among the three nations was weakest in the Czech Republic. In 1999, only 49% of Czechs surveyed supported NATO membership compared to 60% in Poland and 61% in Hungary. The percentage of Czechs and Hungarians favoring NATO membership remained virtually the same in 2000, while increasing slightly among Poles.[32]

According to public opinion research, Czech support for EU membership increased quite dramatically after 1999. In September 2000, a slim majority of Czechs (51%) stated they would vote "yes" in a referendum to decide whether the Czech Republic should join the EU. The percentage of "yes" votes to the same question was 45% in May 1999 and 49% in May 2000.[33] Research results published by the Ministry of Foreign Affairs of the Czech Republic showed that by January 2003 support increased to 61% with voter participation estimated at 73%.[34] Research by the Central European Research Group (CEORG), based in Brussels, placed Czech support for EU membership considerably lower at 55%, with opposition to membership at 25%, and those undecided whether to vote "for" or "against" accession at 19%.[35] Public enthusiasm and support for EU membership is lowest overall in the Czech Republic, compared to Hungary and Poland. In September 2000, 69% of Hungarians and 55% of Poles would have voted "yes" in a referendum on EU membership.

The referendum on EU membership in the Czech Republic took place 16 June 2003, and the results are binding. How does actual voter turnout and voter preference toward membership in the EU compare with the above-mentioned predictions?

Czech voters supported the Czech Republic's membership in the EU by a more than 3:1 margin at 77%, with 23% voting against membership and a voter turnout of 55%. The referendum results are a victory for Czechs who viewed membership in the EU as an incontrovertible sign of the country's reintegration into Europe and a break with its isolation of the past. Prime Minister Vladimír Špidla summarized the sentiment eloquently: "It is as if only now the second World War—which tore us away from a relationship with Western Europe—has ended. In recent years we have returned step by small step. Now it is finally in full swing." [36]

Of the six post-Communist transition states, voter turnout in EU accession referenda was highest in Lithuania with 64% and support for membership at 90%. The lowest voter participation occurred in Hungary where "yes" votes numbered at 84%. Referenda results for six transition states and Malta are summarized in table 4 in the appendix.

Michael Kocáb (chapter four) comments that with the Czech Republic's admission and full integration into both NATO and the EU "nothing can threaten us." But why has public support for the country's membership in both organizations been low historically? What do Czech citizens fear from integration into NATO and the EU?

According to survey data from the year 2000, 47% of Czech respondents described NATO membership as a "new form of our submission to a foreign power." In the same survey, 40% believed that NATO membership increased the possibility of the Czech Republic's involvement in an armed conflict, while only 38% of respondents felt that membership guaranteed the country's independence. Negative responses to all three questions showed an increase over the responses to the same questions in the 1999 survey, the year the Czech Republic joined NATO. [37]

Thomas Szayna offers several explanations for why the Czech public has shown little enthusiasm for NATO membership in contrast to the same issue in Poland and Hungary. The Czech public regards the notion of "security" as the "absence of a threat." The Czech Republic, since the breakup with Slovakia, no longer shares a common border with any former Soviet republic—Slovakia and Ukraine now serve as buffers to any potential security threat from Russia. Moreover, the country's nearest neighbors, Germany, Poland, Hungary, Austria, and indeed Slovakia, pose an unlikely military threat. Therefore, in the absence of any credible threat from neighboring states, both the Czech public and the country's leadership exhibited little enthusiasm for NATO membership. [38]

The national security issue in Hungary and Poland is quite different from that of the Czech Republic, therefore Hungarians and Poles are considerably more enthusiastic toward NATO membership. Both Hungary and Poland share borders with potentially unstable states—Poland with Belarus, and Hungary with Croatia and the former Yugoslav federation. The threat of spillover of the armed conflict in former Yugoslav states in the early and mid-1990s made NATO a very attractive option to Hungarians. [39]

In regard to EU membership, Czech enthusiasm was dampened by the perception that it is the EU member states that benefit most from the EU's current—or "candidacy" period—relations with the Czech Republic (37%), according to the May 2000 survey data. Czech respondents appear to hold a rather high degree of apprehension that wealthy foreigners might begin a land grab after EU membership, with only 48% supporting the right of foreigners to own land in the Czech Republic after accession.[40]

Based on the survey data, the general Czech public demonstrates considerably less enthusiasm for membership in NATO and the EU than Kriseová, Kocáb, or Uhl. The general attitude has been historically more one of indifference, rather than either great support or great opposition toward integration into either organization.

Xenophobia: *Vítejte (kdo není Cikán)!*[41]

One of the prominent issues confronting the societies and governments of the transition states is xenophobia and how to combat it. Indeed, manifestations of xenophobia and racism in the Czech Republic are mentioned a number of times as a concern by the narrators. They register concern not only for the future development of civil society, but also that the perception might develop within the international community, above all in the EU, of Czechs as "racists." The narrators are quick to dispel the notion of Czechs as characteristically racist. In this section, I will discuss xenophobia as a phenomenon in the transition states as a whole and within the Czech Republic in particular, both with regard to the origins of xenophobic attitudes in the region and efforts to deal with the problem.

In the Czech Republic, xenophobic attitudes and acts of aggression have been directed most prominently toward Roma, not "foreigners" but an internal minority group, "citizens" of the country.[42] In 1995, Human Rights Watch reported that since 1989, 27 Roma had been murdered in the Czech Republic and 181 acts of violence toward Roma reported to police. Furthermore, the report states, acts of discrimination against Roma increased since 1989 in the areas of housing, employment, and access to public and private services. After the breakup of Czechoslovakia in 1993, large numbers of Roma were rendered "stateless," many of whose applications for citizenship were subsequently denied.[43]

Entrenched Attitudes

In May 1998, in response to "citizens'" complaints, the mayor of the northern Bohemian city Ústí nad Labem announced that by September, a wall would be built down the center of the town's *Matiční ulice* [Matiční Street] to separate apartment houses inhabited by Roma on one side of the street from three single-family homes of ethnic Czechs on the other side of the street. The wall would protect permanent residents and homeowners *"od hluku a nepořádku"* [from noise and disorder] emanating from the Roma dwellings.[44] Thereafter, for the next year and a half, "Matiční Street" became a catchphrase in the international and domestic media symbolizing Czech xenophobia, some would say even racism.

The original plans called for a four-meter soundproof wall. In September, the authorities changed the design from a partitioning *zed'* [wall] to a 1.8-meter *plot* [fence] of ceramic bricks to form an enclosure around the apartment houses. The international media, the U.S. House of Representatives, and the Council of Europe all denounced the decision by city authorities to construct the wall.

Although postponed several times due to protests by local Roma organizations and other obstacles, and despite appeals even from President Václav Havel and a resolution passed by the lower house of the Czech Parliament overturning the construction order, the wall was ultimately erected in one day on 14 October 1999. The wall's existence proved to be a gigantic embarrassment to the government of the Czech Republic and put accession talks with the EU in jeopardy. "This wall is a wall between us and the European Union," expressed the exasperated minister of foreign affairs Jan Kavan.[45]

The wall in Matiční Street was torn down on 25 November 1999 after negotiations concluded between the central government and Ústí nad Labem officials. The government agreed to allocate CZK 10 million (US$385,000) to the city to improve social conditions, one-third of which the city would use to buy the three homes of Czechs who wished to leave Matiční Street.[46]

The wall in Matiční Street is symbolic of the depth of anti-Roma sentiment in the Czech Republic. The recalcitrance of Ústí nad Labem officials and their defiance of central government authority are an indicator of the strength of entrenched prejudice toward Roma in the Czech Republic. Are acts of violence toward Roma and other dark-skinned people or foreigners in the Czech Republic manifestations of racist or xenophobic attitudes and beliefs?

Czechs are quick to make a distinction between racism on the one hand and xenophobia, or "fear of foreigners," on the other. Michael Kocáb asserts that Czechs lash out at Roma and "other citizens of differently colored skin, students, and so on" out of dissatisfaction and frustration with the required adjustments during transition from Communism, and believes, "Czechs do not have a racist disposition." Accusations of Czechs as racists by Westerners annoy Jiřina Šiklová. "We are not," Šiklová insists (chapter nine), "It is not racism. It is xenophobia. We were closed for a very long time. . . . And we are not prepared for foreigners."

Martin Palouš (chapter eight) argues that alleged racism in the Czech Republic is based not on superiority but "on the Czech feeling of smallness; . . . a complex of inferiority, rather fear, lack of openness, the feeling that we have to struggle not to allow foreigners or disturbers of the peace to enter our territories." Petr Uhl (chapter eleven), commissioner for human rights for the Czech Republic, who visited Ústí nad Labem on more than one occasion during the controversy surrounding the wall, concluded "Matiční Street is neither a political or a racial problem, but a social problem."[47] In light of these remarks, one might pose the question, if the Czechs are not racists but xenophobes, how xenophobic are they?

Origins of Xenophobia in Transition States

Studies of xenophobia in fact support Kocáb's view, at least in part: people become more xenophobic during times of economic uncertainty and falling living standards. Claire Wallace cites research results in Hungary showing that xenophobia increased among all age groups during the period 1989-1993, due to three primary factors: during the Communist era, xenophobia was a taboo subject, there was very little immigration, and the economic crisis was concealed. After Communism, however, politicians and the press openly blamed migrants for rising crime rates. An increase in crime occurred simultaneously with an influx of migrants, linking both in the minds of people.[48]

Survey data indeed show that xenophobic attitudes are particularly strong in Hungary, Poland, the Czech Republic, and Slovakia.[49] In addition to economic pressures, Wallace proposes several factors which can account for the rise in xenophobia and increased, seemingly racially motivated violence in the transition states: 1) xenophobic nationalism provides simple and emotionally satisfying explanations for the complex problems facing post-Communist states; 2) increased migration pressures and the role of transition states as a migration buffer zone between East and West; 3) the lack of an established free press; and 4) lack or weakness of independent human rights groups which could defend the rights of minorities. Wallace asserts that it is journalists who generally champion the causes of Roma and other minorities in "Western" societies and these journalists do not exist in the transition countries of Central and Eastern Europe. Independent human rights organizations are, Wallace maintains, by-products of civil society which is underdeveloped in many transition states.[50]

Pressure from increased migration indeed appears to be a contributing factor in the Czech Republic, as well as in Hungary. Statistics show that among the transition states, the Czech Republic has attracted most of the guest workers, primarily from Ukraine. The country's long border with Germany—the haven sought by enormous numbers of economically disadvantaged Eastern Europeans—also makes it a target for a large population of transit migrants. According to official figures, in 1993 foreigners registered in the Czech Republic numbered more than 44,000, while an almost equal number of illegal transit migrants were stopped at the border with Germany. At the same time, the Czech Republic accepted more than 5,000 asylum seekers.[51]

Xenophobia among Czechs

With the raw numbers of migrants and resident foreigners established, what attitudes do Czechs harbor towards these groups? Researchers conducting the New Democracies Barometer asked a number of questions to find an answer to this question.[52] The survey data revealed that 75% of Czechs felt a threat from migrants and that their numbers should be reduced (Hungarians also 75%). In comparison, Austria has received more migrants than any of the transition states, yet only 27% of Austrians feel a threat from foreigners and argue their numbers should be reduced.[53]

The numbers of migrants and the rise in crime rates are also strongly linked in the minds of Czechs: 82% of Czechs either "agree" or "strongly agree" that the increase in numbers of migrants is directly related to the increase in crime (Hungary, 76%; Slovenia, 52%). In regard to economic opportunity and the competition for jobs between Czechs and migrants, the data are also quite revealing. Among Czechs, 67% "disagree" that migrants are generally good for the economy (Hungary 69%), while 53% believe that migrants take jobs away from people born in the Czech Republic.[54]

In regard to how the state should treat its own national minorities as well as foreign nationals already living and working in the country, Czechs tend to show a high degree of tolerance. While it is true the majority of Czechs would like to reduce the number of migrants in the country, they do not espouse particularly xenophobic attitudes in regard to the treatment of resident working foreigners. For example, 62% of Czechs surveyed "agree" the country and minority groups are better served if minority populations maintain their distinct language, customs, and traditions than if the minority were assimilated.

The majority of Czechs (60%) "agree" the government should take steps to help foreigners in the country learn the Czech language and customs. At the same time, 75% of Czechs "agree," of whom 27% "strongly agree," that foreigners working in the Czech Republic should enjoy social security and other benefits as long as they obey the law. A minority of Czechs (46%) would pass laws limiting the stay of foreigners in the country, and an even smaller minority (26%) would like the state to force foreigners to leave the country.[55]

In order to probe attitudes toward foreigners further, researchers asked Czechs about their preferences for five separate nationalities: Russians, Germans, Jews, Roma, and Austrians. Chinese, Vietnamese, and Arabs together (C/V/A) comprised a sixth group. The questions asked a person's preference for each nationality group as a neighbor, a coworker, a member of the family by marriage, and as a blood donor. Czechs prefer Austrians over the other five nationality groups in three of the four categories: Austrians tie with Germans in the category of an acceptable blood donor with 79% of Czechs answering "like" or "not mind."

In the same category, Roma and C/V/A ranked at the lowest level of preference, "not like," with 36% and 33% respectively. Roma ranked at the lowest level of preference in every other category as well: Czechs would "not like" a Rom as a neighbor (69%), as a coworker (54%), or as a family member by marriage (78%). In the category of family member, the negativity of Czechs toward Roma is surpassed only by Slovaks (85%) and Croats (79%). In fairness, it must be noted that in the blood donor category, perhaps the most personal category, the majority of Czechs would either "like" or "not mind" a blood transfusion from a person of any nationality named, even 53% in regard to Roma.[56] These results are summarized in table 5 in the appendix.

The Profile of a Xenophobe

What then is the political profile of a typical xenophobe? And does the ordinary Czech citizen fit that profile? Answers to the survey produced the following profile: xenophobes feel threatened by international powers, i.e., Russia, Germany, and the United States, as well as by internal minorities and migrants; are likely to support authoritarian political alternatives—including a return to Communism, rule by the army or a strong leader; are sixty years old or older and have low levels of education; prefer assimilation for minorities; exhibit a great deal of national pride and high resistance to multiculturalism; and reject international integration through supranational organizations such as NATO and the European Union.[57]

The previous discussion has shown that Czechs fit the profile of the typical xenophobe only partially. Czechs on the whole do not "agree" that minorities and migrants should be assimilated but should maintain their national identity in language and culture. While the majority of Czechs are proud of their nation, believing the Czech Republic to be "as good or better than most countries" (70%) and preferring Czech citizenship to any other (88%), 79% agree, 45% "strongly," that citizenship should be granted to any person born in the Czech Republic regardless of nationality.[58]

In contrast to the profile of a xenophobe, it is not sixty-year-old nationalist pensioners who generally perpetrate hate crimes against Roma and other foreigners in the Czech Republic but young men generally referred to as "skinheads," as well as others of various economic and social backgrounds. The survey data show that on the whole Czechs are not so much "antiforeigner" or "xenophobic," but rather reserve their prejudice for and direct discriminatory practices toward members of primarily one national minority—Roma.

Government Measures to Combat Xenophobia

The government of the Czech Republic has taken a number of steps to address discrimination against resident foreigners, migrants, and national minorities, including Roma. Since 1996, pressure on the Czech government to comply with EU accession criteria has generated a considerable body of legislation dealing with issues related to minority rights, as well as budgetary appropriations to support legislative mandates, some of which entered into force in August 2001. While the situation of resident foreigners in the Czech Republic—primarily Slovaks, Poles, Germans, Hungarians, and Ukrainians—was declared "satisfactory" by the Commission of the European Communities, Roma still suffer discrimination in housing, education, and employment.[59]

The Czech government has taken positive steps to improve education for Roma children. These measures include the extension of preparatory classes to prepare Roma children for mainstream primary school. From November 2001 to February 2002, the Council of Roma Affairs—a body comprised of an equal number of Roma regional representatives and government ministry officials—received CZK 34 million (US$1.2 million) to administer community projects, support Roma students with scholarships, and to complete a housing project. In

April 2002, the government released another CZK 6 million (US$214,000) to support an antiracism information and media campaign targeted at local and regional levels and an educational campaign in secondary schools.[60]

Efforts by the government to enlighten the populace in regard to Roma appear to have had the hoped-for positive results, especially among the voting public. Party leaders espousing xenophobic views or advocating dramatic government intervention to curb migration have not been successful. In the run-up to the June 2002 elections, position papers of the ODS promised a "crackdown on immigration" and criticized the government of Prime Minister Miloš Zeman for its failure to address "the growing problems" of asylum seekers and illegal immigration.

In response, officials of competing political parties linked the ODS position with the far-right opinions and platform of the French presidential candidate Jean-Marie Le Pen. Hana Marvanová, leader of the Freedom Union-Democratic Union (US-DEU) stated, "The ODS is sending signals that are dangerous and reinforce the xenophobic atmosphere."[61] Klaus and ODS were unable to capitalize on voters' fear, even in the wake of the events of 11 September 2001 and lost the election capturing only 24.5% of the vote. Miroslav Sladek's Republican Party, the most extreme nationalist and far-right "antiforeigner" political organization, appealed to only 1% of Czech voters.[62]

Conclusion

The Czech Republic's transition to a multiparty democracy has to date progressed peacefully. The country has proven that it can conduct free and fair elections, and the political culture demonstrates little or no tendency toward right- or left-wing totalitarianism. The country's economy is stable, growing, and remains viable. Citizens of the Czech Republic enjoy a high standard of living, relative to other post-Communist transition states. There is still work to be done in addressing social inequalities, fighting corruption, and protecting resident foreigners, migrants, and national minorities—especially Roma—from discrimination and violence. The latter, however, are areas requiring constant improvement in all democratic industrialized countries.

In successive elections, Czech voters have made their opinions known concerning which direction they want their democracy and their government's economic and social policy to go. The majority of Czechs is satisfied with the current multiparty system and holds very little nostalgia either for the pre-1989 one-party system or the centralized socialist economy. The majority opposes "turning back the clock."

On the other hand, opinion polls make it clear that voters are concerned that the social welfare net remain intact and supported by the state. They demand higher spending on health care, old-age pensions, education, and environmental protection, even at the cost of higher taxes. In short, they "demand 'less state' than they experienced before 1990, but 'more state' than that which corresponds to the *laissez-faire* capitalist ideal."[63]

The data collected from public opinion surveys and in other research on public trends (Večerník and Matějů) reveal that public concerns intersect with those of the intellectual elite represented by the eleven narrators on a number of levels and to a similar degree on most issues. It might be surprising to the narrators to learn that the public is more in tune with them than it might appear based on their own encounters with the public.

With membership in NATO and accession to the European Union, the Czech Republic's full integration into both the European economy and the Western security apparatus will be complete. One wonders when scholars and researchers might remove the Czech Republic from the list of "transition states."

Barring some kind of global conflagration or a drastic turnaround in voter sentiment which would convert the Czech Republic back to its pre-1989 state, it is difficult to imagine the Czech Republic will not live up to the reality dreamed of by the eleven persons interviewed for this book. These people have worked diligently and with honesty and integrity to rebuild a nation after 1989, nursing it through infancy, nurturing it in adolescence, and now watching it mature into adulthood.

Appendix

Table 13.1. GDP Growth

Country	1995	1996	1997	1998	1999	2000	2001
Czech Rep.	6.4	4.3	-0.8	-1.2	-0.4	2.9	3.5
Estonia	4.2	4.1	10.5	4.7	-1.1	6.9	5.0
Hungary	1.5	1.3	4.6	4.9	4.2	5.2	3.8
Lithuania	3.3	4.7	7.3	5.1	-3.9	3.9	5.9
Poland	7.0	6.0	6.8	4.8	4.1	4.0	1.1
Slovakia	6.5	5.8	5.6	4.0	1.3	2.2	3.3
Slovenia	4.1	3.5	4.6	3.8	5.2	4.6	3.0

Source: *Deutsche Bank Research*, Country Infobase, www.dbresearch.com. Used by permission.

Table 13.2. Unemployment as Percent of Labor Force

Country	1997	1998	1999	2000	2001
Czech Rep.	4.3	5.9	8.5	8.8	8.0
Hungary	9.0	8.9	6.9	6.6	5.7
Lithuania	4.1	12.5	10.2	15.6	16.5
Poland	11.0	9.9	12.3	16.3	18.4
Slovenia	6.6	7.4	7.3	6.9	5.7

Source: Compiled for each country from *2002 Regular Reports on Progress Towards Accession*, Commission of the European Communities.

Table 13.3. Consumer Items

Country	Car	Color TV	VCR	Internet	*Cell Phone
Czech Rep.	62	98	50	33	68
Estonia	45	97	38	38	54
Hungary	42	92	56	14	49
Lithuania	48	90	29	19	29
Poland	52	96	56	18	25
Russia	28	82	39	8	—
Slovakia	45	95	40	19	40
Slovenia	86	96	58	30	76

Source: New Europe Barometer-2001; *Cell phone percent (per 1000 inhabitants) from *2002 Regular Report on Progress Towards Accession.*

Table 13.4. EU Accession Referenda Results

Country	Yes	No	Turnout
Czech Republic	77	23	55
Hungary	84	16	46
Lithuania	90	10	64
Malta	54	46	91
Poland	77	23	59
Slovakia	92	8	52
Slovenia	90	10	60

Numbers in percent. Compiled from *Lidové Noviny*, *Mladá Fronta Dnes*, 16 June 2003.

Table 13.5. Percent of Czech Preferences for Other Nationalities

Group	Neighbor		Coworker		Family Member		Blood Donor	
	+	-	+	-	+	-	+	-
Austrians	86	10	85	9	67	27	79	12
Jews	78	15	80	14	57	35	74	16
Germans	71	24	80	15	59	34	79	12
Russians	56	38	70	28	42	49	75	17
C/V/A	42	51	55	38	19	73	56	33
Roma	25	69	40	54	11	78	53	36

Source: Adapted from Wallace, *Xenophobia in Post-Communist Europe,* appendix. Xenophobia Questions: 1998 New Democracies Barometer. *Note: The "+" column combines percentages of "like" and "not mind"; the "-" represents percentage of "not like."*

Notes

Chapter 1: Dissidence in Czechoslovakia, 1968-1989

1. *Charter 77 Declaration*, English translation published on the occasion of the twentieth anniversary of the original release to the public of the *Charter 77 Declaration* on 1 January 1977, Prague: Radio Free Europe/Radio Liberty, Inc., 1996, http://plato .acadiau.ca/COURSES/POLS/Grieve/3593/Czech/Charter77.html (10 February 2002).

2. Vojtech Mastny, ed., *Czechoslovakia: Crisis in World Communism* (New York: Facts on File, Inc., 1972), 21.

3. Official newspaper of the Czechoslovak Writers Union.

4. An English translation of the entire "Two Thousand Words Manifesto" with a list of signatories is included in Mastny, *Czechoslovakia: Crisis in World Communism*, 28-34.

5. Established by treaty in 1955 in Warsaw, Poland, the Warsaw Pact was a military alliance of the Soviet Union, Poland, Czechoslovakia, East Germany, Hungary, Bulgaria, Romania, and Albania. The alliance disbanded in 1991.

6. Mastny, *Czechoslovakia: Crisis in World Communism*, 36.

7. Philip Windsor and Adam Roberts, *Czechoslovakia 1968: Reform, Repression, and Resistance* (New York: Columbia University Press, 1969), 44.

8. Mastny, *Czechoslovakia: Crisis in World Communism*, 59-60.

9. Robert Littell, ed., *The Czech Black Book* (New York: Frederick A. Praeger, 1969), 10-11.

10. Václav Havel, *Disturbing the Peace: A Conversation with Karel Hvížďala*, trans. Paul Wilson (New York: Vintage Books, 1990), 106. A book-length interview first published in *samizdat* in summer 1986.

11. Bottles containing flammable liquid and a wick, which could be ignited and thrown. Easily improvised from common materials, Molotov cocktails are named after Soviet foreign minister Vyacheslav Molotov (1939-1949) who put them into production in the Soviet Union during World War II.

12. *Oratorio for Prague*. Written and directed by Jan Němec. 26 minutes. 1990. Videocassette.

13. Mastny, *Czechoslovakia: Crisis in World Communism*, 79.

14. For a detailed discussion of the agreement reached between the Soviet and Czechoslovak governments, see Mastny, *Czechoslovakia: Crisis in World Communism*, 93-98.

15. Jaromír Navrátil, ed., "Document No. 62: Meeting Notes Taken by Chief of the Hungarian People's Army General Staff Karoly Csemi on Talks with Soviet Generals in Budapest to Discuss Preparations for 'Operation Danube,' July 24, 1968" in *The Prague Spring 1968: A National Security Archive Documents Reader* (Budapest: Central European University Press, 1998), 277-78.

16. See Clive Barnes's "Public Theater Presents 'Memorandum,'" review of *The Memorandum*, by Václav Havel, as performed by the New York Shakespeare Festival, *New York Times*, 28 April 1968, sec. 2, p. 11. Havel received two other Obies: in 1970 for *The Increased Difficulty of Concentration* in the Distinguished Play category and in 1984 for *A Private View* in the Playwriting category.

17. *Pravda*, September 6. Quoted in Mastny, *Czechoslovakia: Crisis in World Communism*, 130.

18. For a complete English translation of the treaty with introductory notes, see "Document No. 133: Bilateral Treaty on the 'Temporary Presence of Soviet Forces on Czechoslovak Territory,' October 16, 1968" in *The Prague Spring 1968*, 533-36.

19. Alexander Dubček died in Bratislava 7 November 1992, from injuries suffered in a car accident in September of that year.

20. Havel, *Disturbing the Peace*, 119.

21. Jan Hus (1369-1415) was rector of Charles University in Prague (1402-1403) and a translator of Wycliffe's works into Czech. Hus opposed the indulgences announced by the Roman Catholic Church in order to mount a crusade against Ladislaus of Naples. In 1410 the church excommunicated Hus. The church summoned Hus to the Council of Constance, tried and condemned him, then burned him at the stake on 6 July 1415.

22. See more details on Normalization in John Keane, *Václav Havel: A Political Tragedy in Six Acts* (New York: Basic Books, 2000), 227-30.

23. Václav Havel, "The Power of the Powerless," in *Living in Truth*, trans. Paul Wilson (London: Faber and Faber, 1986), 76-80.

24. Term borrowed from Russian, a compound of *sam* [self] and *izdat* [publish] meaning "self-publishing," refers to literature, usually hand-copied or typed in multiple carbon copies, circulated among the population illegally. The term has relevance for virtually every country of the former East Bloc.

25. Details of the beginnings and day-to-day management of *Edice Petlice* are in Vaculík's humorous, yet revealing, essay "A Padlock for Castle Schwarzenberg," trans. A. G. Brain, in *Good-Bye Samizdat: Twenty Years of Czechoslovak Underground Writing*, ed. Marketa Goetz-Stankiewicz (Evanston, Ill.: Northwestern University Press, 1992), 118-26.

26. Kavan became the minister of foreign affairs of the Czech Republic in July 1998.

27. Eda Kriseová, *Václav Havel: The Authorized Biography*, trans. Caleb Crain (New York: St. Martin's Press, 1993), 99.

28. Plastic People of the Universe II, *Vožralej jako slíva* [Drunk as a skunk], Koncerty 1973-1975, words by Egon Bondy, music by Milan Hlavsa, Globus International, 1997. Translation by Michael Long. Used by permission. Globus International in Prague has released the collected recordings of the Plastic People of the Universe, 1969-1986, on ten compact discs.

29. Plastic People of the Universe II, *Vožralej jako slíva*, Koncerty 1973-1975. Translation by Michael Long. Used by permission.

30. Mejla (Milan) Hlavsa and Jan Pelc, *Bez ohňů je underground* [*No Spark in the Underground*] (Praha: Nakladatelství BFS, 1992), 108.

31. Album notes, Plastic People of the Universe II, *Vožralej jako slíva*, Koncerty 1973-1975, 3.

32. See Hlavsa and Pelc, *Bez ohňů je underground*, 124-25; also Eda Kriseová's discussion of the state's persecution of the Plastics in *Václav Havel*, 99-101. In February 2003, the Supreme Court of the Czech Republic repealed the verdict and sentence of the four members of the Plastic People put on trial in 1976. Justice František Hrabec stated "the criminal proceedings at the time can not be regarded as correct or in accordance with the law." See Luděk Navara, "Vězněným muzikantům se otevírá cesta k odškodnění" [Road to compensation opens for imprisoned musicians] *Mladá Fronta Dnes*, 19 February 2003, p. 2.

33. Hlavsa and Pelc, *Bez ohňů je underground*, 111.

34. Havel, *Disturbing the Peace*, 128; see also Hlavsa and Pelc, *Bez ohňů je underground*, 124-25.

35. Havel, *Disturbing the Peace*, 131.

36. Havel, *Disturbing the Peace*, 132.

37. The Helsinki Accords, also known as the Helsinki Final Act, were concluded and signed in Helsinki, Finland, in August 1975. The former Soviet Union and its former Central and East European allies were signatories to the accords.

38. *Charter 77 Declaration*.

39. Kriseová recounts the events of 6 January 1977 as related to her by Pavel Landovský in *Václav Havel*, 114-20. See also Havel, *Disturbing the Peace*, 140-41.

40. Václav Benda (1936) was a founding member of VONS and charter speaker (1984). Otta Bednářová (1927), television editor, was VONS member and longtime copyist for Ludvík Vaculík's *Edice Petlice*. Jiří Dienstbier (1937), reporter, playwright, and translator, was a founding member of VONS and a charter speaker (1985); from 1989 to 1992, minister of foreign affairs, afterwards served as the United Nations special rapporteur for human rights in the former Yugoslavia.

41. See Kriseová for a detailed account of the trial, including partial transcripts, 172-83.

42. Carol Skalnik Leff, *The Czech and Slovak Republics: Nation Versus State* (Boulder, Colo.: Westview Press, 1996), 84.

43. Timothy Garton Ash, *The Magic Lantern: The Revolution of '89 Witnessed in Warsaw, Budapest, Berlin and Prague* (New York: Random House, 1990), 87. Ash provides a day-by-day eyewitness description of the workings of Civic Forum's inner circle during the Velvet Revolution.

44. Jiřina Šiklová, "The 'Gray Zone' and the Future of Dissent in Czechoslovakia," trans. Káča Poláčková-Henley, in *Good-Bye, Samizdat*, 184.

45. Šiklová, "The 'Gray Zone' and the Future of Dissent in Czechoslovakia," 186.

46. Barbara Day provides a thorough treatment of the home seminars in *The Velvet Philosophers* (London: Claridge Press, 1999).

47. Day, *The Velvet Philosophers*, 92-96.

48. See Christopher Marsh, *Russia at the Polls: Voters, Elections, and Democratization* (Washington, D.C.: CQ Press, 2002), 35-36.

49. Leff, *The Czech and Slovak Republics*, 76.

50. Mikhail Gorbachev, "Speech to the United Nations General Assembly," published in *Pravda* 8 December 1988, reprinted in Sylvia Woolby, *Gorbachev and the Decline of Ideology in Soviet Foreign Policy* (Boulder, Colo.: Westview Press, 1989), 109-14.

51. Leff, *The Czech and Slovak Republics*, 78.

52. Imre Nagy (1896-1958), expelled from the Hungarian Communist Party in 1955, was named to the post of prime minister during the Hungarian rebellion of 1956. When the Soviet army put an end to the rebellion, Nagy was taken prisoner, tried in secret two years later, and executed 16 June 1958.

53. See Leff, *The Czech and Slovak Republics*, 79-83.

54. See Ash, *The Magic Lantern*, 82-83.

55. Leff, *The Czech and Slovak Republics*, 80.

56. Leff, *The Czech and Slovak Republics*, 80.

57. Eda Kriseová, conversation with the author, April 1998, San Antonio, Texas.

58. Slovakia separated from the Czech Republic as a free and independent nation on 1 January 1993, an event often referred to as the "Velvet Divorce." See Leff, *The Czech and Slovak Republics*, 126-74. Petr Příhoda discusses the complexities of Czech and Slovak cultural biases which precipitated the formal disintegration of Czechoslovakia in "Mutual Perceptions in Czech-Slovak Relationships," in *The End of Czechoslovakia*, ed. Jiří Musil (Budapest: Central European University Press, 1995), 128-38.

Chapter 2: Ivan Havel

1. Julius Tomin and his wife Zdena ran a philosophy seminar from 1977 until their emigration to Britain in 1980. Zdena Tominová was a Charter 77 speaker in 1979 and 1980. It was Tomin who initiated contact with the Oxford philosophers. See Day, *The Velvet Philosophers* (London: Claridge Press, 1999).

2. Václav Malý, Roman Catholic priest, was among the first charter signatories. The Communist regime banned him from working as a priest in 1979. He served as charter speaker and was a founding member of VONS. In 1996 he was appointed suffragan bishop by Pope John Paul II.

3. Václav Klaus (1941), economist, politician; graduated from the Prague School of Economics (1963); worked as researcher at the Institute of Economics of the Czechoslovak Academy of Sciences until 1970; during Normalization occupied various positions in the Czechoslovak State Bank and later at the Center for Prognostics of the Czechoslovak Academy of Sciences (1971-1986); joined the Civic Forum (1989) and became its leader (1990); cofounder of the Civic Democratic Party (1991), and remained its chairman until he stepped down in December 2002; prime minister (1992-1997); president of the Czech Republic (2003).

4. Addressing a person with the familiar pronoun *ty* [you] rather than with the formal pronoun *vy*.

Chapter 3: Věra Jirousová

1. Founded in 1922 in the Soviet Union, the Pioneers, also known as Young Pioneers, was organized by the Communist Party for children ages 9-15. Membership in the organization was ostensibly voluntary but in practice compulsory. Aside from the heavy emphasis on Communist ideology and propaganda, the Pioneers functioned in many ways similar to scouting in Western democracies and featured summer camps, sing-alongs, craft clubs, and honor guards at monuments to Communist ideology—eternal flames,

statues of Lenin, etc. The Pioneer organization was adopted by and functioned in every country of the East Bloc.

2. During the Communist era, the official Writers' Union literary monthly. Václav Havel served on the editorial board (1965-1967), then again until the magazine's permanent discontinuation (1968-1969).

3. Georg Trakl (1887-1914), playwright and leading Austrian expressionist poet.

4. Pavel Tigrid (1917), writer and publicist; minister of culture of the Czech Republic (1994-1996); advisor to President Václav Havel on Czech-German affairs (1997-1998).

5. *Krajina před bouří* [*The country before the storm*] (Praha: Nakladatelství Lidové Noviny, 1998). Prose collection written 1979-1989.

Chapter 4: Michael Kocáb

1. Miroslav Štěpán was at the time of the Velvet Revolution the Prague Communist Party boss. Civic Forum and students blamed Štěpán for the repression of the 17 November 1989 student demonstration.

2. Marián Čalfa (1946), a Slovak, was a Communist member of the federal government of Czechoslovakia until 1989; prime minister of Czechoslovakia (1990-1992).

3. Miloš Jakeš (1922), first secretary of the Communist Party of Czechoslovakia (1987-1989); acquitted of accusation of collaboration with the Warsaw Pact invasion of 1968 by Prague court 23 September 2002.

4. Lubomír Štrougal (1924), attorney; member of the Presidium of the Communist Party (1958-1989); minister of agriculture (1959-1961); minister of the interior (1961-1965); supporter of Normalization policies and strong supporter of party leadership of Gustáv Husák; prime minister (1970-1988); expelled from the Communist Party (1990).

5. Edvard Shevardnadze (1928), minister of foreign affairs of the Soviet Union (1985-1990); president of the Republic of Georgia (1995-2003).

6. In Czech parliamentary elections, candidates for seats in Parliament are arranged in ordered lists established by each party. Voters may reorder the list of party candidates according to their own preference. In this manner, voters increase the chances that a particular candidate gets a seat in Parliament based on the total number of seats allocated to a given party during an election.

7. Boris Yeltsin (1931), president of the Russian Federation (1991-1999).

8. The Czech Republic, along with Hungary and Poland, joined NATO in March 1999. EU accession took place in 2004. See chapter 13.

9. Roma, an ethnic minority in the Czech Republic known more commonly as "Gypsies." The position of Roma in Czech society is discussed in detail in chapter 13.

Chapter 5: Eda Kriseová

1. Jiří Gruša (1938), novelist; completed doctorate in philosophy at Charles University in Prague (1962); one of the founders of *Tvář* [*Face*]; Charter 77 signatory; Czech citizenship revoked (1982), thereafter lived and wrote in exile in the Federal Republic of Germany; ambassador of Czechoslovakia to the FRG (1990-1997); ambassador of the Czech Republic to Austria (1998).

2. Ivan Klíma (1931), one of the leading Czech novelists, playwright, and publicist; deputy editor of *Literární noviny* and *Listy* in 1960s; works banned in Czechoslovakia (1968-1990).

3. Alexandr "Saša" Kliment (1929), novelist, playwright, and screenwriter; work banned in Czechoslovakia (1970-1989); published in *samizdat* and abroad; received medal "Artis Bohemiae Amicis" for contribution to Czech culture from Ministry of Culture 30 January 2004. Karel Pecka (1928-1997), prose writer; imprisoned for alleged treason in Communist concentration camp (1949-1959); published in *samizdat* and in exile publishing houses; recipient of the Egon Hostovský Prize (1991).

4. Karel Jan Schwarzenberg (1937), entrepreneur and philanthropist, emigrated from Czechoslovakia to Austria with his family in 1948; chair of the International Helsinki Conference for Human Rights (1985-1990) and active supporter of political exiles and opposition movements in Czechoslovakia; returned to the Czech Republic in 1990; served as director of the Office of the President of the Czech Republic (Jan.-July 1990), and chancellor to President Václav Havel (1990-1992).

Chapter 6: Daniel Kummerman

1. *Rudé právo* [*Red Right*] was until 1989 the official daily newspaper of the Communist Party of Czechoslovakia. After 1989, it became the independent newspaper *Právo*.

2. The *Prague Post*, founded in 1991, is the most widely circulated English-language weekly published in the Czech Republic. The paper is also accessible online at: www.praguepost.com.

3. Tomáš Garrigue Masaryk (1850-1937), sociologist, philosopher, and revered statesman; first president of the Republic of Czechoslovakia (1918-1935).

Chapter 7: Dana Němcová

1. Approximately 2.5 million Czechoslovak citizens of German ethnicity were stripped of their citizenship, their property confiscated, and repatriated to the Federal Republic of Germany in the immediate post-World War II years. The controversial removal of ethnic Germans and Hungarians from the territory of Czechoslovakia was established in a set of decrees enacted from 1940 to 1946 by the Czechoslovak government in exile and signed by exiled president Edvard Beneš. See Jolyon Naegele, "Czech Republic: The Beneš Decrees—How Did They Come to Be and What Do They Mandate?" *Radio Free Europe/Radio Liberty*, www.rferl.org (1 March 2002).

2. Olga Havlová (1933-1996) married Václav Havel in 1964; founded the Committee for Good Will (after her death renamed the Olga Havlová Foundation) in 1990 as a charitable organization to finance and promote the restructuring and renovation of state institutions for the disabled.

3. JUDR. Milada Horáková (1901-1950); joined the Czechoslovak resistance against Nazi occupation (1939); was arrested by the Gestapo (1941) and held in a concentration camp until the end of World War II. She was a leading political opponent of the Communist Party. After retiring from politics (1948), she worked in support of families of those persecuted by the Communist regime. Arrested in 1949 for alleged high treason and espionage, Dr. Horáková was executed 27 June 1950 in spite of protests from world lead-

ers, including Winston Churchill, Albert Einstein, and Eleanor Roosevelt. In 1991, Horáková posthumously received the Order of T. G. Masaryk First Class from President Václav Havel.

4. JUDR. Otakar Motejl (1932) served from May 1968 as justice of the Supreme Court in Prague but was forced to leave that position during Normalization (1970). He resumed his law practice and defended the Plastic People of the Universe as well as a number of dissidents; minister of justice of the Czech Republic (September 1998 to October 2000).

5. Frantisek Janouch (1931), leading nuclear physicist; director of the Department of Nuclear Theory at the Institute of Nuclear Research of the Academy of Sciences in Prague (1960-1970); lost position during Normalization, exiled to Sweden (1973), accepted position in the Swedish Academy of Sciences; in retaliation Czechoslovak authorities revoked his citizenship and he became a Swedish citizen; founded the Charter 77 Foundation in Sweden to provide financial aid to dissidents in Czechoslovakia and publish dissident literature (1978).

Chapter 8: Martin Palouš

1. The Czech Republic and the Republic of Slovakia split from each other to form two independent countries as of 1 January 1993.

2. Founded during the Velvet Revolution by chartists, *Respekt* is a leading Czech weekly covering politics and culture. *Respekt* is accessible online at http://respect.inway .cz.

3. In response to the murder of John Lennon in 1980, a group of Prague youth set up a shrine to the Beatle consisting largely of graffiti and impromptu sketches on a section of garden wall in the city's diplomatic quarter. Youth, students, and other admirers of Lennon, including tourists, flocked to the wall in a symbolic act of defiance to the regime. The wall survived numerous whitewashes by city authorities, and more recently the devastating floods of August 2002. Yoko Ono, Lennon's widow, added her own message to the wall in December 2003.

Chapter 9: Jiřina Šiklová

1. Rudi Dutschke (1940-1979), sociologist; leader in the German socialist student organization (SDS) in West Berlin; organizer and participant in a number of student protests in the 1960s in Germany and other European countries; died in Denmark as a result of injuries received in an assassination attempt in Berlin (1968).

2. The *Rote Armee Fraktion* [Red Army Faction] (RAF) is the successor of the Baader-Meinhof Gang (Germany), a terrorist group which emerged from the radical student protest movement in the 1960s; received some support and training from the German Democratic Republic during the 1980s; has carried out a number of bombings, kidnappings, and assassination attempts, primarily directed against U.S. interests.

3. Tomáš Halík (1948), psychologist, philosopher, theologian; studied clinical psychology and philosophy at Charles University, a student under Jan Patočka, later also at the Pontifical Lateran University in the Vatican; ordained into the Roman Catholic priesthood in secret in Erfurt (former East Germany) (1978); active in *samizdat* literature and underground activities of the Catholic Church, assistant to Cardinal Tomášek; presi-

dent of the Czech Christian Academy. Miroslav "Merek" Tyl (1943), agronomist, expert in the cultivation of medicinal herbs; studied philosophy (under Jan Patočka) and sociology at Charles University; founded the Independent Student Movement [*Samostatné studentské hnutí*] (1965-1969); Charter 77 signatory (1977) and charter speaker (1990); member of Parliament of the Czech Republic (1990-1992; 1996-1998).

4. JUDR. Petr Pithart (1941), political scientist, historian, attorney; among first signatories of Charter 77; member of editorial board of *samizdat Lidové noviny*; prime minister of the Czech Republic (1990-1992); president of the Senate (1996-1998; 1998-2000; 2000-).

5. Ľuboš Holeček and Jiří Müller were both active in the student movement of the 1960s and the Prague Spring (1968). Müller was expelled from the university (1966), then rehabilitated by the Dubček regime (1968); arrested (1971) for distributing leaflets explaining voters' rights, tried for subversion of the republic (Article 98) (1972), and sentenced to five and one-half years in prison.

6. Jiří Pelikan (1923-1999), politician, journalist; active in the Communist youth movement; imprisoned for several months by the Gestapo (1940); member of the Czechoslovak National Assembly (1949-1954); director of Czechoslovak national television (1963-1968); supported reforms of Prague Spring, emigrated to Italy following the Warsaw Pact invasion of Czechoslovakia (1969), and became an Italian citizen (1977); editor of leftist oriented émigré journal *Listy*; elected twice to the European Parliament from the Italian Socialist Party (1979-1989).

7. Vilem Prečan (1933), historian, political essayist; researcher at the History Institute of the Czechoslovak Academy of Sciences in Prague (1957), expelled (1970); persecuted by the StB for his part in the publication of the Czech Black Book of the Warsaw Pact invasion, *Sedm pražských dnů, 21.-27.8.1968* [*Seven Days of Prague, 21-27.8.1968*]; emigrated to Germany (1976); director and caretaker of the Documentation Center for Independent Czechoslovak Literature in Scheinfeld, Germany (1986-1990), a repository of *samizdat* literature smuggled from Czechoslovakia; director of the Institute for Contemporary History of the Academy of Sciences of the Czech Republic (1990-1998).

8. Established in 1986, the Documentation Center for Independent Czechoslovak Literature was housed in rooms of Karel Schwarzenberg's ancestral home, Castle Schwarzenberg in Scheinfeld, Germany.

9. Pavel Kohout (1928), playwright, prose writer, poet, dramaturge, theater director, and translator; former member of the Communist Party; cultural attaché in the Czechoslovak embassy in Moscow (1949-1950); leading proponent of Prague Spring reforms and Communist Party chair in the Prague branch of the Writers' Union (1968-1969); persecuted by StB since 1970, one of the founders of Charter 77; exiled to Austria (1978) and Austrian citizen (1980). Zdeněk Mlynář (1930-1997), attorney, political scientist, and politician; studied law at Moscow State University (classmate of Mikhail Sergeevich Gorbachev) (1950-1955); member of the Communist Party (1946-1970) and one of the authors of the Action Program of the Czechoslovak Communist Party which established the reform agenda of the Prague Spring (1968); signatory to the Moscow Protocol; member of the Presidium of the Communist Party of Czechoslovakia (1968-1969); signatory of Charter 77, emigrated to Austria after several months of house arrest (1977); since 1989, professor of political science at Innsbruck University.

10. Bruno Kreisky (1911-1990); chancellor of Austria (1970-1983).

11. Jan Ruml (1953), journalist, politician; excluded from higher education due to political activities of his parents (cf. Jiří Ruml), worked in various areas of manual labor; signatory of Charter 77 and charter speaker (1990); member of VONS (1979); in investigative confinement on suspicion of subversion of the republic (1981-1982); minister of

the interior of the Czech Republic (1993-1997); founded the political party Freedom Union [*Unie Svobody*] (1998) which later merged with Democratic Union (DEU).

12. Jaroslav Šedivý (1929), historian and diplomat; archivist at the Institute for International Politics and Economics in Prague (1957-1970); sentenced to eighteen months in prison for alleged subversion (1971); signatory of Charter 77; ambassador to France, ambassador to Belgium; ambassador to NATO (1997); minister of foreign affairs (1997-1998).

13. Milan Šimečka (1930-1990), philosopher, essayist, and translator; imprisoned for one year (1981); chairman of the board of advisors to President Václav Havel. Jiří Ruml (1923-2004), journalist, political writer; coeditor of *samizdat Lidové noviny*; Charter 77 speaker (1984); member of the Federal Assembly (1990-1992).

14. Jiří Hájek (1913), politician and diplomat; served as Czechoslovakia's ambassador to Great Britain and the United Nations; minister of foreign affairs under Dubček (1968) but forced into official political retirement during Normalization; one of the founders of Charter 77 and one of the first three charter speakers with Václav Havel and Jan Patočka.

15. François Mitterrand (1916-1996); president of France (1981-1995). Margaret Thatcher (1925); prime minister of Great Britain (1979-1990). Jimmy Carter (1924); governor of the state of Georgia (1971-1975), thirty-ninth president of the United States (1977-1981).

16. Klaus Nellen (1948), since 1984 the director of the Patočka Archive and permanent fellow at the *Institut für die Wissenschaft vom Menschen* [Institute for Human Sciences (IWM)] in Vienna; editor of *Transit* and the cofounder of *eurozine*, an Internet magazine; coeditor of *Jan Patočka: Ausgewählte Schriften* [*Jan Patočka: Selected Writings*] (five vols. 1987-1992).

17. Eva Kantůrková (1930), journalist and writer; former member of the Communist Party; work banned after the invasion of 1968 during Normalization; Charter 77 signatory and charter speaker (1985); arrested and imprisoned for almost a year after the Palach Press truck carrying smuggled literature was intercepted by the StB (1981).

18. See Václav Havel, *Letters to Olga: June 1979-September 1982* (*Dopisy Olze*), trans. Paul Wilson (New York: Henry Holt and Company, 1983). The collected letters from prison of Václav Havel to his wife Olga.

19. During the Cold War (1948-1991), a number of well-known dissidents from the Soviet Union and countries of the East Bloc walked to freedom across the Glienicker Bridge between Potsdam (East Germany) and West Berlin in exchange for captured "spies" held in the West. Natan Sharansky, a prominent Soviet dissident, was exchanged at the bridge in 1986.

20. Leonid Brezhnev (1906-1982); chairman of the Presidium of the Supreme Soviet of the Soviet Union (1960-1964); following Nikita Khrushchev's fall from power (1964), became the general secretary of the Communist Party; one of the chief engineers of the Warsaw Pact invasion of Czechoslovakia (1968); formulated the "Brezhnev Doctrine" in Soviet foreign policy, which asserted that the Soviet Union could intervene in the domestic policy of any of the satellite nations of Central and Eastern Europe in order to maintain Soviet hegemony; president of the Soviet Union (1977-1982).

21. Dagmar Veškrňová Havlová (1953), theater and film actress; married President Václav Havel in 1997; established VIZE 97 Foundation with Havel.

22. "Backlash," *Social Research*, Vol. 60, No. 4 (Winter 1993), 737-49.

23. "What Did We Lose after 1989?" *Social Research*, Vol. 63, No. 2 (Summer 1996), 531-41.

24. In *Good-Bye Samizdat*, 181-92.

25. *Nomenklatura* (from Russian номенклатура, via Latin *nomenclatura*), originally referred to the list of names of Communist Party members; later designated the system of patronage for the privileged elite class of Communist Party officials, government functionaries, and bureaucrats in the Soviet Union and the satellite states of Central and Eastern Europe.

Chapter 10: Petruška Šustrová

1. Started by Petr Uhl in 1977, *Informace o Chartě 77*, commonly known as *Infoch*, published documents produced by speakers of Charter 77.

2. Roger Scruton, a former lecturer in philosophy at Birkbeck College, London University, made several trips to Czechoslovakia beginning in 1979 to lecture in the home seminars. For his efforts, President Václav Havel awarded Scruton the Medal of Merit, First Class, of the Czech Republic in 1998.

3. Alexandr "Saša" Vondra (1961), geographer; Charter 77 speaker (1989); deputy foreign minister of the Czech Republic (1993-1997), subsequently ambassador to the United States until September 2001.

Chapter 11: Petr Uhl

1. Anna Šabatová (1951) as a student of philosophy was sentenced to three years in prison (1971); founding member of VONS; during her husband's imprisonment, continued the publication of *Informace o Chartě* (1979-1984); charter speaker (1986) with Martin Palouš and Jan Štern. Daughter of Jaroslav Šabata (see below).

2. "Memorial," in Russian *Pamiat'*, was a grassroots movement begun in 1988 in the Soviet Union to memorialize the victims of Stalinism by erecting monuments and opening research centers devoted to Stalin's reign of terror.

3. Marta Kubišová (1942), singer; Charter 77 speaker (1978); officially banned from public performances (1970-1989).

4. Jaroslav Šabata (1927), philosopher, psychologist, politician; chair of the southern Moravian regional committee of the Communist Party (1968-1969); one of the leading reformers within the Communist Party (1968); during Normalization, relieved of all official duties (1969) and expelled from the Communist Party (1970); imprisoned (1971-1976); Charter 77 signatory (1977) and charter speaker (1978, 1982); speaker for Civic Forum in Brno (1989-1990).

5. Pavel Landovský (1936), actor and playwright; a close associate of Václav Havel; heavily persecuted by the StB in the 1970s; after an official visit to Austria, denied reentry into Czechoslovakia and since 1978 resident in Vienna and employed as an actor at the Burgtheater; returned to Czechoslovakia only in 1989.

6. Jiří Gruntorád (1951), publisher; currently curator, archivist, director of *Libri Prohibiti* (Prague), a library and archive of Charter 77 documents and *samizdat* literature; Charter 77 signatory (1979); imprisoned for "subversion of the republic" (Article 98) (1980-1984).

7. General Wojciech Jaruzelski (1923); Poland's minister of defense in 1968; appointed prime minister of Poland (Feb. 1981) and first secretary of the Communist Party of Poland (Oct. 1981). Due to tension and unrest in light of Solidarity's increasing influ-

ence, declared a state of martial law in December 1981. Resigned from his positions in 1990 in capitulation to the government established by Solidarity.

8. Ladislav Lis (1926-2000), secretary of the Prague Municipal Committee of the Communist Party (1968); expelled from the party (1969); imprisoned a number of times (1978-1984); Charter 77 signatory (1977) and Charter 77 speaker (1980).

9. Ján Čarnogurský (1944), Slovak religious dissident jailed by the Communist regime for his religious writings (1989); founded the Christian Democratic Party in Slovakia and served as Slovakia's prime minister (1991-1992); since 1998, minister of justice.

10. Jozef Tiso (1887-1947), doctor of Theology and Roman Catholic priest; as president of the independent state of Slovakia established as a German protectorate (1939-1945) presided over the "aryanization" of Jewish businesses and the deportation of Slovak Jews; fled to Austria after the liberation of Slovakia by the Red Army (1945), but was captured, tried, and executed in Bratislava two years later.

11. Pavel Bratinka (1946); studied nuclear physics (1964-1970); held a number of odd jobs (1981-1989); member of Parliament of the Czech and Slovak Federated Republic (1990-1992); deputy foreign minister for the Czech Repubic (1992-1996); member of Parliament (1996-1998).

12. Vladimír Mlynář (1966), member of Parliament and minister of informatik (2002); as a student, participated in the seminars of the "flying university"; aided Jiřina Šiklová in the collection and distribution of literature and messages to and from Palach Press; aided in the distribution of *samizdat Lidové noviny*, later became an editor of the legal *Lidové noviny* (1990); editor in chief of *Respekt* (1994-1997).

Chapter 12: Jan Urban

1. Gleb Yakunin (1934), Russian Orthodox priest, spent more than five years in Soviet labor camps and exile for human rights activities; deputy to Supreme Soviet of the Russian Federation (1990); elected to Russian Federation Duma (1993); defrocked by Russian Orthodox Church (1994); heads Social Committee to Defend Freedom of Conscience.

2. Sergei Kovalev (1930), biologist, leading human rights advocate during the Soviet era; in labor camp for political prisoners (1975-1987); twice elected to Duma from Russia's Choice Party (1991, 1993); presided over Duma's Human Rights Commission (1994-1996); remains an ardent activist, especially critical of Russian policy and action in Chechnya.

3. Zviad Gamsakhurdia (1939-1993), linguist; founded a human rights organization (1955) for which he was imprisoned; member of the Union of Writers of the Georgian SSR (1966-1977; 1981-1992); founded the Georgian Helsinki Committee (1976); elected president of the Republic of Georgia by the Supreme Council (1991); fled into exile in face of coup d'état (1991); died under mysterious circumstances (1993).

4. Andrei Sakharov (1921-1989), nuclear physicist, primary developer of the Soviet nuclear weapons arsenal; protested against weapons testing and from then on lived as a dissident (1962); awarded the Nobel Peace Prize (1975); exiled to Gorky (Nizhniy Novgorod) (1980); at Gorbachev's personal invitation returned to Moscow (1986). Yelena Bonner (1923), pediatrician; married Andrei Sakharov in 1972; served as Sakharov's secretary and spokesperson to the world; with Sakharov under house arrest in Gorky (1984); continues to campaign for democracy and human rights in Russia.

5. In August 1998, Russia experienced a severe financial crisis. While revenues from oil and other commodities declined—the government's main source of revenue—spending continued unabated. The government had been financing its debt through the issuance of short-term treasury bills (GKOs). As the Central Bank's hard currency reserves became depleted, investor confidence declined. On 17 August, the government announced that it would default on its GKOs amounting to approximately US$43 billion. By May 1999, the ruble had been devalued by 70 percent of its precrisis value, while purchasing power declined by 35 percent. The IMF loaned Russia US$22.6 billion to ease the country through the crisis.

6. Richard C. Holbrooke (1941); appointed assistant secretary of state for European and Canadian Affairs by U.S. president Bill Clinton (1994); chief U.S. negotiator for the Dayton Peace Accords that ended the war in Bosnia (1995); served as U.S. special envoy in Bosnia and Kosovo (1998).

7. Slobodan Milošević (1941); president of Serbia since 1989 and president of the Federal Republic of Yugoslavia (1997-2000); considered to be the main instigator of two wars in the region and the "mastermind" behind the practice of ethnic cleansing in Bosnia and Kosovo, Milošević was indicted by the International War Crimes Tribunal in The Hague (1999) and arrested to stand trial for war crimes (2001).

Chapter 13: Reality Czech

1. John Keane, *Václav Havel: A Political Tragedy in Six Acts* (New York: Basic Books, 2000), 233.

2. Václav Havel, "The Power of the Powerless," in *Living in Truth: Twenty-six Essays Published on the Occasion of the Award of the Erasmus Prize to Václav Havel*, ed. Jan Vladislav (London: Faber and Faber, 1986), 78.

3. Keane, *Václav Havel*, 251.

4. Eda Kriseová, conversation with the author, April 1998, San Antonio, Texas.

5. Havel, "The Power of the Powerless," in *Living in Truth*, 87.

6. Barbara Falk, *The Dilemmas of Dissidence in East-Central Europe* (Budapest: Central European University Press, 2003), 181.

7. Richard Rose, *A Bottom Up Evaluation of Enlargement Countries: New Europe Barometer 1*. Studies in Public Policy Number 364 (Glasgow: Centre for the Study of Public Policy, University of Strathclyde, 2002), 2.

8. *Freedom House*, www.freedomhouse.org/ratings/congo.htm (Czech Republic) and http://www.freedomhouse.org/ratings/phil.htm (Slovakia) (17 February 2003).

9. Rose, *A Bottom Up Evaluation of Enlargement Countries*, 33-34.

10. Rose, *A Bottom Up Evaluation of Enlargement Countries*, 34.

11. Rose, *A Bottom Up Evaluation of Enlargement Countries*, 44.

12. Richard Rose, Neil Munro, and Tom Mackie, *Elections in Central and Eastern Europe since 1990*, Studies in Public Policy Number 300 (Glasgow: Centre for the Study of Public Policy, University of Strathclyde, 1998), 37; also W. Derksen, *Electionworld.org*, www.electionworld.org/czech.htm (12 February 2003); also Wolfram Nordsieck, *Parties and Elections in Europe*, www.parties-and-elections.de/index.html (12 February 2003).

13. Rose, *A Bottom Up Evaluation of Enlargement Countries*, 10.

14. Jiří Večerník and Petr Matějů, eds., *Ten Years of Rebuilding Capitalism: Czech Society after 1989* (Prague: Academia, 1999), 260.

15. Janos Simon, *Popular Conceptions of Democracy in Post-Communist Europe*, Studies in Public Policy Number 273 (Glasgow: Centre for the Study of Public Policy, University of Strathclyde, 1996), 11, 16.

16. Simon, *Popular Conceptions of Democracy in Post-Communist Europe*, 42.

17. *Economic Survey of Europe 2002*, United Nations Economic Commission for Europe (UNECE), No. 2, 167, www.unece.org/ead/survey (18 February 2003).

18. *Economic Survey of Europe 2002*, No. 2, 167.

19. Derksen, *Electionworld.org*, www.electionworld.org/czech.htm (8 October 2002).

20. Richard Rose, Neil Munro, and Tom Mackie, *Elections in Central and Eastern Europe since 1990*, www.cspp.strath.ac.uk/polelec.html (16 February 2003).

21. Robert J. Gitter and Markus Scheuer, "Low Unemployment in the Czech Republic: 'Miracle' or 'Mirage'?" *Monthly Labor Review*, August 1998, 31-37, www.bls.gov (17 February 2003).

22. Gitter and Scheuer, "Low Unemployment in the Czech Republic: 'Miracle' or 'Mirage'?" *Monthly Labor Review*, 32.

23. Figures from table 1, Gitter and Scheuer, "Low Unemployment in the Czech Republic: 'Miracle' or 'Mirage'?" *Monthly Labor Review*, 32.

24. See Leff, *The Czech and Slovak Republics*, table 6.1, 183; also *Deutsche Bank Research*, Country Infobase, www.dbresearch.com (16 February 2003). Used by permission.

25. *2002 Regular Report on the Czech Republic's Progress towards Accession*, Commission of the European Communities, 36, http://europa.eu.int/comm/enlargement/report2002/cz_en.pdf (18 February 2003).

26. Nordsieck, *Parties and Elections in Europe*, www.parties-and-elections.de/index.html (16 February 2003).

27. Rose, *A Bottom Up Evaluation of Enlargement Countries*, 18, 20.

28. Rose, *A Bottom Up Evaluation of Enlargement Countries*, table 3, 17.

29. *2002 Regular Report on the Czech Republic's Progress towards Accession*, 152. Reports also for Hungary, Slovenia, Lithuania, and Poland.

30. Thomas A. Szayna, "The Czech Republic: A Small Contributor or a 'Free Rider'?" in *America's New Allies: Poland, Hungary, and the Czech Republic in NATO*, ed. Andrew A. Michta (Seattle: University of Washington Press, 1999), 112.

31. The remaining five countries are Estonia, Hungary, Poland, Slovenia, and Cyprus.

32. *The Attitudes to Nato Membership*, Brussels: Central European Opinion Research Group Foundation (CEORG), www.ceorg-europe.org/research/2000_02.html (20 February 2003).

33. "Trends in EU, Czech, Hungarian and Polish Public Opinion on Enlargement: Implications for EU Institutions and Industry," *Joint Omnibus Survey*, September 2000: Poland, Czech Republic, Hungary, Brussels: Central European Opinion Research Group Foundation (CEORG), 1-19, http://ceorg-europe.org/sept2000.pdf (19 February 2003).

34. *The Czech Republic and the European Union*, Mission of the Czech Republic to the European Communities, Prague: Ministry of Foreign Affairs of the Czech Republic, www.mzv.cz/missionEU/public_support.htm (19 February 2003).

35. "EU Accession Referenda: High Participation, Growing Support in Poland and in the Czech Republic, Decrease in Hungarian Support," *January 2003 Omnibus Survey*, Brussels: Central European Opinion Research Group Foundation (CEORG), 4, www.ceorg-europe.org/research/2003_01.html (12 April 2003).

36. In Czech, "Teprve nyní pomyslně skončila druhá světová valka, která nás vytrhla ze vztahu k západní Evropě. V posledních letech jsme se vraceli krůček po krůčku. Teď je to konečně naplno." *Mladá Fronta Dnes*, 16 June 2003, p. A2. Translation by Michael Long.

37. *The Attitudes to Nato Membership*, 2.

38. Szayna, "The Czech Republic: A Small Contributor or a 'Free Rider'?" in *America's New Allies*, 115.

39. Szayna, "The Czech Republic: A Small Contributor or a 'Free Rider'?" in *America's New Allies*, 113.

40. *Joint Omnibus Survey, September 2000*, 16.

41. Czech for "Welcome (whoever isn't a Gypsy)!"

42. *Rom* and its plural form *Roma* are the native designations for the ethnic group commonly referred to in English as "Gypsy" (also "Romany"), in Czech as *Cikán*, in German *Zigeuner*. Sources place Roma migration into Europe from India as early as the eleventh century. See David M. Crowe, *A History of the Gypsies of Eastern Europe and Russia* (New York: Palgrave Macmillan, 1995).

43. "Roma in the Czech Republic: Foreigners in Their Own Land," *Human Rights Watch/Helsinki Watch*, June 1996, Vol. 8, No. 11, www.hrw.org/reports/1996/Czech .htm (14 February 2003). Human Rights Watch began in the United States as Helsinki Watch with the purpose of monitoring the compliance of Soviet Bloc countries with the human rights provisions of the Helsinki Accords.

44. Dagmar Cestrová and Vít Lukáš, "V Matiční ulici už dávno nejde o zed'" [In Matiční Street the wall hasn't been the issue for a long time], *Mladá Fronta Dnes* (Prague), 30 April 1999, 14, http://mfd.newton.cz (29 January 2003).

45. "Vláda bude mluvit do stavby plotu," [Government to intervene in construction of fence], *Mladá Fronta Dnes* (Prague), 11 October 1999, 1, http://mfd.newton.cz (29 January 2003). Translation by Michael Long.

46. "Plot v Matiční se bude nakonec bourat," [Fence in Matiční to be demolished], *Mladá Fronta Dnes* (Prague), 24 November 1999, 1, http://mfd.newton.cz (29 January 2003).

47. "Matiční ulice je sociální problém, prohlásil Uhl" [Uhl declares Matiční Street a social problem], *Mladá Fronta Dnes* (Prague), 28 January 1999, 1, http://mfd.newton.cz (29 January 2003). Translation by Michael Long.

48. Claire Wallace, *Xenophobia in Post-Communist Europe*, Studies in Public Policy, Number 323 (Glasgow: Centre for the Study of Public Policy, University of Strathclyde, 1999), 5. Wallace cites research by Csepeli and Sik (1995) and Csepeli and Orkney (1996) on xenophobia in Hungary.

49. Wallace, *Xenophobia in Post-Communist Europe*, 2.

50. Wallace, *Xenophobia in Post-Communist Europe*, 2-8.

51. Reported in Wallace, *Xenophobia in Post-Communist Europe*, 15

52. Data quoted is taken from the 1998 New Democracies Barometer V (NDB), Xenophobia Questions, reported in Wallace, appendix, 53-70. In addition to Austria, the NDB was conducted in eleven transition states: Poland, Hungary, Czech Republic, Slovakia, Slovenia, Croatia, Federal Republic of Yugoslavia, Bulgaria, Romania, Ukraine, and Belarus.

53. Wallace, *Xenophobia in Post-Communist Europe*, appendix, 54.

54. Wallace, *Xenophobia in Post-Communist Europe*, appendix, 54-55.

55. Wallace, *Xenophobia in Post-Communist Europe*, appendix, 56.

56. Wallace, *Xenophobia in Post-Communist Europe*, appendix, 59-66.

57. Wallace, *Xenophobia in Post-Communist Europe*, 47-48.

58. Wallace, *Xenophobia in Post-Communist Europe*, appendix, 53 and 69.

59. *2002 Regular Report on the Czech Republic's Progress towards Accession*, 30.

60. *2002 Regular Report on the Czech Republic's Progress towards Accession*, 31.

61. Michael Mainville (with Petr Kašpar), "Klaus Promises to Rein in Foreigners," *Prague Post*, 22-28 May 2002, 1.

62. Derksen, *Electionworld.org*, www.electionworld.org/czech.htm (10 April 2003).

63. Večerník and Matějů, *Ten Years of Rebuilding Capitalism*, 196.

Bibliography

2002 Regular Report on the Czech Republic's Progress towards Accession, Commission of the European Communities. 10 September 2002. www.europa.eu.int/comm./enlargement/report2002 (18 February 2003).

Ash, Timothy Garton. *The Magic Lantern: The Revolution of '89 Witnessed in Warsaw, Budapest, Berlin, and Prague.* New York: Random House, 1990.

The Attitudes to Nato Membership. Brussels: Central European Opinion Research Group Foundation (CEORG). www.ceorg-europe.org/research/2000_02.html (20 February 2003).

Barnes, Clive. "Public Theater Presents 'Memorandum.'" Review of *The Memorandum* by Václav Havel. New York Shakespeare Festival. *New York Times*, 28 April 1968, sec. 2, p. 11.

Cestrová, Dagmar, and Vít Lukáš. "V Matiční ulici už dávno nejde o zeď'." [In Matiční Street the wall hasn't been the issue for a long time.] *Mladá Fronta Dnes* (Prague). 30 April 1999, p. 14. www.mfd.newton.cz (29 January 2003).

Crowe, David M. *A History of the Gypsies of Eastern Europe and Russia.* New York: Palgrave Macmillan, 1995.

The Czech Republic and the European Union. Mission of the Czech Republic to the European Communities. Prague: Ministry of Foreign Affairs of the Czech Republic. www.mzv.cz/missionEU/public_support.htm (19 February 2003).

Day, Barbara. *The Velvet Philosophers.* London: Claridge Press, 1999.

Derksen, W. *Electionworld.org.* www.electionworld.org (8 October 2002).

Deutsche Bank Research. Country infobase. www.dbresearch.com (14 April 2003).

Economic Survey of Europe 2002, No. 2. United Nations Economic Commission for Europe (UNECE). www.unec.org/ead/survey (18 Febraury 2003).

"EU Accession Referenda: High Participation, Growing Support in Poland and in the Czech Republic, Decrease in Hungarian Support." *January 2003 Omnibus Survey.* Brussels: Central European Opinion Research Group Foundation (CEORG), 4. www.ceorg-europe.org/research/2003_01.html (12 April 2003).

Falk, Barbara J. *The Dilemmas of Dissidence in East-Central Europe: Citizen Intellectuals and Philosopher Kings.* Budapest: Central European University Press, 2003.

Freedom House. www.freedomhouse.org/ratings (17 February 2003).

Gitter, Robert J., and Markus Scheuer. "Low Unemployment in the Czech Republic: 'Miracle' or 'Mirage'?" *Monthly Labor Review*, August 1998, 31-37. www.bls.gov (17 February 2003).

Havel, Václav. *Disturbing the Peace: A Conversation with Karel Hvížďala*. Trans. Paul Wilson. New York: Vintage Books, 1990.

———."The Power of the Powerless." Trans. Paul Wilson. In *Living in Truth: Twenty-two Essays Published on the Occasion of the Award of the Erasmus Prize to Václav Havel*. London: Faber and Faber Limited, 1986.

Hlavsa, Mejla, and Jan Pelc. *Bez ohňů je underground* [*No Spark in the Underground*]. Praha: Nakldatelství BFS, 1992.

Informace o Chartě 77 (1978-1990): Článková bibliographie [*Infoch*]. [*Information about Charter 77 (1978-1990): A Bibliography of Articles*]. Compiled by Jiří Gruntorád. Brno: Doplněk, 1998.

Keane, John. *Václav Havel: A Political Tragedy in Six Acts*. New York: Basic Books, 2000.

Kriseová, Eda. *Václav Havel: The Authorized Biography*. Trans. Caleb Crain. New York: St. Martin's Press, 1993.

Leff, Carol Skalnik. *The Czech and Slovak Republics: Nation versus State*. Boulder, Colo.: Westview, 1996.

Littell, Robert, ed. *The Czech Black Book*. New York: Frederick A. Praeger, 1969.

Mainville, Michael. "Klaus Promises to Rein in Foreigners," *Prague Post*, 22-28 May 2002, p. 1.

Marsh, Christopher. *Russia at the Polls: Voters, Elections, and Democratization*. Washington, D.C.: CQ Press, 2002.

Mastny, Vojtech, ed. *Czechoslovakia: Crisis in World Communism*. New York: Facts on File, Inc., 1972.

"Matiční ulice je sociální problém, prohlásil Uhl." [Uhl declares Matiční Street a social problem.] *Mladá Fronta Dnes* (Prague), 28 January 1999, p. 1. www.mfd.newton.cz (29 January 2003).

Naegele, Jolyon. "Czech Republic: The Beneš Decrees—How Did They Come to Be and What Do They Mandate?" *Radio Free Europe/ Radio Liberty*, www.rferl.org (1 March 2002).

Navara, Luděk. "Vězněným muzikantům se otevírá cesta k odškodnění: Soud zrušil 26 let starý verdikt nad čtyřmi hudebníky ze skupin Plastic People of the Universe a DG 307" [Road to compensation opens for imprisoned musicians: Court repeals verdict of 26 years ago of four musicians from the groups Plastic People of the Universe and DG 307.] *Mladá Fronta Dnes*, 19 February 2003, p. 2.

Návratil, Jaromír, ed. *The Prague Spring 1968: A National Security Archive Documents Reader*. Budapest: Central European University Press, 1998.

Nordsieck, Wolfram. *Parties and Elections in Europe*. www.parties-and-elections.de/ indexe.html (12 February 2003).

The Plastic People of the Universe II. *Vožralej jako slíva*, Koncerty 1973-1975. Globus International, 1997. Compact disc.

"Plot v Matiční se bude nakonec bourat" [Fence in Matiční to be demolished.] *Mladá Fronta Dnes* (Prague), 24 November 1999, p. 1. www.mfd.newton.cz (29 January 2003).

Příhoda, Petr. "Mutual Perceptions in Czech-Slovak Relationships." *The End of Czechoslovakia*. Ed. Jiří Musil. Budapest: Central European University Press, 1995, 128-38.

"Roma in the Czech Republic: Foreigners in Their Own Land." *Human Rights Watch/ Helsinki Watch*. June 1996, Vol. 8, No. 11. www.hrw.org/reports/1996/Czech.htm (14 February 2003).

Rose, Richard. *A Bottom Up Evaluation of Enlargement Countries: New Europe Barometer 1*, Studies in Public Policy Number 364. Glasgow: Centre for the Study of Public Policy, University of Strathclyde, 1998.

Rose, Richard, Neil Munro, and Tom Mackie. *Elections in Central and Eastern Europe since 1990*. Studies in Public Policy Number 300. Glasgow: Centre for the Study of Public Policy, University of Strathclyde, 1998.

———. *Elections in Central Europe since 1990*. www.cspp.strath.ac.uk/polelec.html (16 February 2003).

Šiklová, Jiřina. "Backlash." *Social Research*, Vol. 60, No. 4 (Winter 1993): 737-49.

———. "The 'Gray Zone' and the Future of Dissent in Czechoslovakia." *Good-Bye Samizdat: Twenty Years of Czechoslovak Underground Writing*. Ed. Marketa Goetz-Stankiewicz. Evanston, Ill.: Northwestern University Press, 1992, 181-92.

Simon, Janos. *Popular Conceptions of Democracy in Post-Communist Europe*. Studies in Public Policy Number 273. Glasgow: Centre for the Study of Public Policy, University of Strathclyde, 1996.

Szayna, Thomas S. "The Czech Republic: A Small Contributor or a 'Free Rider'?" *America's New Allies: Poland, Hungary, and the Czech Republic in NATO*. Ed. Andrew A. Michta. Seattle: University of Washington Press, 1999, 112-48.

"Trends in EU, Czech, Hungarian and Polish Public Opinion on Enlargement: Implications for EU Institutions and Industry." *Joint Omnibus Survey, September 2000: Poland, Czech Republic, Hungary*, 1-19. Brussels: Central European Opinion Research Group Foundation (CEORG). www.ceorg-europe.org/sept2000.pdf (19 February 2003).

Večerník, Jiří, and Petr Matějů, eds. *Ten Years of Rebuilding Capitalism: Czech Society after 1989*. Prague: Academia, 1999.

"Vláda bude mluvit do stavby plotu." [Government to intervene in construction of fence.] *Mladá Fronta Dnes* (Prague), 11 October 1999, p. 1. www.mfd.newton.cz (29 January 2003).

Wallace, Claire. *Xenophobia in Post-Communist Europe*. Studies in Public Policy Number 323. Glasgow: Centre for the Study of Public Policy, University of Strathclyde, 1999.

Windsor, Philip, and Adam Roberts. *Czechoslovakia 1968: Reform, Repression, and Resistance*. New York: Columbia University Press, 1969.

Index

About the Author

Michael Long completed his Master of Arts in Russian language and area studies (1986) and his Doctor of Philosophy in Slavic linguistics (1994) at Indiana University in Bloomington, Indiana. He is associate professor of Russian and director of Slavic and East European Studies at Baylor University. His research focuses on Czech morphology, as well as cultural topics concerned with human rights in the former East Bloc, the transition of post-Communist states of Central and Eastern Europe, and Communist Party policy toward the preservation of cultural monuments in Russia and the Republic of Georgia.